# TRANSITIONS from DICTATORSHIP to DEMOCRACY

## Comparative Studies of Spain, Portugal, and Greece

Ronald H. Chilcote
Stylianos Hadjiyannis
Fred A. López III
Daniel Nataf
Elizabeth Sammis

CRANE RUSSAK A Member of the Taylor & Francis Group New York · Philadelphia · Washington, DC · London

| | | |
|---|---|---|
| **USA** | Publishing Office: | Taylor & Francis New York Inc.<br>79 Madison Ave., New York, NY 10016-7892 |
| | Sales Office: | Taylor & Francis Inc.<br>1900 Frost Road, Bristol, PA 19007-1598 |
| **UK** | | Taylor & Francis Ltd.<br>4 John St., London WC1N 2ET |

**Transitions from Dictatorship to Democracy:**
Comparative Studies of Spain, Portugal, and Greece



First published 1990
Printed in the United States of America

**Library of Congress Cataloging in Publication Data**

Transitions from dictatorship to democracy : comparative studies of
Spain, Portugal, and Greece / by Ronald H. Chilcote . . . [et al.].
p. cm.
Includes bibliographical references.
ISBN 0-8448-1675-2. -- ISBN 0-8448-1676-0 (pbk.)
1. Europe, Southern--Politics and goverment.
2. Authoritarianism. 3. Democracy. I. Chilcote, Ronald H.
D1058.T725 1990 90-32110
320.5'3'094--dc20 CIP

# Contents

# Preface

In the late 1970s, Nicos Poulantzas, in *Crisis of the Dictatorships: Portugal, Spain, Greece,* applied his well-known theoretical perspectives to a concrete analysis of the major transformations that occurred in those three countries during 1974 and 1975. His provocative and interpretative analysis not only provided a basis for comparative study but also examined several important theoretical questions about transition from dictatorship to representative democracy and on to socialism. The present essays offer a retrospective assessment of this transition and examine current developments with particular attention to the role of the state and social classes in the overthrow of the old dictatorships, the evolution of representative democracy and political parties, and the formal integration of these countries into the European Economic Community and the international capitalist system.

Among the issues raised by Poulantzas and analyzed in this volume are: (1) whether a domestic bourgeoisie (largely national capital) achieves hegemony and dominance over a comprador bourgeoisie (compromised with foreign capital), (2) the question of the exceptional capitalist state (dictatorship) in a crisis of capital accumulation and political legitimacy and why the exceptional state persists when it faces severe internal contradictions, (3) emphasis on the strategic importance of bourgeois hegemony in the democratic transition, which must be balanced with an analysis of the strategies and tactics of the parties of the left, and (4) the Leninist strategy of dual power and frontal assault on the state contrasted with the movement of the popular classes within the apparatuses of the state, winning parliamentary elections, and gaining control of government. This analysis leads to an understanding of why a transition to socialism was not achieved in these countries even though the alliance of labor and a fraction of the capitalist class opened up and extended democracy as an initial step in the path toward socialism.

The essays in this volume are based on fieldwork in Southern Europe. As a graduate student during the early 1960s, I devoted nearly two years to research and study in Spain and Portugal. A series of journalistic reports and a book on Portuguese Africa (1967) resulted in the Salazar dictatorship declaring me persona non grata. My return to Portugal and Africa in the summer of 1975 and 1983 was associated with a desire to study in depth the exciting revolutionary developments of 1974 and 1975. Thanks to a sabbatical leave during 1985–86 and research visits during June–July 1987 and June–July 1988, I was able to carry out this task. The basic research is being published by the Centro de Documentação 25 de Abril of the University of Coimbra.

Prior to my sabbatical year I supervised the doctoral dissertations of Fred López, who carried out his research on the transition to democracy in Spain, and Stylianos Hadjiyannis, who returned to his native Greece on four occasions to study the transition there. I also served on the dissertation committee of Elizabeth Sammis of UCLA whose work focused on the transition up to the April 25, 1974, coup in Portugal. Sammis joined with Dan Nataf who had written his dissertation on Portugal, and all of us decided to combine our research in a collective work to reassess and update the analysis of Poulantzas.

The writing of these essays has evolved through several drafts and a process of criticism and self-criticism in an effort to ensure balance in terms of presentation, organization, and length thereby allowing the reader a basis for comparison of recent theory and experience in Southern Europe.

Ronald H. Chilcote

# Chapter 1

# Southern European Transitions in Comparative Perspective

*Ronald H. Chilcote*

---

During 1974 and 1975 Southern Europe was shaken by the overthrow of military dictatorships. On April 25, 1974, the nearly 50-year-old Portuguese regime, initiated by coup in 1926 and sustained under António de Oliveira Salazar and Marcello Caetano, fell to progressive elements in the armed forces long disenchanted with the debilitating colonial wars in Africa and desiring change at home. On July 24, the seven-year-old military Greek junta fell, the consequence of an abortive intervention in Cyprus and disillusionment among both bourgeois and popular classes. A year later began the gradual dismantling of the regime of Francisco Franco, who had ruled since victorious in the Spanish civil war in 1939.

Acompanying these dramatic events were popular euphoria and expectations and demands for reforms and substantial change from the authoritarian practices of the old regimes. A transition from precapitalist to capitalist relations of production had been evident for some time in all three countries despite their obvious backwardness when contrasted to the advanced industrial nations of Western Europe. The immediate objective was achievement of a transition from the old dictatorships to democracy, but the problematic of attaining a democracy involved alternative courses of action: on the one hand, the establishment of formal representative or parliamentary democracy, the preservation of bourgeois capitalist hegemony, and the further consolidation and expansion of capitalism; on the other, the struggle toward socialism, the implementation of democratic socialism, participatory democracy, and ultimately the socialization of the means of production.

During the middle of the nineteenth century in his analysis of the state and class struggle in revolutionary France, Karl Marx, in *The Eighteenth*

*Brumaire of Napoleon Bonaparte* (1852), focused on this problem of a transition to democracy. In the late 1970s Marxist academics set forth to unravel the intricacies of the transition in Spain, Portugal, and Greece. In a series of published letters, French philosopher Louis Althusser reflected briefly on the need of fascist states to establish a mass base, including not only the monopolistic and nonmonopolistic bourgeoisies but also the middle classes, poor and small peasant farmers, and a fraction of the working class (Althusser and Rebello 1976, 21). In a more elaborate and insightful analysis, Greek political sociologist and theorist Nicos Poulantzas played upon this theme and also offered a comparative study of the three cases. His *The Crisis of the Dictatorships* (1976a) departs from prior theory, concentrates on an elaboration and analysis of causes and their repercussions, and assumes a relatively informed readership. He was especially interested in the experience "of popular movements confronting the exceptional capitalist regimes" (1976a, 8). Poulantzas was the first social scientist to study these transitions. His pioneering comparative work serves as a point of departure for our own essays. My introduction focuses on his work, first, by examining the theoretical foundations of important thinkers such as Marx, Engels, Lenin, and Gramsci who preceded and influenced him; second, with a brief synthesis of what he wrote about the transitions in Spain, Portugal, and Greece; and, third, through an assessment of his analysis in light of the ensuing decade, as drawn from the three case studies in this volume.

## THEORETICAL FOUNDATIONS

State and class are essential concepts employed by these Marxist thinkers, and they provide the framework of analysis for Poulantzas as well as our own essays. Poulantzas affirmed: "I think that in Marx and Engels, and also in Lenin, not to mention Gramsci, whose contribution is very important, there are certainly elements of what I am trying to develop" (1978a, 14). The ensuing discussion examines their ideas before turning to Poulantzas.

Through a critique of Hegel in *Contribution to the Critique of Hegel's Philosophy of Law* (1843), Marx acknowledged the separation of state from civil society and provided a rudimentary theory of the state, although he did not elaborate his theory in a systematic manner. Whereas the state is conceptualized briefly in later works with Engels such as *The German Ideology* (1845–46) and *Manifesto of the Communist Party* (1848), Marx works out a more complex class theory of the state in *Class Struggles in France, 1848 to 1850* (1850), *The Eighteenth Brumaire* (1852), and "Critique of the Gotha Programme" (1875). Several themes appear in these works: the distinction between the economic base and the political superstructure in which the state is a reflection of the capitalist economy and where political struggles are but illusions of the real conflict among classes; the state as an instrument of the ruling class, a perspective found in the *Manifesto* where the executive of the modern state is recognized as a committee that manages the affairs of the bourgeoisie; the perspective that the state is a means of cohesion of socially necessary and class interests in the social formation; and the assumption that the state is an "institutional ensemble," allowing the adoption of "an institutional approach in combination with a firm grasp of Marxist political economy and an historical appreciation of the nature of class and popular-democratic struggles" (Jessop 1982, 23). It is possible to identify theoretical fragments, but no unitary and coherent theory of the state is discernible in the thought of Marx.

In *On the Origins of the Family, Private Property, and the State* (1884), Engels emphasized that "a power, apparently standing above society, became necessary for the purpose of moderating the conflict and keeping it within the bounds of 'order'; and this power, arising out of society, but placing itself above it and increasingly alienating itself from it, is the state . . . ." (Engels, n.d., 148). Under capitalism the state assumes many of the functions necessary in society because of the estrangement between public and private life, the division of labor resulting in social classes, and the fragmentation of society into competing private interests. The state legitimizes the right of individuals to pursue particular interests through the possession of private property, which promotes inequality and disunity among people.

Lenin extended this analysis in *State and Revolution* (1918) by insisting that the state does not reconcile class conflict but ensures the oppression of one class by another. He believed that state power must be destroyed through violent revolution and that reformist solutions would not mitigate class antagonisms. Gramsci defined the state as "the entire complex of practical and theoretical activities with which the ruling class not only justifies and maintains its dominance, but manages to win the active consent of those over whom it rules" (Gramsci 1971, 244).

Gramsci (1957) focused on bourgeois hegemony in civil society, an idea that one writer has characterized as "the ideological predominance of bourgeois values and norms over the subordinate classes" (Carnoy 1984, 66). He located the hegemony of the bourgeoisie in such a manner as to show that the state functioned as a coercive apparatus of the bourgoisie to the extent of being "involved in reproducing the relations of production" (Carnoy 1984, 66). Hegemony thus became the means whereby the dominant class established its view and shaped the interests and needs of other classes. It also became "a process in civil society whereby a fraction of the dominant class exercises control through its moral and intellectual leadership over other allied fractions of the dominant class" (Carnoy 1984, 70).

Contemporary Marxist thinkers extrapolate various interpretations from these theories of the state. First, the state is viewed as an instrument of the ruling class, which influences public policies through its control and ownership of production; the work of English scholar Ralph Miliband (1969), exemplified this perspective. Second, the state is often seen as autonomous and not a passive tool of the ruling class. Autonomy is apparent especially in "exceptional" periods such as during the empire of Louis Napoleon Bonaparte from 1852 to 1870. Poulantzas (1973, 1975) combined this notion with a structural interpretation that was popular among French social theorists of his time. The contrasting views of Poulantzas (1969, 1976) and Miliband (1970, 1973) stimulated widespread debate over the nature of the state during the 1970s. Third, in opposition to instrumentalist and structuralist theories, the state may be seen as consisting of institutional apparatuses and bureaucratic organizations, norms, and rules that represent legitimate authority and a monopoly of coercive force in regulating the public and private spheres of society; influenced by the Frankfurt School and by the Weberian understanding of bureaucracy, Claus Offe (1972, 1975) represented this "political" view. A fourth perspective is "derived" from Marx's theory of capital and political economy and assumes that through intervention and policy the state can build infrastructure that stimulates and ensures capital accumulation. Analysis of the state depends on the constraints and limitations that capitalist accumulation places on the state; German writers such as Joachim Hirsch (1978) advanced this position. Finally, emphasis is given to politics and democracy; whereas bourgeois democracy involves representation of the bourgeoisie in or direct control over parliament so as to mystify the actions of the state administration and deceive the masses, proletarian democracy allows the direct and continuous participation of people in the affairs of society and government—struggle over these positions was evident, especially in the Portuguese revolutionary period of 1974 and 1975. Given the lack of a unified theory, a class theory of the state can employ these various approaches as relevant to conditions of particular states, their forms and apparatuses (see Carnoy 1984; Jessop 1982, for elaboration of these and other approaches).

Marx also did not delineate an explicit theory of class. In the *Manifesto* he and Engels emphasized two classes under capitalism; capitalist owners of the means of production and wage laborers who sell their labor power in order to subsist. The conception of class in the studies of midnineteenth-century France embraced a variety of classes, including the aristocracy, financial bourgeoisie, industrial bourgeoisie, petty bourgeoisie, peasantry, lumpenproletariat, industrial proletariat, bourgeois monarchy, and big bourgeoisie. In the last chapter of the third volume of *Capital,* Marx referred to three big classes—landowners, industrial capitalists, and workers—yet he also identified less important groups. These categories of class may assist in a class analysis of the state, and some of them are employed in our analysis of Spain, Portugal, and Greece.

Contemporary Marxist thinkers also develop different and conflicting theories of class from the analysis of Marx. One of the important controversies focuses on the class position of salaried intermediary workers (who Marx identifies in his brief last chapter of volume three of *Capital*) and their role in the class struggle, how to define the boundary between the intermediate class and the working class, and the political question of whether the intermediate classes will align with the proletariat or bourgeoisie or find a third position. Poulantzas was particularly interested in this question, and his analysis stimulated considerable debate. Among the perspectives are Poulantzas' theory of the new petty bourgeoisie (1975); Erik Olin Wright's theory of class structure and exploitation (1985); Guglielmo Carchedi's theory of the new middle class (1977); and Barbara and John Ehrenreich's theory of the professional-managerial class (1977) (see Burris, 1987, for a useful analysis of these various theories).

Another controversy addresses the issues of deterministic and reductionist class analysis by insisting that Marxian theory is class theory in terms of overdetermination: "the Marxian view assigns no priority to economic over noneconomic aspects of society as determinants of one another. All the different aspects shape and are shaped by all the others. No one part of a society, neither the economy nor any other part, determines the whole society. Every aspect of society, including the economic, is overdetermined by all the others" (Wolff and Resnick 1987, 134). In the concluding chapter I return to this theme because Poulantzas, although faithful to Marxism, offered a revision of his class theory of the state, and I believe that the shift in his thinking was based on his personal experience and interpretation of the transition to democracy in Southern Europe. This in turn led many scholars to a movement away from class analysis, and Wolff and Resnick help to bring the entire debate back into perspective by sharply distinguishing between Marxian and neoclassical theory: "what differentiates Marxists is their view that theories and explanations are all partial, their own included, while neoclassical theorists presume that final causes of events exist and that their theory can and will disclose them in a finished and completed explanation" (Wolff and Resnick 1987, 21).

The search for a class theory of the state in the study of transitions from dictatorship to democracy suggests a focus on the form of the state that evolves from the relations of production in a capitalist society where the state is the political expression of the class structure and the contributions of accumulation inherent in production. I believe it important to avoid economistic analysis that concentrates on the economic base or infrastructure of society in isolation from class relations of production, at the same time being careful not to overemphasize political concepts or to examine superstructure (the state and its apparatuses) without recognizing the need for a materialist critique of political economy. Concentration on political institutions may lead to static analysis; the appearance of political parties, for example, may divert attention from the locus of power in the state and economy. This search for a class theory of the state prompts a number of questions, however. For example, to what extent are the form and function of the state determined by relations of class within the capitalist mode of production and what determines how successful it will be? Must the capitalist class mobilize the state as a counterforce to the crises of capitalism, and what determines how successful it will be? Does the state bureaucracy operate independently of the capitalist class, yet serve the interests of that class because of dependence on capitalist accumulation? Is the state an arena for class conflict? Does the bourgeoisie in certain instances delegate power to the bureaucracy to act on behalf of the ruling class and preserve political interests? Or is autonomy the rule in "exceptional" periods when all classes are unable to rule and a Bonapartist personality assumes power and plays off the classes against each other? What of the contradictions between the constraints of an autonomous state and a bourgeoisie that no longer is content with Bonapartist rule or a restless proletariat that threatens revolt? Can the state successfully manage and implement programs and policies that represent competing and contradictory interests of different classes? Can the state serve to permit and stimulate direct and continuous participation of the populace in government and society? If bourgeois and proletarian democracy are incompatible, must workers seize the state and its apparatuses, as Lenin advocated? Can workers find their place within the bourgeois state or should they establish a parallel organization to exert demands for participatory democracy?

These questions help in understanding the events of 1974 and 1975, and although they guide us in the case studies of Spain, Portugal, and Greece, we have not found answers to all of them. They remain central to theoretical debates today in Europe and in other parts of the world where democratic openings have appeared. They are important because in many countries social democratic and democratic socialist regimes have come to power through an electoral process. Once in power these regimes must decide whether their systems will transcend representative and bourgeois forms of government and institutionalize direct participation of all people in their own affairs. In their advocacy of some form of socialism, they must also face the question of to what extent the means of production can be socialized.

As is evident in our ensuing analysis, we initiate our search for a class theory of the state through careful examination of the Poulantzas approach, which yielded a useful but controversial interpretation in the heat of complex and rapidly changing events; in hindsight our own analysis reveals problems with that interpretation, and we are inclined not to settle at the outset on a rigid theoretical formulation to guide us in our own work but to test various theories through the experience in Southern Europe. Whatever his faults, Poulantzas demonstrated that theory can lead to a basis for comparison as well as insights and understandings beyond the descriptive accounts that characterize most studies of the region. At minimum, we hope to be able to suggest a theoretical approach that could lead to a more definitive analysis of the cases under study.

We believe that, whereas the Marxist tradition yields a variety of approaches and that one need not rely on a particular "correct" theory, our work differs substantially from other comparative studies of Southern Europe. For example, Beate Kohler (1982) focused on political developments in Spain, Portugal, and Greece with attention to political parties and parliaments that acted to counter the authoritarian forces that continued to dominate in the democratic period. He noted that only in Portugal had any transformation of social power taken hold, but he explained the shift to the right after the revolutionary period of 1974–75 as a reaction to the economic crisis and despair over unrealistic socialist aspirations, which led to increasingly conservative politics. He believed that links with the European Economic Community gave support to the domestic political configuration. His analysis of the Greek transition was based on the ties binding civil service, power groups, and the army, which opposed social change. Political stability in Spain he saw as threatened by regional disparities. His account tends to be descriptive, with particular attention to institutional forces; there is little theoretical perspective, and the comparative discussion looks to common patterns emerging from the experience of the three cases.

Likewise, most of the essays edited by Geoffrey Pridham (1984) tend to present overviews of major events and historical processes in the nascent democracies, with attention to political parties, monarchies, armed forces, and so on. No common theoretical basis underlies the descriptive analysis, although Pridham has drawn briefly upon a model of transition to democracy suggested by Dankwart Rustow (in the form of preparatory, decision, and habituation phases), but the model is not examined in specific cases. He also showed the usefulness and limitations of historical and political science approaches, identified a number of mainstream approaches that might be useful in comparative political analysis, offered comparisons within Southern Europe and between that region and the rest of the continent, suggested the need to look at political culture as well as institutions, and confirmed the viability of a Mediterranean model of "liberal democracy."

Guillermo O'Donnell, Philippe C. Schmitter, and Laurence Whitehead (1986) have provided some elements of theory with the recent historical experience of regime change and transitions from democratic rule. Schmitter argued that most countries of Southern Europe (Spain, Portugal, Greece, and Italy, with Turkey the exception) generally conform to "the range of institutional variation and patterns of political conflict characteristic of Western Europe as a whole" (1986, I:3). Regime transitions are the outcome of replacing authoritarian rule with political democracies. A mainstream liberal bourgeois or social democratic consensus has supplanted illusions of popular democracy or Mediterranean socialism, terrorist movements have failed, and the Soviet model has been discarded by most Communist parties: "Western Europe offers a variety of experiences and formulas from which prospective democratizers can learn and all provide some assurance of legitimate acceptance." (O'Donnell et al. 1986, I:9). Although Schmitter believes that authoritarian rule always remains a threat and much of the Left rejects political democracy in principle, "four of the five Southern European countries have been belatedly entering into the range of institutional and behavioral variation characteristic of contemporary Western Europe" (O'Donnell et al. 1986, I:10). In his essay, O'Donnell affirmed that their "project had from the outset a normative bias . . . We have considered political democracy as desirable per se . . . [a revolutionary path is unlikely] for countries that have reached some minimal degree of stateness and social complexity, and concomitantly, of expansion of capitalist social relations" (1986, II:10).

Thus advocacy of political democracy in its liberal and social democratic variants pervades both the Pridham and O'Donnell et al. essays and gives them a common theme in this collection. Salvador Giner modified the theme slightly with an analysis of socialism in the world of corporate liberalism and of democratic socialism in contrast to the Marxism-Leninism advocated by the Communist parties. He saw socialists in Southern Europe as attaining a process of modernizing reformism in which socialism has meant the democratic transition to constitutional consolidation (in Pridham 1984, 155–56). Further, socialism also has been integrated with corporate society, its pluralism, civil rights, and democratic organization and growth of the state bureaucracy and other large formal organizations such as trade unions, employer associations, and so on: "It is also a society in which class conflict, market trends, and personal and collective social integration are nearly always mediated by the presence of the all-pervading 'corporations': they are redefined, filtered, and governed by them" (O'Donnell et al. 1986, II:40). He suggested that socialism must transcend the constraints that result in "a displacement of its immediate goals from revolution to the rationalization and modernization of the existing society. This shift is not only the result of fears of a violent reaction by the rightwing opposition and its powerful reactionary allies but is also the consequence of far-reaching changes in the very texture of those societies" (O'Donnell et al. 1986, II:43). Advocating a stronger position, Arthur MacEwan insisted that O'Donnell and colleagues push for political democratic rules and procedures without serious attention to social and economic inequalities that face these countries; he favors democracy in the form of popular power: "Building popular movements that are themselves democratic would seem to be the only way to get where we want to go, even if success seems improbable" (1988, 23). Finally, Nancy Bermeo (1987) looked at redemocratization and elections during the transition in Spain and Portugal. Similar to other comparative studies, she delved into the nature of the regime transformation and the strength of the opposition before the coups, but she also noted the configuration of the class structure during the authoritarian period. Thus Giner, MacEwan, and Bermeo move their discussion toward theory and in the direction of a class analysis, a principal concern of Poulantzas as well as ourselves.

## POULANTZAS' CONTRIBUTION

In an effort to guide the reader into the thinking of Poulantzas, the following summary draws from *The Crisis of the Dictatorships* his ideas on imperialism and the dependent state, dominant and popular classes, state and state apparatuses, hegemony, transitions, and socialism.

During the period of dictatorship, according to Poulantzas, Spain, Portugal, and Greece were dependent on the imperialist metropoles and characterized by exceptional capitalist regimes of fascism, Bonapartism, and military dictatorship. However, he believed that these countries were not underdeveloped because of their relevance to Europe; their dependence affected "a new phase of imperialism" because of the relationship to the United States and the European Economic Community (EEC) (Poulantzas 1976b, 7–8). However, Spain and Portugal historically benefitted from exploitation of their colonies, whereas Greece exploited the Eastern Mediterranean. In turn, their "backwardness" was not the consequence of "underdevelopment" but of delayed industrialization because of attention to agriculture and raw material extraction. The internationalization of capital on a worldscale and the dominance of North American multinationals resulted in the production of most finished goods in these three countries because of a cheap labor and the low cost of production. Poulantzas referred to Spain, Portugal, and Greece as examples of a new organization of the imperialist chain and its associated dependence or dependent industrialization characterized by industry based on low-cost technology, low level of labor productivity, and mostly expatriated profits (1976b, 13–14).

Poulantzas identified the dominant classes as a power bloc of big landed proprietors allied with a comprador big bourgeoisie or "oligarchy" whose interests were tied entirely to those of foreign capital; its economic base was weak, and it functioned as the commercial and financial intermediary for the penetration of foreign capital. In all three countries (Portugal to a lesser extent) the domestic bourgeoisie was dependent on foreign capital and experienced contradictions within its ranks because the rewards of exploitation tended to go to foreign, not domestic, capital.

This domestic bourgeoisie was largely dependent on the internationalization of capital and unable to oppose imperialism. Economically it was "dependent on technological processes and labor productivity, on a complex network of subcontracting for foreign capital, on the sector of light industry and consumer goods"; politically it was weak and unable "to wield long-term political hegemony over the other fractions of the bourgeoisie and the dominant classes, i.e. over the power bloc" (Poulantzas 1976a, 44). Additionally, the contradictions between U.S. and European capitals were "reflected and reproduced actually within the domestic bourgeoisie itself" (1976a, 45). Consequently, the bourgeoisies in these three countries failed to carry out their bourgeois-democratic revolutions and "to establish a bourgeois-ideological discourse with hegemonic character in their social formations" (1976a, 46). At the same time the domestic bourgeoisie, especially in Greece and Portugal, was able to distance itself from the military dictatorship, thereby undermining the compromise between the big comprador bourgeoisie and the state; in particular the domestic bourgeoisie challenged agrarian interests and the power bloc alliance between the comprador bourgeoisie and the large landowners. However, Poulantzas showed that the overthrow of the dictatorships and the ensuing process of democratization under the hegemony of the domestic bourgeoisie was possible without "being telescoped together with a process of transition to socialism and national liberation" (1976a, 66). He argued that the domestic bourgeoisie is doubly underestimated, not just as a force favoring change through the overthrow of the dictatorship and implementation of democracy but as an adversary to popular involvement, especially by the working class, so that "the forms of "democratic" regime that replace the dictatorships run the risk of remaining compromised, for a long period, by the way in which these regimes have been overthrown . . . It is this process that contributes to the characteristic instability of the democratization process in the countries in question" (1976a, 67).

In opposition to the dominant classes the dominated popular classes comprise the numerically weak working class, which exercises little political influence; the peasantry, which is 'subordinated to precapitalist relations of production; the petty bourgeoisie, including traditional interests in small-scale manufacturing and production, handicrafts, and commerce; and the state petty bourgeoisie, which represents the state apparatuses. Poulantzas identified various popular struggles (strikes and absenteeism, and low productivity in disputes over wages and job security; struggle against increases in productivity demanded by the multinationals; struggle for health and services by the new urban middle class; struggle by peasants against proletarianization in the countryside; women's liberation; struggle of intellectuals where the bourgeoisie is weak and unable to establish ideological hegemony) that contributed to but were not decisive nor able to mount a mass movement against the dictatorship. He characterized the new petty bourgeoisie as manifesting a national orientation and being mobilized by the domestic bourgeoisie: "The domestic bourgeoisie has successfully exploited the new petty bourgeoisie's nationalism in its own contradictions with the comprador bourgeoisie (1976a, 73). He examined the ideological domination of the working class and the popular masses manifested through the state apparatuses, their "leading circles," and the "hierarchy" below them—the army, judiciary, or civil administration that maintains touch with the popular masses: "the middle and lower levels of the hierarchy are thus ultimately squeezed between the popular masses and leaders," thus accentuating "very strong internal contradictions between the lower and intermediate levels and the top" (1976a, 85).

In examination of the state and the state apparatuses, Poulantzas made clear that exceptional forms of the state such as fascism, dictatorship, and Bonapartism are incapable of reforming themselves into parliamentary democracies. He argued that one of the functions of the parliamentary form of democratic state is to allow a balance of forces within the power bloc to change without a disruption of the state apparatuses; the exceptional state serves to resolve crises of hegemony within the power bloc and in the relationship of the bloc with the popular masses. He suggested that whereas political parties may serve as a means for organization of the bourgeois state, their role is supplemented by the ideological and repressive apparatuses of the capitalist state that form "strongholds and privileged organizational bulwarks of this or that fraction of the bourgeoisie or component of the power bloc" (1976a, 103). The ideological apparatuses function to elaborate and inculcate ideology, whereas the repressive apparatuses such as the army, police, judiciary, and administration maintain control. Contradictions are apparent within the state: "every bourgeois state is riven by contradictions between its various apparatuses and branches . . . as the organizational bases of one or other fraction and component of the power bloc" (1976a, 104). He noted contradictions in the religious apparatus (the relationship of the church hierarchy to the power bloc was affected by the decline of the landlords, whereas lower levels of the church were influenced by the disaffection of the poor and middle peasantry, the working class, and the petty bourgoisie); the administrative apparatus (entrenched bureaucratic elements affected by technocracy and efforts to rationalize administration); and educational apparatus (influenced by technocratic "liberal" reforms).

Poulantzas emphasized hegemony to explain how unity of state power is maintained within the power bloc: "The unity of the state power, which in the last analysis is that of the hegemonic class or fraction within the power bloc, is expressed in a very complex fashion, by way of a contradictory domination of the branch or apparatus that particularly embodies this class or fraction's power and organization, over the other branches or apparatuses of the state" (1976a, 104). Under the exceptional state and the absence of political parties, the military may serve as the privileged apparatus of the power bloc and becomes "the de facto political party of the bourgeoisie as a whole, under the direction of the hegemonic fraction" (1976a, 106). Under the parliamentary democratic state, a multiparty system may undermine the development of a hegemonic fraction and result in political crisis and unstable government, as in the case of Portugal after 1975.

Poulantzas assumed that transitions to capitalism have occurred in Spain, Portugal, and Greece. Within capitalism he referred to transitions from one form of state (exceptional forms such as fascism, dictatorship, and Bonapartism) to parliamentary democratic forms; changes in state forms thus coincide with changes in regimes, but he did not systematically examine whether other institutional forms changed in any substantial fashion. These transitions do not occur in continuous processes but coincide with political crises or "conjunctures in which contradictions are condensed together and punctuate the rhythm of development of the class struggle" (1976a 90–91). He recognized that a state network tends to persist through the various forms of the bourgeois state, which ultimately must be smashed in order to effect a transition to socialism. In his postscript and reassessment, he confirmed that no transition to socialism was likely, even in revolutionary Portugal, but that there was a possibility of democratization under the hegemony and leadership of the popular masses and their class organizations: "What was really at stake in Portugal . . . was . . . the hegemony and leadership of this democratization process by the popular masses" (1976a, 136). At this point he acknowledged his neglect of "the relative autonomy of the political superstructure in relation to the various classes in struggle" (1976a, 143). He attributed the defeat of popular forces in Portugal to lack of coordination and absence of an alliance among organizations on the Left. He believed that the popular masses must organize forms of popular power at the base (factory councils and peasant committees); they cannot rely on a dual power strategy and a framework of a parallel state, but must win power within the state apparatuses. This "lesson" of the Portuguese experience thus constituted a theoretical revision and suggested in the modern period that a more evolutionary approach to transition was in order. In similar fashion he related the relative autonomy of the Spanish state after the death of Franco to the delayed transition to parliamentary democracy (1976a, 157). Likewise, relative political autonomy contributed to the more advanced democratization process in Greece where a crisis of representation and divisions among left organization also were evident (1976a, 159–61).

The conditions of the late 1970s in these three countries were not conducive to the transition to socialism, according to Poulantzas. First, because of the low level of consciousness of the popular masses under the dictatorships, the politicized segments of the masses lacked the historical experience of open class struggle. Second, the radicalization of the popular masses affected only a minority of the population; in Portugal the domestic bourgoisie broke away as did a good share of professional people, whereas the working class began to divide in the face of an anti-Communist campaign by the Socialists. Third, it was difficult to modify arrangements with NATO and its military bases, and nationalizations did not affect foreign capital. Fourth, the state apparatuses showed resistance to demands of the popular masses, whereas the masses lacked a revolutionary party with a consistent line.

In *Crisis* (1976a) and in his last book, *State, Power, Socialism* (1978b), Poulantzas believed he had resolved the problems of a theory of the capitalist state and that he had contributed significantly to Marxism. Jessop affirms that Poulantzas was "a theorist who claimed to have completed (if not to have discovered) the Marxist theory of the state. . . . Moreover his work reveals shifts in theoretical object that are remarkably similar to those of Marx himself. Both men moved from law to the state and thence to political economy. . . . From an existential-Marxist approach, he attempted to combine Althusserian and Gramscian positions within an essentially Marxist-Leninist outlook and then went on to adopt a left Eurocommunist position similar to that of prewar Austro-Marxism" (Jessop 1985, 314). Jessop believes that Poulantzas provided a breakthrough in state theory by combining three contrasting theoretical tendencies: "French philosophy, Italian politics, and Romano-German law; and he went on to synthesize them in a unique manner within the overarching framework of Marxist political economy" (1985, 332). Jessop's appreciative account is not uncritical, however; he feels Poulantzas exaggerated political elements and that the "politicist" potential is found in each of the three intellectual sources: "the Althusserian notion of relative autonomy and the Foucauldian emphasis on power; the concern with the global role of the state and party in Italian politics; the focus of Romano-German law on juridico-political institutions" (1985, 334). Poulantzas failed to implement a Gramscian approach to political class struggle by focusing instead on structural determinants of state power; he did not effectively apply his legal training to determine how juridico-political institutions and practices affect relative state autonomy; and he could have drawn on Foucault's approach to power and strategy (1985, 334–35).

In summary, his "theory was based on the idea that the state is the material condensation of a relation of forces between classes" (1985, 336). The state is not neutral among classes nor does it represent a general will or a national interest in a rational manner. It is "an institutional ensemble . . . shot through with contradictions and has no political power of its own. The power of the state is the power of the class forces which act in and through the state" (1985, 337). The legacy of this thinking serves as a foundation for the essays in this volume. The task ahead involves a close examination of a class theory of the state and an assessment of how Poulantzas understood Spain, Portugal, and Greece in an important moment of conjuncture and transition. We also update the analysis with attention to such issues as capitalist accumulation and the crisis in the political system; the rise of political parties and representative democracy in tandem with the decline of popular mobilization and direct forms of democracy; and the decline of both right and left political forces and the shift to a mainstream reformulation of the socialist project so emphatically manifested in the years of transitions.

## References

Althusser, Louis, and Luiz Francisco Rebello. 1976. *Cartas sobre a revolução portuguesa*. Lisbon: Seara Nova.

Bermeo, Nancy. 1987. Redemocratization and transition elections: A comparison of Spain and Portugal. *Comparative Politics* 19 (12): 213–31.

Burris, Val. 1987. Class structure and political ideology. *Insurgent Sociologist* 14 (Summer): 5–46.

Carchedi, Guglielmo. 1977. *On the Economic Identification of Social Classes*. London: Routledge and Kegan Paul.

Carnoy, Martin. 1984. *The State and Political Theory*. Princeton, NJ: Princeton University Press.

Claudín, Fernando. 1978. *Eurocommunism and Socialism*. London: NLB.

Ehrenreich, Barbara, and John Ehrenreich. 1977. The professional managerial class. *Radical America* 11 (2).

Engels, Frederick. (n.d.) *The Origins of the Family, Private Property, and the State*. New York: International Publishers.

Gramsci, Antonio. 1957. *The Modern Prince and other Writings*. New York: New York University Press.

———. 1971. *Selections from Prison Notebooks*. New York: International Publishers.

Hirsch, Joaquim. 1978. The state apparatus and social reproduction: Elements of a theory of the bourgeois state," in Holloway and Picciotto.

Holloway, John, and Sol Picciotto (eds.). 1978. *State and Capital: A Marxist Debate*. London: Edward Arnold.

Jessop, Bob. 1977. Recent theories of the capitalist state. *Cambridge Journal of Economics* (4): 353–73.

———. 1982. *The Capitalist State: Marxist Theories and Methods*. New York: New York University Press.

———. 1985. *Nicos Poulantzas: Marxist Theory and Political Strategy*. London: Macmillan.

Kohler, Beate. 1982. *Political Forces in Spain, Greece, and Portugal*. London: Butterworth.

MacEwan, Arthur. 1988. Transitions from authoritarian rule: A review essay, *Latin American Perspectives* 15 (Summer).

Miliband, Ralph. 1969. *The State in Capitalist Society*. New York: Basic Books.

———. 1970. The capitalist state: Reply to Nicos Poulantzas. *New Left Review* No. 59 (January–February): 53–60.

———. 1973. Poulantzas and the capitalist state. *New Left Review* No. 82 (November–December): 83–92.

O'Donnell, Guillermo, Philippe Schmitter, and Laurence Whitehead (eds.). 1986. *Transitions from Authoritarian Rule: Prospects for Democracy,* Baltimore: Johns Hopkins University Press. Citations to volume on Southern Europe.

Offe, Claus. 1972. "Political authority and class structures—An analysis of late capitalist societies. *International Journal of Sociology* 2 (Spring): 73–108.

———. 1975. Theses on the theory of the state. *New German Critique* No. 6 (Fall), 137–47.

Poulantzas, Nicos. 1969. The problem of the capitalist state. *New Left Review* No. 58 (November–December): 67–78.

———. 1973. *Political Power and Social Classes*. London: NLB.

———. 1975. *Classes in Contemporary Capitalism*. London, NLB.

———. 1976a. The capitalist state: A reply to Miliband and Laclau. *New Left Review* 95 (January–February): 63–83.

———. 1976b. *The Crisis of the Dictatorships: Portugal, Greece, Spain*. London: NLB.

———. 1978a. The state and the transition to socialism. *Socialist Review* 7 (March–April): 9–36. Interview with Henri Weber.

———. 1978b. *State, Power, Socialism*. London: NLB.

Pridham, Geoffrey (ed.). 1984. *The New Mediterranean Democracies: Regime Transition in Spain, Greece, and Portugal*. London: Frank Cass and Co.

Wolff, Richard D., and Stephen Resnick. 1987. *Economics: Marxian versus Neoclassical*. Baltimore: Johns Hopkins Press.

Wright, Erik Olin. 1985. *Classes*. London: NLB.

# Chapter 2

# Bourgeois State and the Rise of Social Democracy in Spain

*Fred A. López III*

---

Spain has witnessed a remarkable series of events: the decay and dismantling of the military dictatorship of Francisco Franco in 1975 after 36 years of rule; its replacement by a democratically elected government under a new constitution in 1979; and the election of the Socialist party to a majority in the Spanish Parliament in 1982, 1986, and most recently in 1989. In the short span of fourteen years, Spain transformed itself from military dictatorship to one of the most stable parliamentary democracies in Europe.

Nicos Poulantzas* offered one of the first theoretical and comparative studies of this transition (1976).[1] Early in 1975 he realized the importance of the transitions taking place in Southern Europe. At first Poulantzas separated important political and strategic questions from his more general theoretical interests, but later he realized the connection between such questions and more general problems in a Marxist theory of the state (Jessop 1985, 263). This led him to write his fourth book, *The Crisis of the Dictatorships*, where he attempted to answer those questions that he felt were important not only for Spain, Portugal, and Greece, but for several other countries, particularly in Latin America, that are similarly marked by authoritarian rule.

Comparative theorizing among scholars in an attempt to explain these transitions includes work by O'Donnell, Schmitter, Whitehead 1987; Balroya 1987; Cammack 1986; Drake and Silva 1986; Herman and Petras 1985; Nef 1986; Richards 1985, 1986; and Needler 1980, 1987.

In this chapter I summarize the main ideas of Poulantzas regarding the

*Unless noted otherwise, all page numbers in parentheses in this chapter refer to Poulantzas 1976 (see References).

transition to democracy in Spain and critically analyze the validity of his assertions as related to events that occurred there in the years since the publication of *The Crisis of the Dictatorships*. I examine the role of the opposition during the transition and offer my thoughts on Spanish democracy today and the prospects of a deepening of the democratization process.

Poulantzas began his analysis of the dictatorships by considering three interrelated areas: the class character of the Spanish military dictatorship as a society undergoing a process of dependent industrialization; the various causes of the regime collapse; and the nature of democratization and its relation to antimonopoly and national liberation struggles in dependent capitalist systems (Jessop 1985, 264–65).

Poulantzas began his analysis of the transition to democracy by locating Spain in what he called the "new world context," or the new phase of imperialism within which a nation tries to modernize and develop. He believed that Spain could no longer be classified as "underdeveloped" in the traditional sense, because it exhibited economic and social features approximating a developed capitalist nation. However, he distinguished it from developed capitalist nations by a particular form of dependence, which he felt was a function of Spain's particular history (p. 10).

This form of dependence was a product of the primitive accumulation of capital deriving from Spain's exploitation of its colonies, and uneven and late industrialization. It was the Catalans who were interested in developing trade and commerce, but who suffered from the politically dominant Castilians and their anticapitalist spirit. Thus Spanish industrial development suffered from a lack of capital investment, inefficient agrarian policies, and a general neofeudal attitude. This led the ruling class to become overly dependent upon exogenous sources of capital accumulation, for example, the gold and silver mines in the New World. Add to this the Hidalgo (nobility) aversion to manual labor and business activities, and the state and church's anticapitalist spirit, and the result was a very weak base for endogenous capital accumulation. Thus from very early on the Spanish economy was dependent upon foreign sources of capital.

Spanish dependence on New World wealth (gold and silver), coupled with the anticapitalist spirit fostered by the clerical state, had a substantial impact upon the socioeconomic structures of the society. The working class in Spain was relatively weak economically and politically due to the preponderance of agriculture and the corresponding delay in the process of industrialization and the primacy placed on the extraction of raw materials. The peasantry, a politically more weighty class, was still subject to precapitalist relations of production. The two other classes were the petty bourgeoisie (composed of small-scale producers and owners, independent craftsmen, and traders) and the bureaucracy or the agents of the state apparatus that are typical of this kind of dependent situation (pp. 11–12).

Under the Franco dictatorship, the ruling class could be characterized by its manifestation in a particular configuration of the power bloc, commonly referred to as the "oligarchy" (see Fig. 2.1). The oligarchy comprised the large land-owning aristocracy, allied to a comprador bourgeoisie concentrated in finance, banking, and commerce. The political weight of the landed aristocracy was very substantial, whereas its economic base in the country was very weak. The comprador bourgeoisie functioned chiefly as a commercial and financial intermediary aiding the penetration of foreign capital, and in turn is controlled by its interests (p. 12).

Poulantzas believed that the present phase of imperialism had its beginnings in the immediate postwar years, consolidating and expanding after 1960. But he noted the changed nature of its function. He believed that the principal function of the export of capital today derives from the need for imperialist monopoly capital to valorize itself on a worldscale by turning to profit every relative advantage in the direct exploitation of labor. This he believed was directly related to a characteristic contradiction of capitalism leading to a long-term decline in the rate of profit. To counteract this tendency, the metropolitan countries seek other means by which to extract relative surplus value. This usually takes the form of exploiting every possible relative advantage that core countries have vis à vis the periphery such as raising labor productivity or through technological innovation. It also leads to a reproduction of capitalist relations of production within the dependent country itself, and the increased subordination of labor power. Within the country labor power is exploited because capitalists buy workers' labor power

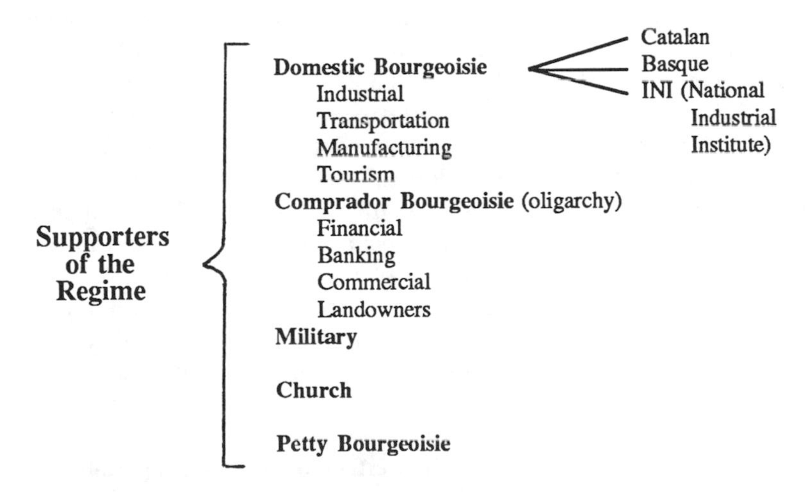


**Figure 2.1** Poulantzas' view of the power bloc (dominant classes) under the Franco dictatorship.

at a wage equal to its value, but extract labor greater than the equivalent of that wage (pp. 12–13).

Poulantzas believed that these changes in the current phase of imperialism have serious implications for Spain and other dominated or dependent countries. He noted that foreign capital in Spain since 1959 had taken the form of direct investment in the sector of productive industrial capital (p. 13). He cited an increase of foreign investment from $36.1 million in 1960 to approximately $180 million in 1968, concentrated in the chemical industry, electrical equipment and heavy engineering, and various other manufacturing industries (p. 16). He argued that the Franco dictatorship favored the path of dependent industrialization under the aegis of foreign capital, because of the interests that it represented (the comprador-agrarian bloc, or oligarchy), which benefitted greatly from this type of dependent development.

Initially, U.S. capital dominated the process of dependent industrialization in Spain, following an upward curve from 1961 to 1965, rising from 27.8 percent to 48.3 percent of the total (p. 25). But the U.S. position later was challenged by European Economic Community (EEC) capital investment so that by 1970 U.S. capital in the total volume of foreign investment had fallen to 29.2 percent of the total (p. 25). Poulantzas believed that this created a substantial contradiction between the United States and the European Common Market, which were competing for raw materials, export opportunities, protected markets, and staging posts (Jessop 1985, 265). This led to a polarization of various fractions of the ruling class toward either American or European capital, causing a "destabilized hegemony" within the power bloc and eventually led to the crisis of the dictatorship.

The percentage of American capital in the total volume of foreign investment followed an upward curve from 1960 to around 1965, rising from 27.8 percent to 48.3 percent of the total. Table 2.1 reveals that by the end of 1975 the U.S. investment was 40.6 percent of total foreign investment in Spain. By 1980 this figure had dropped to 29.4 percent. The countries of the EEC, especially France, Holland, and Germany, accounted for the difference in the decline of U.S. investment during the 1975–80 period.

This led Poulantzas to question the contradiction between the United States and the EEC in the decline and fall of the dictatorship (pp. 26, 28). He believed that the contradiction did not contribute directly to the breakdown of the regime because it was not between two equivalent counterimperialisms contending for hegemony step by step; rather the contradiction revolved around a rearrangement in the balance of forces, but always under the hegemony of the United States (p. 28).

Thus he believed that the principal effect of the interimperialist contradictions was to create an instability of hegemony for the power bloc, stemming from intensified struggle between competing fractions of the bourgeoi-

**Table 2.1**
**Distribution of foreign investments according to county of origin in the 1960s and 1970s[a]**

| | Countries of Destination | | | | |
|---|---|---|---|---|---|
| Countries Capital Origin | Italy 1974 % | U.K. 1974 % | Germany 1974 % | Spain 1960–75 % | Spain 1976–80 % |
| Great Britain | 6.2 | — | 10.2 | 10.1 | 4.5 |
| Germany | 3.3 | 2.6 | — | 10.6 | 12.0 |
| Belgium & Luxembourg | 7.2 | 3.2 | 5.5 | 2.1 | 1.1 |
| France | 3.8 | 2.5 | 6.3 | 5.4 | 10.4 |
| Italy | — | 1.5 | 1.1 | 2.1 | 1.8 |
| Holland | 3.4 | 5.1 | 12.8 | 4.4 | 6.9 |
| Other Countries of Europe | 12.1 | 5.5 | 3.2 | 3.5 | 7.3 |
| Switzerland | 35.1 | 7.5 | 15.4 | 16.7 | 13.3 |
| U.S. | 24.3 | 55.6 | 44.1 | 40.6 | 29.4 |
| Rest | 4.5 | — | 15.4 | 4.5 | 13.3 |
| TOTAL | 100.0 | 100.0 | 100.0 | 100.0 | 100.0 |

[a] Cited in Banco Urquijo, *La economía española en la década de los 80* (Madrid: Alianza Editorial, S.A., 1982), p. 349.

*Source:* Libre Empresa, *La industria española ante la CEE,* May–August 1978.

sie. This instability allowed the domestic bourgeoisie (primarily located in Catalonia and the Basque country) to distance itself from the dictatorship and to seek closer links with the EEC as a counterweight to the United States (pp. 26–40). The domestic bourgeoisie is distinguished from both the comprador and national bourgeoisie fractions by being neither totally subordinated to foreign capital, as is the comprador fraction, nor totally independent of foreign capital, as is a truly "national bourgeoisie." Thus Poulantzas believed that the decay of the Franco regime corresponded to a redistribution of the balance of forces within the power bloc in favor of the fraction of capital polarized toward the European Common Market; in this case the domestic bourgeoisie encompassed the indigenous bourgeoisie, under the leadership of the Catalan and Basque bourgeoisies, but also included a section of public capital under the control of the National Industrial Institute, or Instituto Nacional de Industria (INI).

On June 29, 1970, Spain signed a treaty granting it special treatment in its trade with the Common Market countries. The treaty granted Spain substantial tariff concessions and reciprocated with practically negligible tariff reductions (Lieberman 1985, 43; Biescas 1980, 100–103). Spain formally requested full participation and membership in the EEC on July 28, 1977, because integration held out the promise of over 250 million new consumers for Spanish exporters. Yet, exports from Spain to Common Market countries increased only 1.1 percent between 1973 and 1980 from 47.8 percent of total exports to 48.9 percent (Servicio de Estudios del Banco Urquijo 1980, 312, 313, 317). Imports to Spain from the Common Market during the same period fell slowly from 42.9 percent of total imports to 30.7 percent (Servicio 1980, 312–13, 317). Spanish exports to the United States fell from 13.9 percent in 1973 to 5.3 percent in 1980; imports from the United States to Spain also fell from 16.1 percent to 13.0 percent (Servicio 1980, 314, 317).

These data call into question Poulantzas' assertion that the decline of the dictatorships corresponded to a redistribution of the balance of forces within the power bloc in favor of the fraction of capital polarized toward the Common Market. It is thus useful to ask why there was no substantial increase in trade with the Common Market or a marked decline in trade with the United States.

According to Poulantzas, the domestic bourgeoisie enjoyed a significant degree of autonomy from foreign capital, which the comprador bourgeoisie did not due to its complete dependence on foreign capital. The comprador bourgeoisie functioned as a staging post or direct intermediary for the implantation and reproduction of foreign capital in the country (p. 42). The comprador bourgeoisie, he believed, was represented by a highly concentrated banking and financial sector, with industrial banks in the lead. This sector of the bourgeoisie was the true support and agent of foreign imperialist capital (primarily American), and these fractions of the Spanish bourgeoisie support and maintain the military dictatorship (pp. 42–43).

Located primarily in the industrial and manufacturing centers of Catalonia and the Basque country, and to a lesser extent Madrid, the domestic bourgeoisie favored European capital and democracy as a counterweight to the privileged position of the comprador bourgeoisie and foreign capital, both of which preferred an exceptional capitalist state, i.e., dictatorship. The domestic bourgeoisie felt cheated in its share of the exploitation of the masses, preferring industrial development less polarized toward the exploitation of the country by foreign capital, state protected markets at home, and an extension of the home market (p. 43). The domestic bourgeoisie pressed for a return to democracy so that it could achieve more effective representation of its specific interests, secure long-term political gains from its economic concessions to the popular masses, and enhance its prospects of reorganizing the power bloc under its own hegemony (pp. 41–47, 57–58).

Poulantzas emphasized the weaknesses of the Spanish domestic bourgeoisie and its inability to lead a truly anti-imperialist struggle, because it was not truly independent of foreign capital. In fact, the development of the domestic bourgeoisie coincided with the new phase of imperialism and the induced reproduction of the dominant relations of production within Spain. So to a great extent the domestic bourgeoisie was itself dependent upon the process of internationalization under the aegis of foreign capital (pp. 43–44), which explains why this fraction of the bourgeoisie was unable to wield long-term political hegemony over other fractions of the bourgeoisie within the power bloc. In light of the internal contradictions between the domestic bourgeoisie and the comprador bourgeoisie, and the many weaknesses of the former, Poulantzas questions what role the domestic bourgeoisie played in the transition to democracy in Spain.

In 1957 General Franco reshuffled his cabinet by bringing in a team of Opus Dei technocrats; their ostensible aim was to reorganize and reintegrate the Spanish economy back into the capitalist world economy, and bring it out of its state of crisis. In 1959 these technocrats implemented a stabilization plan, which achieved that objective and reduced the political weight of the landed oligarchy to the benefit of the financial and commercial fractions of the comprador bourgeoisie. Finance capital soon reached a position of economic and political hegemony leading to a deepening of the contradictions within the power bloc and a need for a form of state that would permit the circulation of hegemony through forms of organic representation such as parliamentary government and other democratic forms (p. 48).

Initially, the Spanish domestic bourgeoisie opted for a strategy of "normalization" or "liberalization," or a policy of internal evolution. The first government of Arias Navarro was unable to implement this, according to Poulantzas, due to the specific structure of the regime and its apparatuses. There did not exist any mechanisms for the regulated and orderly functioning of class representation as the political organizations of the power bloc such as political parties had been eliminated (pp. 48–49).

As a result, the domestic bourgeoisie opted for a strategy of shifting the weight of dependence toward the EEC in an effort to readjust the balance of forces to their advantage. Part of this strategy included a new partial alliance with the subordinated classes. Poulantzas noted that the general policy of the Spanish domestic bourgeoisie toward the popular masses, and the working class in particular, evolved into a more open and conciliatory position with regard to their demands. In Spain, this took the form of acceptance of trade unionism as a necessary evil by the domestic bourgeoisie, specifically the recognition of two new institutions: the *jurados de empresa* (shop steward committees) and *convenios colectivos* (a system of collective bargaining) (pp. 54–55; Maravall 1978, 26–29). The primary purpose of this shift in policy by the domestic bourgeoisie was to increase productivity within industry and the rationalization in organization of work methods (Maravall 1978, 27). The Spanish domestic bourgeoisie, according to Poulantzas, needed genuine representatives of the working class with which to negotiate and thereby resolve wage disputes. This led to the semilegal existence of the Spanish Communist party, or Partido Comunista de España (PCE)-dominated Workers' Commissions or Comisiones Obreras (CCOO), which originally constituted a movement of autonomous shop floor committees and later an organized trade union (Maravall 1978, 30–32; Ariza 1976). The Workers' Commissions were regarded by the domestic bourgeoisie as a potentially promising development of the official trade unions.

Added to this was the desire of the domestic bourgeoisie to win the support of the popular masses and working class in the struggle against the "oligarchy." Poulantzas believed that the Spanish domestic bourgeoisie was willing to pay the price of democratization, especially if that coincided with its own aspirations, which was to tilt the balance of forces within the power bloc to its relative advantage (p. 56). As proof of this, Poulantzas cited the formation in 1974 of the Democratic junta, or Junta Democrática, a coalition consisting of the PCE, the Workers' Commissions, the Popular Socialist party, or Partido Socialista Popular (PSP), the Carlist party, or Partido Carlista, the Andalucian Socialist Alliance, or Alianza Socialista Andaluza, and such independents as Rafael Calvo Serér, Antonio García Trevijano, and José Vidal Beneyto (p. 58). Some of the principal aims of this coalition were the establishment of a provisional government, total amnesty, the legalization of all political parties, union liberties, separation of church and state, and eventual Spanish entry into the EEC (Mujal León 1983, 138). Poulantzas believed that the monopoly sectors of the domestic bourgeoisie would lead the struggle, drawing the nonmonopoly sectors in their wake (p. 57).

Poulantzas identified a relationship of the domestic and comprador bourgeoisie to the Spanish ruling bloc: between a domestic bourgeoisie oriented toward Common Market capital and democracy, and a comprador bourgeoisie oriented toward U.S. capital and maintenance of the dictatorship (see Fig. 2.2). He maintained that after 1959 modernization and development under the aegis of foreign capital created two dichotomous sectors in the bourgeoisie; one, the domestic bourgeoisie, oriented toward an industrial development less polarized in the exploitation of the country by foreign capital; and the other, the comprador bourgeoisie (or oligarchy) entirely subordinated to the interests of foreign capital (primarily American), serving as a direct intermediary for its implantation and reproduction within the country (pp. 41–43). By virtue of its hegemonic position within the power bloc, the comprador bourgeoisie captured most of the surplus value extracted from the exploited masses at the expense of the domestic bourgeoisie. This provoked the domestic bourgeoisie into an uneasy alliance with the popular classes in an effort to "liberalize" the regime and shift the balance of forces in their favor. Also, progressive sectors of the comprador bourgeoisie, the military, and the church weakened the hegemonic alliance by openly advocating a return to democracy. At the same time, Poulantzas warned that

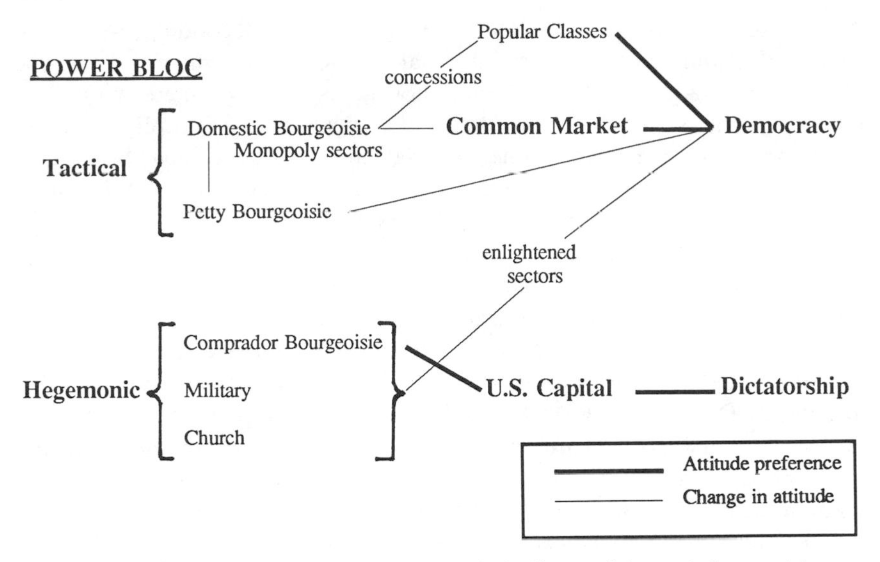


**Figure 2.2** Poulantzas' view of the new tactical alliance of domestic bourgeoisie.

the domestic bourgeoisie was not a genuine national bourgeoisie, a bourgeoisie independent of the influence of foreign capital that could promote an independent national development (p. 43).

One prominent Spanish author has noted the importance of the fragmentation of the ruling class in Spain, the plans for liberalization stemming from a fraction of these classes within a context of popular pressure, and the attempt to form a bourgeois party and the limits within which this fraction attempts to contain the process of democratization (Maravall 1981, 21, 1982, 7). He and several other scholars have noted that the division between comprador and domestic fractions of the bourgeoisie does not square with Spanish reality (Maravall 1982, 7–8, 1981, 20–21; Giner and Salcedo 1976, 360–62; Jessop 1985, 280–81; Aramberri 1979, 174–75).

In a penetrating critique and analysis of the work of Nicos Poulantzas, Salvador Giner and Juan Salcedo (1976, 344–65) concluded that the duality of comprador and domestic bourgeoisie could be "somewhat applicable" to both Greece and Portugal, and could "more or less" fit some aspects of the Spanish bourgeoisie during the nineteenth century, up to the outbreak of World War I. They suggested that the empirically testable truth was that the comprador bourgeoisie was actually "internal" (oriented toward internal development, and the "internal" or domestic bourgeoisie is really external (oriented toward external demand) (Giner and Salcedo 1976, 362). They stated that the so-called comprador bourgeoisie in the Basque country and Catalonia was largely responsible for the creation of the industrial infrastructure of those regions and the Catalan bourgeoisie was independent, self-sufficient, and stimulated their own industrial development (Giner and Salcedo 1976, 361). In addition, the "internal" bourgeoisie, represented by interests linked to light or semiheavy industry, was dependent on foreign capital, technology, and investment. Giner and Salcedo concluded that "Spain now finally possesses a single and unified upper class, in contrast with its structured pluralism in other respects" (1976, 362).

Julio Rodríquez Aramberri similarly called into question Poulantzas' structured and economic division of the ruling bloc into comprador and domestic bourgeoisie fractions as artificial and not corresponding to reality. He felt that this dichotomy did nothing to explain why banking capital moved toward Suárez's Union of Democratic Center, or Unión de Centro Democrático (UCD), which in Poulantzas' terms would represent the domestic bourgeoisie, and not toward the right-wing Popular Alliance, or Alianza Popular (AP) (Aramberri 1979, 175).

Poulantzas warns that the distinction between comprador and domestic bourgeoisie is not a statistical and empirical distinction, permanently fixed for all time. Rather, it is a tedential differentiation whose concrete configuration depends on the conjuncture (p. 45). In this way Poulantzas explains how a fraction of capital, originally dependent upon foreign capital, may acquire a relative autonomy and gradually become a part of the domestic bourgeoisie. The reverse process is also possible. The autochtonic bourgeoisie may gradually "fall under the thumb of foreign capital" (p. 45). It seems clear that Poultanzas believed that a constant reclassification should take place to take into account the various moments and phases of the process of internationalization of capital, and its expression in each social formation.

Maravall denied that the economic development that took place in Spain after 1957 was under the aegis of foreign capital. Nor did he believe that this gave rise to a powerful "comprador" bourgeoisie that supports the dictatorship, or a "national" bourgeoisie that led the fight for democratization of the regime due to its "strategic" interests. Rather, drawing on the model outlined by C. Moya in *El poder económico en España,* Maravall argued that Spanish economic development from 1939 on resembled the "Prussian" model of economic growth in which a "financial aristocracy" allies with the state and takes advantage of an economically and politically weak bourgeoisie (1982, 7). Maravall highlighted four main aspects of the role played by the financial aristocracy and its connection with the Spanish state. First, the symbiotic relationship between the banks and large industrial concerns results from the control of industrial capital by financial capital. To support this claim, Maravall recalled that in 1956 five banks controlled 51 percent of Spanish capital, and in the 1960s, seven of the 112 banks in the country managed 70 percent of all foreign resources, granted 60 percent of all loans, held 90 percent of all private assets, and exercised direct control over a fourth of Spain's 200 largest industrial enterprises (1982, 7–8). Even after the government passed a comprehensive reform law for commercial and industrial banks in 1962, the *Ley de Bases,* there was very little change, and those changes brought about by the reform law seemed more of form than substance and in many areas could be interpreted only as a strengthening of state intervention (Wright 1977, 103–4).

The second aspect noted by Maravall regarded the link between the aristocracy and the financiers. He believed that beginning with the liberal disentailment of the midnineteenth century, the financial elite of the bourgeoisie was coopted by the aristocracy and thus formed a "national ruling class" (Maravall 1982, 8).

Third, Maravall believed that the political significance of this financial aristocracy was demonstrated by the economic support this national ruling class gave to Francisco Franco and the nationalists. The Bank of Spain played a major role in support of the nationalists, and its board of directors was dominated by the financial oligarchy (Maravall 1982, 8).

Finally, the Francoist state promoted capital formation through the Spanish state's holding company, the INI. Created in 1941, the INI cooperated very closely with the financial aristocracy in an effort to encourage and supplement development within the private sector, which was reluctant to diversify and modernize production without substantial state guarantees. Citing Moya, Maravall noted that half of the important board positions of the INI were occupied by members of the financial aristocracy (1982, 18: fn. 19). This may account for nearly 90 percent of the INI's investments being financed by direct grants of credit from the Bank of Spain in 1960 (Medhurst 1973, 154). The aforementioned denials of the existence of a dichotomous comprador and a domestic bourgeoisie and Maravall's assertion that a financial oligarchy wields economic power in Spain were supported by many facts that Poulantzas seems to have overlooked.

The Spanish banking system is dominated by seven major banks or banking groups frequently referred to as *los siete grandes* (the seven giants). These banks are consistently profitable and pay out large dividend payments. Part of the reason for the Spanish banking communities' high profitability in the 1970s when all seven major banks between 1977 and 1979 recorded double-digit profits stems from bank linkages with the Spanish energy industry as attested in an interesting essay by Thomas D. Lancaster (1985, 168–201). He identified overlapping directorates and showed how major banks dominate several of the electricity company's boards, and have direct representation on the Nuclear Energy Council (JEN), and control private petroleum refineries:

> The Spanish bank's overlapping directorates with the electricity companies, the refineries, CAMPSA, JEN, and other non-energy-related companies rein-

> forces the banking industry's own cohesion. The banking officials' common interests in maximizing profits and their working relationship in electricity, refining, and other enterprises in which they share information and common perspectives motivates oligarchical tendencies. This oligarchical behavior is continually reinforced (Lancaster 1985, 190).

Poulantzas incorrectly distinguished the interests in the INI, which he believed was part of the domestic bourgeoisie (p. 42), from the interests of the financial, banking, and commercial sectors, or the comprador fractions of the bourgeoisie (pp. 42–43). After 1939 the financial aristocracy played an important role in the creation of Spain's national industry. The Spanish state under Franco was largely responsible for the creation of a new industrial infrastructure through the INI. The INI, therefore, was a close collaborator of the financial aristocracy throughout the Franco regime.

## POLITICAL AND STRATEGIC QUESTIONS

The above observations of the transition to democracy in Spain led Poulantzas to consider some very important political and strategic questions for the European Left regarding the correct strategy in the struggle for democracy and socialism. Among the questions was whether it is correct for the main resistance organizations of the popular masses, and the Communist parties in particular, to accept an alliance with the domestic bourgeoisie, with the precise and limited objective of overthrowing the dictatorship, and under whose hegemony would this alliance be made? The answer to the first question was an emphatic yes. Poulantzas believed that a tactical alliance with the domestic bourgeoisie at particular conjunctures was possible and necessary in Spain. He also felt that the process occurring in Spain was clearly directed under the hegemony of the domestic bourgeoisie, due to particular historical circumstances (pp. 59–60).

The above political and strategic questions led Poulantzas to consider the more general problem in Marxist state theory of whether the process of democratization, under the hegemony of the domestic bourgeoisie, was compatible with a process of transition to socialism and national liberation. Or, whether the process of democratization was possible because the possibility of a transition to socialism and national liberation was excluded (p. 60).

Poulantzas addressed those questions with a focus on Portugal, although he thought the process taking place in Spain also was applicable. He believed that the transition to democracy in Spain and eventual overthrow of the Franco regime was possible and did not have to correspond with a process of transition to socialism and national liberation, or what he called "telescoping." Poulantzas perhaps thought that the alliance between the popular masses and domestic bourgeoisie in Spain, around the limited objective of the overthrow of the dictatorship, was made possible by the exclusion of this latter possibility. He clearly warned that the domestic bourgeoisie was often doubly underestimated: not just as a possible ally but, more importantly, as an adversary (pp. 66–67). He believed that the transition to bourgeois democracy in Spain represented a victory for the domestic bourgeoisie, and in this respect a weakening of the workers' movement. The transition to democracy in Spain, therefore, was a particularly conditioned democracy and was characterized by a certain degree of instability due to the way in which this regime was dismantled. This instability was highlighted by the trial of two military officers in late 1978 for plotting a coup d'etat (Operation Galaxy) against the young democratic government and the attempted coup of February 23, 1981, where the entire Spanish Córtes, or parliament, was held hostage (Fernandez 1982, 257–99).

Poulantzas seems to have misjudged the anomalous Spanish transition to democracy because he neglected an analysis of the specific strategies and tactics of the parties of the Left (Jessop 1985, 282). Later in this chapter, I address this issue.

## THE ECONOMIC TRANSFORMATION

In 1957, responding to a severe crisis of accumulation marked by a growing balance of payment deficit, Franco reorganized his cabinet and brought in a group of technocrats. Their objective was the reintegration of Spain back into the world capitalist economy. The new government introduced many neocapitalist economic reforms, which culminated in the 1959 Stabilization Plan. It called for a freeze on wages in the public sector, the reduction of governmental spending, tightening of commercial credit, reform of tax laws, the elimination of subsidies, and the adoption of a single exchange rate (Arango 1978, 143; Biescas 1980, 64–68). The participation of Spain in the international capitalist economy also increased with its entry into the International Monetary Fund (IMF), the World Bank (IBRD), and the Organization for Economic Cooperation and Development (OECD).

The reinsertion of Spain into the world capitalist economy resulted in a period of rapid "dependent industrialization" marked by high GNP growth rates (the annual GNP growth was 9.2 between 1960 and 1965) and increasing consumer purchasing power (the annual rate of growth of per capita income between 1960 and 1966 was 7.5) (Maravall 1978, 25). This process of "externally centered" dependent industrialization had a profound impact upon the Spanish social structure, especially the popular classes. The proportion of active population employed in agriculture fell from 42 percent in 1960 to 23 percent in 1974. A process of unprecedented urbanization began, resulting in an increase of people living in cities of over 100,000 inhabitants, from 19.1 percent in 1960 to 32.7 percent in 1965 (Maravall 1978, 25). Industrialization resulted in the proletarianization of the peasantry, an increase in the new middle class of civil servants and liberal professionals, and the decline of the handicraft, manufacturing, and petty bourgeoisie (p. 68).

Poulantzas asserted that the structural changes in the dependent economy gave rise to an increase in class struggle, usually around wages and job security (p. 68). Between 1966 and 1975 the number of industrial disputes increased from 179 to 3,156, and the number of hours lost through strikes increased tenfold (Maravall 1978, 32–33). For Poulantzas these struggles were not always expressed in the form of open strikes, but also in more subtle forms of class resistance—absenteeism, low productivity, and laziness. He noted the increase in struggles over health and social facilities, women's liberation, student demands in education, and thr rise in the struggles of intellectuals (pp. 70–71). He stressed the important role played in these struggles by the new petty bourgeoisie, or nonproductive wage earners, which he distinguished from the traditional petty bourgeoisie, or small-scale producers and owners; he notes that the ideological and political relations between the new petty bourgeoisie and traditional petty bourgeoisie are distinct. He believed this resulted from the convergence of the subjective class positions of the white collar workers with those of the working class. In Spain this convergence was founded on the basis of nationalism, in particular manifested by the nationalist movements of the Basque, Catalan, and Galician petty bourgeoisies.

The Spanish domestic bourgeoisie was able to exploit the nationalism of the petty bourgeoisie in its contradictions with the comprador bourgeoisie. The domestic bourgeoisie also enticed the petty bourgeoisie by advocating policies to which it was particularly sensitive, due to its class position, such as: technocracy, Europeanization, and modernization (p. 73). This contrasted sharply with the role played by the petty bourgeoisie under fascism (p. 72). In sum, the new petty bourgeoisie of liberal professionals and intellectuals played a decisive role in the struggle for democracy because of its major repercussions within the state apparatus (Jessop 1985, 267).

The ties between the Spanish new petty bourgeoisie and state apparatus (repressive and administrative) were very close due to the class origin of its members and the low level of pay, which necessitated that a majority of officers have a second job (Busquets 1967, 132–33). This was significant, according to Poulantzas, because the contradiction between petty bourgeoisie and bourgeoisie cut through the armed forces in a far more direct way than that between the bourgeoisie and working class. This situation was intensified by the upper echelons of the military who tended to act as the political representatives of the bourgeoisie in the absence of parties (pp. 107–8).

Poulantzas believed that the contradictions of the Spanish dictatorship were reflected in the state apparatuses, especially the army, which in an exceptional form of regime such as a military dictatorship was the principal organizer of the power bloc. The unity of the Spanish state was that of the hegemonic fraction of the power bloc (landed oligarchy) expressed through the contradictory domination of the army, which embodied this fraction's power and organization, over the other state apparatuses (ideological and repressive) (pp. 104–5).

Poulantzas believed that the contradictions of the power bloc were particularly acute within the army, precisely because the army was a heirarchic, disciplined, and centralized organization that encountered difficulty in acting as an alternative to a pluralist party state where dominant class disputes are negotiated through a process of bargaining, compromise, and accommodation (Fernández 1982). Thus progressive shifts in strategy, as the balance of forces changes, becomes nearly impossible, resulting in incoherent policies and arbitrary and jerky changes in direction (Jessop 1985, 269). Moreover, whole sections of the armed forces followed the various vertical clans, which represented the contradictions of the power bloc (Fernández 1982). In Spain this opposition was reflected by the split between the Civil Guard and the army. The Civil Guard was the most reactionary, antidemocratic force of the repressive apparatus in Spain, as proved in the unsuccessful coup of February 23, 1981.

Poulantzas extended his analysis of the impact of the internal contradictions on the state apparatus to include the great majority of ideological apparatuses, for example, the church, bureaucracy, schools, trade unions, political parties, and the electronic and print media (p. 117). Recalling the theory developed by Antonio Gramsci, Poulantzas stressed that the state had not only a "coercive" role but also an ideological role, as the "organizer of hegemony." He believed the state included not only public institutions but also those organizations normally referred to as "private." He believed that the same principles that govern the analysis of the military also govern the analysis of the other state apparatuses.

A major section of the Catholic church changed its attitude toward the Franco regime, advocating a return to democracy and civil liberties, a trend particularly evident after the Second Vatican Council (Payne 1984; Cooper 1975, 28–44; Giner 1973, 490–92). A minority of active laymen in Catholic Action or Acción Católica, inspired by French-Catholic thought, promoted a process of self-criticism and self-renewal (Carr and Fusi 1979, 151). This progressive movement represented the internal contradictions of the regime, whereas the upper echelon of the church, the bishops, remained staunchly Francoist and antidemocratic (Giner 1973, 492; Ruíz Rico 1977, 182–275). Many of them were from poor rural families and exhibited the rigid conservatism of the old traditional petty bourgeoisie. The progressive elements of the church came from the major urban centers and often chose to live as worker priests in the industrial suburbs. Poulantzas believed that it was the decline of the political and economic position of the landed oligarchy within the power bloc that led to the church's relative disaffection (Poulantzas 1976, 118) and that incorporation of members of Opus Dei, the semisecret Catholic lay organization, into the Franco governments after 1957 represented a compromise between the comprador bourgeoisie and the domestic bourgeoisie, with great repercussions within the church (pp. 118–19).

Poulantzas believed that the contradictions within the power bloc were manifested in the top ranks of the administrative apparatus; he noted the impact of a shift in the dominant ideology from the political domain to the economic domain, or from the general will and civil liberties to the apolitical ideology of technocracy. This allowed the top ranks of the bureaucracy to provide massive support for the regime in the name of "progress" and "modernization" (p. 120). Eventually the inherent contradictions of dependent industrialization led certain sectors of the bureaucracy to distance themselves from the dictatorship (López Pintor 1982, 64–65).

Attempts to "rationalize" the operation of the bureaucracy created certain contradictions; the Spanish dictatorship was based upon strict disciplinary control of the administration by a 'bureaucratic,' centralized, and archaic mode of operation (p. 121). Given the difficulty of reforming this type of regime, it was not surprising that the hostility of the domestic bourgeoisie intensified toward the dictatorship. The domestic bourgeoisie was interested in a genuine need for "rationalization," or the adaptation of the state administration to the new phase of imperialism. This would require the formation of a "technocratic-authoritarian" state (p. 121), yet the process was bitterly resisted by the proletarianized peasants and old petty bourgeoisie who man the bureaucracy and found security in their corporate privileges (p. 121).

According to Poulantzas, the educational apparatus in the form of the universities was similarly affected by the contradictions of the regime. There was a very substantial rift between the upper sector of the universities and the intermediate and lower levels of the teaching staff (p. 122). This was due largely to the upsurge in the student movement after 1960. In 1960 and 1961 students were successfully mobilized around the issue of the increasing control of the Opus Dei over higher education and the high unemployment that affected certain branches of study, such as law and philosophy (Maravall 1978, 106–7). The contradictions of the regime were particularly acute for this ideological apparatus due to the almost feudal structure of the Spanish universities. The system of promotion in Spain gave tremendous power to senior ranking professors over the rest of the teaching staff. The intermediate and lower level teaching staff, recruited mainly from the domestic bourgeoisie and working classes and reinforced by the changing attitude of the church, demanded a return to democracy in the universities. Between

1955 and 1960 there was an upsurge in the struggle between the Falangist-dominated Spanish University Syndicate, or Sindicato Español Universitario (SEU), and the democratic opposition. The increase in democratic opposition in the universities was due to policy changes brought on by the economic liberalization and political thaw advocated by the domestic bourgeoisie (in this case the Opus Dei technocrats). These sectors of the bourgeoisie were the most negatively affected by the dictatorship.

Finally, Poulantzas briefly turned his attention to the legal system, the press and publishing, and trade unions. Consistent with his earlier analysis, he maintained that the contradictions of the regime, particularly those between the comprador and domestic bourgeoisie, brought on by the process of dependent industrialization, were also present within these ideological apparatuses. He pointed to the vanguard role played by the lawyers' associations in Spain in opposition to the dictatorship, the consequence of their abhorrance of the regime's arbitrary system of justice. The liberalization of the press and media in Spain, which began with the reforms of Minister of Culture Manuel Fraga Iribarne in 1962, created other contradictions for the regime. The domestic bourgeoisie turned to this ideological apparatus as a means of expression and autonomous political organization. In 1963 a group of young Christian Democrats initiated publication of *Cuadernos para el Diálogo,* a monthly on contemporary political issues that brought together Christian Democrats, Marxists, and other opposition intellectuals into a pro-democracy dialogue. The trade unions were in a constant crisis due to the contradictions related to working class struggles and strategies of the power bloc toward them (pp. 122–23).

In his postscript, Poulantzas added some thoughts on the transition to democracy in Spain from March 1975 to June 1976. The tone of his thoughts reflected a certain frustration on the transition. He reaffirmed his hypothesis that military regimes were incapable of reforming themselves and making a continuous and linear internal evolution toward parliamentary-democracy as events in Spain during this period seemed to underscore (p. 156). He argued that the process of transition was somewhat tardy due to his underestimation of the popular support of the Franco right wing; that a significant section of the domestic bourgeoisie seemed to be opting for conservative Fraga Iribarne's "reformist" way out of the authoritarian regime; and that the relative autonomy of the Franco state vis-a-vis the power bloc was greater than he had estimated, as attested to by the considerable institutional weight that the "bunker" (Franco hardliners) enjoyed within the state apparatus (pp. 156–57). He added that the Spanish Communist party (PCE) was the leading element in the popular movement and left-wing organizations and would be the determinant element in the democratic break. Poulantzas believed that the moderation of the Communist party and its willingness to work within a progressive coalition of center and center-right forces (after the fusion in

March 1976 of the Democratic Junta, or Junta Democrática, and the Platform of Democratic Convergence, or Platforma de Convergencia Democrática, into a single organization, the Democratic Coordination, or Coordinación Democrática (CD)) was largely responsible for diffusing government attempts to divide the opposition and isolate the Communist party (p. 158).

Poulantzas believed that the state was neither a thing ("state-object") subordinate to the power of a single fraction of the bourgeoisie—monopoly capitalists—nor a subject ("state-subject") with its own power and an absolute autonomy independent of any social classes. Rather, the state served a particular function derived from its relationship to society as a whole. In a capitalist society the state functions to provide "order" in political class conflicts (Poulantzas 1978, 50). It acts to mute class conflict and prevent the capitalist social formation from bursting apart. Following Marx's formulation of the state in *The Poverty of Philosophy,* Poulantzas saw the state as "the official resume of society" (Poulantzas 1978, 49).

Poulantzas envisaged the state's principal role as one of organization that represents and organizes the dominant class or class fractions. But more importantly, the state represents and organizes the long-term political interest of the power bloc, which is composed of several competing bourgeois class fractions and is able to do this when it enjoys relative autonomy of given fractions of the power bloc (Poulantzas 1980, 127). So the state's policy is the result of the class contradictions inscribed in the very structure of the state (Poulantzas 1980, 132). The state then is the condensation of a relationship of forces between classes and class fractions (Poulantzas 1980, 132). When class contradictions reach certain critical conjunctures due to the particular historical period and the level of economic development, a crisis of hegemony ensues. A crisis affects not only the various fractions of the ruling bloc, but the relationship between the ruling bloc and the dominated classes. This becomes a crisis of the specific condensation of the relationship of forces between classes and class fractions, i.e., a crisis of the capitalist state itself.

According to Poulantzas, capitalism throughout the world had reached a phase of worldwide crisis. This was due to the intensity and sharpness of class struggle during the new historical period of capitalist formations, specifically the imperialist stage of capitalism or the monopoly stage. He argued that capitalist states react differently to this political crisis depending on their position within the imperialist chain and the particular historical period that affects the conjuncture of the class struggle (Poulantzas 1979, 16). He coined the term "exceptional capitalist state" to distinguish these regimes from the normal capitalist state. He identified three specific forms of exceptional capitalist state: fascism, Bonapartism, and military dictatorship, each resulting from a crisis of hegemony within the power bloc, which also is linked to a crisis of hegemony over the society as a whole. Within this crisis an exceptional capitalist state emerges whose role becomes one of reorganizing hegemony within the power bloc and over society.

In the case of Spain, his concept of an exceptional capitalist state can be criticized in at least two respects: first, the assumption of the nonmodal capitalist state and conversely of parliamentary democracy as the modal type; second, the functionalist argument that parliamentary democracy would fulfill the "normal" requirements of capitalism and that an exceptional capitalist state emerges only to meet the abnormal requirements resulting from a crisis of capital accumulation or political legitimation (Maravall 1978, 3). Nor did Poulantzas adequately explain why these regimes persist once the abnormal requirements have been met. The two Fascist regimes of Germany and Italy came to an end only after they were defeated militarily, and the Franco regime persisted for more than 35 years.

Bob Jessop notes that in *Crisis* Poulantzas inverts the approach of his work, *Fascism and Dictatorship* (1979). Jessop argues that Poulantzas was trying to demonstrate that fascism was functional for monopoly capital and that the internal contradictions of these regimes were insignificant in their collapse. Poulantzas did not address the question of whether the internal contradictions of Fascist Italy and Germany played an important part in their downfall (Jessop 1985, 279), but the core of *Crisis* revolved around the internal contradictions of the military dictatorships and their eventual collapse in order to explain why these regimes transformed themselves without being directly confronted by the popular masses (Jessop 1985, 279). Poulantzas fails to explain why the internal contradictions of the military dictatorships in Spain and Portugal survived for so many decades and why these contradictions were not important for fascist regimes. This was due to his underestimating the syncretic authoritarian ideology of Francoism, which is analyzed below. The concept of exceptional capitalist state results from this confusion so that in some instances there may appear a functionalist capitalist state and in others a dysfunctionalist capitalist state, according to Poulantzas. In his analysis, the Franco dictatorship became dysfunctional for capital accumulation due to the internal contradictions of the regime. Capitalist economic growth after the reinsertion of Spain into the world capitalist economy created new requirements that could not be met by the highly restrictive and ordered Franco corporatist state.

The democratization of Spain, according to Poulantzas, was not the result of a mass movement leading to a direct assault on the dictatorship, although he believed that the popular struggles were the "determining factor." Rather, the impact of the popular struggles operated "at a distance," intensifying the contradictions of the regime, especially within the repressive apparatuses (pp. 76–78). In this way, Poulantzas believed that the popular masses were indirectly determinant in so far as they shaped the internal contradictions of the dictatorship itself.

The decomposition of the dictatorship in Spain was the result of the crisis of hegemony within the power bloc itself and the marked increase in popular struggles. Both of these factors acted together to weaken the regime's ability to respond with a coherent, consistent approach to the popular classes. The resulting policy of the regime toward the popular classes was a combination of concessions (liberalization of press and media) and repression (arrest and prosecution of labor, student, and nationalist leaders). This growing political instability within the power bloc, and between the power bloc and the dominated classes, manifested itself in internal splits within the ideological state apparatuses (the church, universities, media, trade unions, etc.) and the repressive state apparatuses (the army, police, administration, etc.), leading key sectors to support the democratization of the regime.

Poulantzas also questioned the possibility of the regime reforming itself. He did not believe that a continuous and linear evolution toward a "parliamentary-democratic" form of state was possible; similarly, he did not believe that an exceptional form of state can develop in a linear fashion out of a parliamentary-democratic state (pp. 90–93, 102). This was due to the differences between these forms of the bourgeois state concerning their structure and the balance of forces between the classes. Thus the process of democratization, or the breakdown of democracy into an exceptional form of capitalist state, coincided with political crises, or periods of acute class struggle (pp. 90–91). He correctly maintained that a transition from dictatorship to democracy would not necessarily result in an automatic transition to socialism. He believed that the transition to socialism would require the state apparatus to be smashed, due to the specific weight and role of the apparatus expressed as a resistance to such a transformation (p. 93). This was particularly true in Spain where the majority of the Left opposition—Socialists, or Partido Socialista Obrero Español (PSOE), and Communists (PCE)—never seriously led an antimonopoly, anti-imperialist struggle (Vilar 1984, 422–30). The reasons for this, and the possibility of a different opposition strategy was never addressed by Poulantzas (pp. 73, 89). Instead, the major issue was under whose hegemony would the struggle for democracy be waged and how far the democratization process would be taken (pp. 66–67, 87–88). Poulantzas' neglect of an analysis of the strategies and tactics of the Left opposition, and the possibility of an alternate strategy, can be seen as one of his greatest shortcomings, which led him to several erroneous conclusions.

## BOURGEOIS HEGEMONY AND THE TRANSITION TO DEMOCRACY

One of the most important—if not *the* most important for socialist strategy—aspects of the transition to democracy in Spain is the control by the ruling class over the democratization process. It was not a transition that was led and controlled by the popular classes, although their input through political parties and associations and trade unions was crucial; it was a process of a series of pacts and reforms initiated from above. This fact, confirmed by many scholars (San Miguel 1981; Maravall 1978, 1982; Maravall and Santamaria 1986; Kohler, 1982; Carr and Fust 1979; Lancaster and Prevost 1985; Mujal-León 1983; Share, 1986a, b; Pérez Díaz 1987; Roca 1987), poses a significant problem or question for Poulantzas, socialist strategy, and Marxist state theory. Should the overthrow of a military dictatorship and its replacement by some form of democracy (pluralist or socialist) be accomplished by pacts and reforms from above or what Adam Przeworski refers to as a "contingent institutional compromise" (1986, 59) initiated by the ruling class, or by a direct frontal assault by the popular masses ("via revolucionaria")?

This question caused repeated problems for Poulantzas' analysis. He firmly believed that the working class should be in the vanguard of popular struggles against the regime, but he did not believe that a process of democratization could be coupled with a transition to socialism and national liberation under the exclusive hegemony of the domestic bourgeoisie (p. 66). This would require a far more radical antimonopoly democratization process, one that could only be led by the working class and that would require a genuine break with the previous regime. Recent events in Spain seem to confirm this hypothesis.

Poulantzas was often very contradictory in his analysis of whether a military dictatorship was capable of reforming itself, whether a continuous and linear evolution toward democracy was possible by way of controlled succession, a question addressed later in this chapter.

Poulantzas believed that the role of the working class in the transition to democracy in Spain was vague and contradictory. He stated that there was no frontal mass movement against the dictatorship by the popular classes and that the popular struggles were not the direct or principal factor in their overthrow (p. 78). Nevertheless, he argued that the popular classes played the "determining" role in the democratization process, not just as a result of the internal contradictions produced by the changing composition of the popular classes and rise in class struggle, but also the increasing disaffection of the masses toward the dictatorship (p. 79), an assertion supported by many studies of public opinion and the opposition at that time (Informe 1981, 7–13). This was due in large part to the difference between military dictatorships and fascist regimes, that is, the former's lack of success in implanting its ideology into the masses (pp. 79–80). In Spain an attempt was made in this direction by the Falange in the early 1940s and again in 1956, but the attempts to create a genuine mass party were defeated by conservative monarchists (Carr and Fusi 1979, 26, 172–73; Tusell 1977, 30–63).

Poulantzas was incorrect in his analysis of the ideology of the Franco dictatorship. He underestimated the extent to which the regime was able to neutralize the masses through a national-popular ideology, which "cemented" together the social formation. As Jessop points out, this was probably due to his incorrectly extrapolating from the Greek case (Jessop 1985, 281).

## THE IDEOLOGICAL CONTENT OF FRANCOISM

The Franco military dictatorship was characterized by profound changes in ideology, specifically the *dominant ideology* (Vilar 1977, 31–40). It is a common assumption of mainstream political science that military dictatorships, or "authoritarian regimes" as they are called, are noted for their lack of ideology. Rather than an elaborate ideology, what these regimes possess is a specific mentality, which is defined here as a way of thinking and feeling, more emotional than rational. Juan Linz (1975) was the first to characterize the Franco regime as authoritarian, situated on a continuum equally distant from "totalitarian" and "democratic" regimes. Another variant of this model looks toward the "apolitical" ideology of modernization and the technocratic elites who advocate it (O'Donnell 1973). I believe the Franco regime represented the outcome of an intense ideological struggle between the forces of the Left and of the Right, and that the emergence of the regime from the intense political crisis (of hegemony) of the republic would have been impossible without a pre-existing ideological base.

Max Weber drew our attention to the function of ideology in the determination of political action. He believed that ideology is the "rationalized" product of social forces, that ideology and practice are not separated in history:

> Not ideas, but material and ideal interests, directly govern men's conduct. Yet very frequently the "world images" that have been created by "ideas" have, like switchmen, determined the tracks along which action, has been pushed by the dynamic of interest. "From what" and "for what" one wished to be redeemed and, let us not forget, "could" be redeemed, depended upon one's image of the world (Weber 1958, 280).

When Weber speaks of action being pushed by the dynamic of interest, he was not referring only to economic interests but to cultural, political, and religious interests. Every potential ruling class tends to nationalize their objectives. For this they create their own intellectuals. As Gramsci stated:

> Every social class, coming into existence on the original basis of an essential function in the world of economic production, creates with itself, organically,

> one or more groups of intellectuals who give it homogeneity and consciousness of its function not only in the economic field but in the social and political field as well . . . (1980a, 18).

The "organic intellectual," according to Gramsci, performs the function of cohesion and consensus for a given class. During the Spanish Second Republic (1931–36) diverse ideological groups of the Right (Falangists, monarchists, accidentalists, technocrats) virulently criticized the republic and performed this function, providing cohesion and consensus for the forces of the Right, guaranteeing their social, political, and economic position and their social hegemony.

In an interesting essay on the ideological origins of the Franco regime, Amando de Miguel and Benjamin Oltra (1978) employed an analysis that accounts for the relationship between ideology and class interests. They very carefully delineated the relationship between ideologies and intellectuals, and the political groups that represent various class interests. They believed, following Gramsci, that the relation between ideology and interests was not a simple mechanical one; that it was, on the contrary, complex and difficult to explain and that every social class, either in or out of power, needs a legitimizing ideology to organize and give definition to their political practices. They demonstrated how the origins of Francoism lay with the intellectuals of the nationalist bloc. These intellectuals were either sympathetic or politically active in the political parties of the Right during the republic (de Miguel and Oltra 1978, 57). The political activity of the intellectuals of the Right during the republic, through political parties of the nationalist bloc, gave coherence to the ideology and politics that emerged.

In the period immediately preceding the military rebellion and the civil war, the intellectuals of the Right explained and justified the need for a military coup. As Amando de Miguel explains, they did this not just in negative and critical terms but by offering different alternatives for the Right. By the February 1936 elections, which brought the Left back into power, the national bloc was in agreement on one essential point: to overthrow the republic by force of arms, to stop and destroy the "revolution," and to install the political and cultural form of Catholic and eternal Spain (de Miguel and Oltra 1978, 59). This was the culmination of a long process that started with the ideological crisis of the republic.

There was also the relation between ideological change and the process of crisis. Before the Spanish civil war, an intense ideological battle of ideas waged between parties of the Left and of the Right. Parties of both sides tended toward extremism because they were part of the crisis of hegemony that plagued the Second Republic, a crisis of political power and ideological consent.

In a similar fashion, Salvador Giner and Eduardo Sevilla (1980) classified the Franco dictatorship as "reactionary despotism" brought about by a reactionary coalition. They noted that this type of regime was able to neutralize, not mobilize, the popular classes through its control of the collective means of emotional production. This was accomplished by the manipulation of the materials and techniques used to stage rituals producing strong emotional bonds such as political and religious ceremonies (Giner 1980, 228 fn. 71).

The Franco regime was characterized by its limited ideological sphere and a very limited political pluralism. The officially sanctioned ideology included ideological components from all sections of the ruling bloc, at the same time excluding ideologies and values of the popular classes (Giner 1980, 204). Franco could freely choose between fascism, Catholicism, monarchism, or any of the ideologies that composed the syncretic ideological substratum, and his choice depended on the particular political conjuncture.

Several authors have noted the limited political pluralism that was part of the Franco regime (Giner and Sevilla 1980, 200–120; Maravall 1978, 2–3; Linz 1973, 171–259; Carr and Fusi 1979, 47; Share 1986a, 57–58; Preston 1986, 5; Juarégui and Vega 1984). Most authors drew on the pioneering work of Juan Linz, one of the first scholars to classify the Franco dictatorship as an authoritarian regime resembling a "near-pluralistic" hegemony. He defined the regime as a political system with limited, not responsible, political pluralism, not only within the governing group but within institutions and social forces (Linz 1973, 185, 188).

In studying the transition to democracy in Spain, it is important to consider the politics and strategies of both the popular classes and the ruling class, for the transformation of the Spanish regime was a process of reform "from above" and pressure and demand "from below" (Maravall 1982, 5). Poulantzas was one of the few scholars to attempt an analysis of the transition from the point of view of the composition and politics of the ruling class, yet he failed to consider how the intrabloc relations varied across the three regimes (Jessop 1985, 281). For instance, he never sufficiently explained why the Greek and Portuguese regimes collapsed and the Spanish regime "decomposed."

Given his emphasis on the role of the popular classes in the transition to democracy, Poulantzas neglected an analysis of the strategies and tactics of the major parties of the Left (Jessop 1985, 282). In the remainder of this chapter I analyze the role played by the opposition movement in Spain during the transition to democracy and explore the connection between the economic and political contradictions produced by the miracle economic growth in Spain during the 1960s, and the development of such organized opposition movements as trade unions, political parties and organizations, students, autonomy movements, and the church. I believe that an analysis of the strategies and tactics of the major opposition groups before and during the transition to democracy helps to explain the dynamics of the transformation of the Spanish regime.

## THE OPPOSITION AND REFORM "FROM ABOVE"

One inescapable feature of the Spanish transition to parliamentary democracy was that it could not be completed until after the death of General Francisco Franco on November 20, 1975. King Juan Carlos became the new head of state. Franco had groomed the young king to be the protector of the institutions and spirit of Francoism. With his first official act, Juan Carlos seemed to confirm Franco's intent; he reappointed Carlos Arias Navarro as prime minister and included many Francoists in the new Arias government. The government, from January 1974 to July 1976, was a failure for several reasons, principally because Arias was unable to initiate reform or control the process of change. The process of transition lay in the hands of the ruling class, which proved unable to initiate reform and a true transition to democracy. Juan Carlos sensed that the pace of reform under Arias was too slow. In addition, the economy was deteriorating, working class discontent was on the rise, and Basque terrorism racked the nation.

Throughout the early 1970s the opposition was organizing and gathering strength so that by March 1976 there were two rival opposition "associations," the Democratic Junta and the Platform of Democratic Convergence. The Junta, formed in Paris in 1974 when Franco's death seemed imminent, was originally comprised of members of the PCE and politicians linked to Don Juan, the father of Juan Carlos, but later came to include the Socialists of Enrique Tierno Galván, the Carlists of the young pretender Carlos Hugo, the Workers' Commissions, and other splinter groups. The Platform group was formed as an alternative to the "Communist-dominated" Junta. The moderate opposition of Christian-Democrats, Social-Democrats, Socialists, and liberals objected to several features of the Junta such as: the similarity of the Junta to the "Front" organizations of the republic; the presence of Tierno Galván's Socialist group; and the role played by individuals such as Rafael Calvo Serér and Antonio García Trevijano, who were linked to Don Juan.

The king, sensing that the opposition held the initiative and desiring to retain the strategy of reform "from above," chose as prime minister Adolfo Suárez González, a former civil governor and director of Spanish television and president of a political association committed to the politics of continuity. Most people were caught off guard by the king's choice and many branded it "an immense error." He probably chose Suárez because of his age (43 at the time), his loyalty to Juan Carlos, and his willingness to initiate reform through the already existing Franco institutions.

Suárez imposed a strategy of reform "from above," moving in the direction of *ruptura pactada,* or negotiated break (Maravall 1982, 11; Pérez Díaz 1987, 216–46; Roca 1987, 247–68). He emphasized cooperation and coordination with the left and a strategy of cooptation. His aim was to limit the demands of the popular classes, during a time of acute economic crisis, concerning issues such as redistribution of wealth, restraints on property rights, and changes in labor relations; at the same time maintaining the confidence of the bourgeoisie during the transition to democracy. Suárez was determined not to let the popular classes control or dominate the transition.

On September 11, 1976, Suárez appeared on national television to introduce his plan of political reform. He stressed the need for popular sovereignty and a freely elected parliament in the solving of Spain's economic problems. A political reform bill was presented to the Córtes the next day; it called for a bicameral legislature, elected through direct, secret, and universal suffrage and allowing the king to choose one-sixth of the senators. After considerable opposition and debate, the last Franco Córtes voted itself out of existence and approved the reform measures by a vote of 426 in favor, 59 against, and 13 abstentions.

The opposition rejected the political reform bill, not becauase of its content but because of its origin. They feared that if Suárez continued to act on his own initiative, they would be excluded from the process. This contradiction within the opposition (Communists, Socialists, regional nationalists, and some Christian-Democrats), led them to campaign in favor of abstention only halfheartedly.

On December 15, 1976, the reform measures passed in a national referendum: 77.4 percent of the electorate went to the polls; 94.2 percent voted for the reform bill; 2.6 percent against; 22.6 percent abstained (*Informe* 1981). The stunning victory for Suárez greatly strengthened his reform "from above" strategy, and the opposition was forced to negotiate with Suárez upon his terms.

Most observers agree that the transition to democracy in Spain was a process controlled and dominated by the ruling class or a process of "reform from above." Poulantzas correctly highlighted the strategic importance of bourgeois hegemony, but tended to discount the crucial role played by the opposition during the transition process. Whereas Poulantzas emphasized the popular classes as the "determining factor" in the overthrow of the dictatorship (pp. 78, 85), in the same breath he affirmed that the popular struggles were not decisive in their overthrow (p. 85). This emphasis on the internal divisions of the ruling class led Poulantzas to neglect the strategies and tactics of the parties of the Left. He scarcely mentions the PCE and PSOE strategies or errors during the democratization process. He never addresses whether the opposition made more concessions than necessary or demonstrated more moderation than was needed.

A significant amount of social unrest and demands for democractic reform marked the last 15 years of the Franco regime, making a strategy of "mere liberalization" impossible (Maravall 1982, 12; Biescas and Lara 1980, 337–421; Vilar 1984, 289–473). I am convinced that the opposition significantly influenced the direction of reform as suggested by Maravall who argues that "this pressure must be borne in mind in order to understand the development of the strategy 'from above' in favor of negotiation" (Maravall 1982, 13). This position is supported in the remainder of this chapter by focusing on the strategy and tactics of the opposition during the transition to democracy in Spain in an effort to understand the anomalous Spanish case. I focus on the PCE, PSOE, the trade unions, and church because of the importance of these groups in the initial stages of the transition. The student movement, the media, and the autonomy movements also played a crucial role in the transition to democracy in Spain.

## THE OPPOSITION AND THE POLITICS OF THE TRANSITION

At the end of the Spanish civil war (1936–39) the opposition was defeated or fled to exile. Franco repressed opposition political parties. The PCE entered the postcivil war era with its organization shattered and its leaders dispersed. The PSOE was decimated with its leaders and activists dead, imprisoned, or in exile (Vilar 1984, 33–44).

In the Spanish case, various groups comprise the opposition. Juan Linz believes that in democracies we should distinguish between "loyal" or "constitutional" opposition and "disloyal" opposition, whereas in authoritarian regimes we have to distinguish between "opponents" *within* and *outside* the system (1973, 230). He also distinguished a semiopposition from "opposition" in these regimes. Semiopposition consists of those groups that are not dominant or represented in the governing group but are willing to participate in power without fundamentally challenging the regime (Linz 1973b, 191). In the case of Spain, the semiopposition was comprised of the directors, administrators, professionals, and technocrats of the modern country. Nancy Bermeo has highlighted the fact that Spain produced a resilient semiopposition, whereas Portugal produced a highly vulnerable one. She believes that the success of the Right and center-Right parties in Spain, in contrast with Portugal, in the postauthoritarian period was due in large part to the role played by the young technocrats. They created a constituency for capitalism and were able to attract the modern middle classes (Bermeo 1987, 221–28). For our purposes here, opposition is limited to those groups that operate outside the system, including groups that Linz labels "alegal" and "illegal" opposition. By alegal, he refers to those groups (for example, the church) in limbo between legality and illegality but unwilling to conspire in overthrowing the government by revolution. Illegal opposition comprises those groups actively committed to illegal forms of protest—from political strikes to terrorism, such as the PCE and the Basque nationalists.

## THREE PERIODS OF OPPOSITION

E. Ramón Arango divided opposition to the Franco regime into three periods: during the civil war; after the war until the 1950s; and from the 1950s to the present (1978, 219). During the first two periods opposition came largely from opponents "within" the regime, such as the Falange, the Spanish Confederation of Autonomous Rights, or Confederación Española de Derechas Autónomas (CEDA), the Carlists, and the Alphonsine Monarchists—or what Linz would refer to as the semiopposition. In the third period the new opposition emerged out of the contradictions of an archaic, atavistic political system and the requirements of an expanding capitalist economy. The third period of opposition is marked by three phases.

The first phase, from the late 1950s until the constituent elections in June 1977, saw increased student activism and the predominance of the PCE within the opposition, especially within the newly emerging labor movement in Spain. Also of significance was the very high level of working class mobilization after the death of General Franco and the high number of hours lost and workers affected by strikes, as reflected in Table 2.

After the 1977 elections, popular mobilization decreased significantly even though strikes remained high a year later (68 million working hours lost), half of what it was in 1976 (Maravall 1982, 13). Issues motivating workers were no longer political but also economic. Strikes after 1977 were a sign of organizational weakness within the unions, because the number of workers affected by strikes increased, although the worker's parties and unions did not carry out an active mobilization policy after the summer of 1977 (Maravall 1982, 13).

The second phase began after the June 1977 elections and lasted until the parliamentary elections of March 1979, which marked the end of the transition and a move away from a consensus-seeking style of government. This new circumstance forced a change in the strategy of the opposition forces, particularly within the PCE and the PSOE. The PCE developed a working relationship with Suárez and his party, the UCD, who needed PCE support for his minority government. After the March 1979 election, Suárez was

**Table 2.2**
**Hours lost and workers affected by strikes during the transition**

| | 1976 | 1977 | 1978 |
|---|---|---|---|
| Working hours lost (in millions) | 156 | 110 | 68 |
| Workers affected (in thousands) | 2,956 | 3,265 | 4,183 |

*Source:* José Maravall, *The Transition to Democracy in Spain* (New York: St. Martins, 1982), p. 13.

less interested in cooperation with the PCE and believed that he could now count on the support of Manual Fraga Iribarne's Democratic Coalition, or Coalición Democrática (CD), and the Basque and Catalan nationalist parties (Mujal-León 1983, 187). This led to an increase in competition between the opposition parties, particularly between the PSOE and the PCE.

The third phase, a period of "crisis and retrenchment," began immediately after the 1979 parliamentary elections. Parliamentary democracy had finally arrived in Spain and opposition forces were forced to find their place within the democratic system (Gunther, Sani, and Shabad 1985, 2, 389–418). At its Ninth Congress in April 1978, the PCE dropped its Leninist label for the epithet "revolutionary and democratic." This marked the triumph of Santiago Carrillo's Eurocommunist strategy and the embracing of "revolutionary reformism" through electoral competition. The PSOE was also experiencing changes. Their failure to defeat Suárez and the UCD caused much internal debate. At issue was whether the PSOE should enter into electoral alliances. In addition, in May 1979 at the PSOE's congress, Felipe González proposed to drop the term "Marxism" from the party program and introduced several organizational reforms aimed at solidifying a more moderate majority within the party. These changes were easily approved by the delegates, although resistance from the left wing of the party provoked the temporary resignation of González and the convening of a special party congress in September 1979. Eventually the PSOE and the PCE would agree to a postmunicipal election pact.

The result of the special congress was an endorsement of the González leadership within the party. This signaled the beginning of a dramatic ideological shift to the right (Share 1986b, 19). The PSOE's evolution toward social democracy can be explained as the result of the contradiction of its efforts at becoming a credible petty-bourgeois party and its historical claim of representing the working class. The electoral benefit of its move toward the right was substantial, whereas the political cost from the left was minimal due to the extreme disarray of the Communist camp (Share 1986b, 24). The PSOE was no longer just a working class party and was increasingly viewed by Spaniards as representing all classes (Gunther et al. 1985, 191–202).

## THE SPANISH COMMUNIST PARTY AND THE CHURCH

The role played by the PCE in the transition to parliamentary democracy is pivotal. The PCE was the major opposition force during the first phase from the late 1950s to the March 1977 constituent elections. Not only was the PCE the best organized and most efficacious opposition force, but its collaboration with Catholics within the labor movement and the cultural domain (media) was crucial to the development of a unified opposition movement.

The Catholic church in Spain has always regarded the PCE as anti-Catholic, and the Second Republic and ensuing civil war did much to reinforce this image. In an effort to broaden the appeal of the PCE to liberal sectors of the Catholic church, in June 1956 the Communists issued a call for National Reconciliation. The thrust of the document was to put behind the divisions of the war and concentrate on building a more democratic and liberal Spain. The more liberal sectors of the church were very receptive to these ideas, although there was skepticism on both sides about the incorporation of Catholics into a Communisit-dominated opposition.

There were several reasons for the change in PCE policy toward the Catholic church in Spain, all stemming from the fact that the church in Spain is a politically powerful institution. Thus the PCE could continue to make a frontal assault upon church dogmas and its privileged position within Spanish society, or it could seek an alternative strategy, found in the writings of the Italian Marxist Antonio Gramsci.

Gramsci believed (1980b, 229–38) that in advanced capitalist societies the state can be transformed into a social democracy only by first democratizing civil society comprising the ideological apparatuses of the state or such private organizations as the church, universities, trade unions, political parties, media (newspapers, radio, TV), cultural domain (publishing), and the family. This was because of the immense power of the state to resist a revolutionary thrust, due to the hegemony of ruling class ideology within the private institutions of society.

Santiago Carrillo believed that it was essential to establish a new cultural hegemony in Spain before a transition to democratic socialism would be possible: "a flourishing culture does not tolerate prohibitions, and the flowering and extension of culture is the sphere in which revolutionary and progressive ideas can establish themselves, become hegemonic and have even more influence in the march of humanity, penetrating and transforming the ideological apparatuses" (Carrillo 1978, 44).

This belief led the PCE to change its strategy toward the church and work toward an historical compromise. As Carrillo states in his book *Eurocommunism and the State,* "the strategy of the revolutions of today, in the developed capitalist countries, must be oriented to turning these ideological apparatuses round, to transform and utilize them—if not wholly then partly—against the state power of monopoly capitalism" (1978, 27–28). Carrillo believed that the church in Spain was entering a crisis due to "the decline of bourgeois society and the birth of socialism" (1978, 28). A new generation of theologians was turning away from rigid dogmatism to a more humane Catholicism. This phenomenon was, in my view, confirmed and given greater impetus by the Second Vatican Council in 1964 when Pope John

XXIII and his successor Paul VI undermined the legitimacy of the Franco regime by defending ideological pluralism, human rights, freedom of religious expression and association, and even supporting dialogue with the Communists (Carr and Fusi 1979, 152). The effect was to undermine the church heirarchy in Spain. As Mujal-León points out, "the shift away from identification with conservative social and political systems and toward the reassertion of Church independence from even the most 'Catholic' of states had a most profound impact on Spanish Catholicism" (1983, 33). Church critics within Spain now had an authoritative source upon which to base their attacks on the regime.

There also was an historical paradox of certain sectors of the clergy and Catholic layleaders associating themselves with working class protest and nationalist movements: "nobody would have expected that in Spain the majority approval for the activities of priests in politics and trade unions would come from those situated on the extreme left . . . and that they would defend the use of churches and convents for political meetings" (Informe 1981, 299). The church was the only institution permitted, by virtue of the 1953 Concordat, to run independent labor organizations such as the *Hermandad Obrera Acción Católica* (HOAC) and *Juventud Obrera Católica* (JOC). Therefore, it was logical for the Left opposition to look toward these organizations as they began to compete with the official, Falange-dominated Sindical Organization, or Organización Sindical (OS).

## THE LABOR MOVEMENT

The labor movement played a major opposition role by pressing for a democratization of the regime. Prior to the civil war, the labor movement was dominated by the Socialist-influenced, General Union of Workers, or Unión General de Trabajadores (UGT), and the anarchosyndicalist National Confederation of Work, or Confederación Nacional del Trabajo (CNT). At the end of the war, all trade unions were brutally repressed by the Franco regime, and in their place Franco set up the OS, a vertically organized sindicate fashioned along Italian corporatist lines and designed to function as an integral part of the state, ostensibly eliminating class struggle and replacing it with cooperation among all those involved in the process of production. The syndicate would constitute an "organic whole." The OS came to be dominated by the Falange; Franco allowed this largely as a consolation prize for their support during the civil war, but "this was a useless gift (except to the 34,000 bureaucrats it employed), given the failure to create a parallel Falangist corporatist state" (Carr and Fusi 1979, 27). The OS became an insignificant bureaucratic shell.

At the end of the civil war, Franco reorganized the Spanish capitalist economy along autarchic lines so that the economy would become self-capitalizing and self-sufficient. This was accomplished through intervention and a labor-repressive system of industrial relations. Strikes were illegal in Franco's Spain, collective bargaining did not exist, and wages and working conditions were set by the labor ministry. This system functioned for roughly the first half of the Franco regime. The reactivation of the Spanish economy in the latter part of the 1950s abruptly influenced industrial relations.

As mentioned earlier, Franco reshuffled his cabinet in 1957 by bringing in a group of technocrats whose charge was to bring Spain out of its economic crisis (stagnation and inflation) and reintegrate it back into the world capitalist economy. These men forged policies to develop and modernize the economy. This change in economic policy signaled a shift in the balance of forces within the power bloc as the finance capitalist fraction of the bourgeoisie reached a dominant position within the ruling bloc, whereas the political weight of the landowning oligarchy was reduced in disproportion to their economic position.

The new team of technocrats introduced many reforms: reform of the tax system, a unified foreign exchange, wage and price controls, and setting up a system of collective bargaining. Spain also joined the IMF, the World Bank, and the OECD. Finally, in 1959 the government instituted an IMF-imposed stabilization plan. It consisted of a devaluation of the peseta, restriction on imports, a reduction in public spending, a credit squeeze, and price and wage freezes (Biescas 1980, 64–67).

The change in industrial relations of production and the general reorientation of the Spanish economy after 1957 led to the growth of an independent labor movement and contradictions within the Franco system of industrial relations crucial to the transition to democracy, as Maravall has documented in his study of the working class movement (1978, 18–43). The development of two new institutions—the *jurado de empresa,* or shop committees, and *convenios colectivos,* or collective bargaining—became the dominant means for the regulation of work, wages, productivity, and industrial relations so that the Left was able to penetrate and organize a powerful opposition labor movement.

## THE WORKERS' COMMISSIONS (CCOO)

The CCOO became the largest and most important trade union in Spain. Developed in the late 1950s among locally organized assemblies of workers, consisting of anarchists, Socialists, Communists, Catholics, and left-wing Falangists, the CCOO soon became a major force within the emerging labor movement (Ariza 1976). It was no secret that the PCE was influential within the leadership of the CCOO, especially after government persecution began in 1966, but many Catholic labor activists also were exposed to the ideas of Marx and, more specifically, of the PCE (Mujal-León 1983, 36). This contact between Catholics and Communists in the labor movement was important because "it allowed the party to develop an organizational structure and presence in a crucial sector of Spanish society . . ." and it had "an impact on otherwise sectarian working-class militants . . ." who could not deny ". . . the visible successes achieved through cooperation in the nascent CCOO" (Mujal-León 1983, 37).

The CCOO was not the only trade union that developed in this period. The Socialist UGT made a remarkable comeback, given its limited constituency in Asturias and the Basque country, to become the second-ranking trade union in Spain. The Sindical Worker Union, or Unión Sindical Obrera (USO), was the third largest trade union in Spain. Composed of Socialist and Catholic labor activists, it adopted an independent position in favor of self-management socialism. Eventually the USO divided internally over the issue of whether to join forces with the UGT.

The role played by the PCE, PSOE, the trade unions, and the church is the key to understanding the anomolous Spanish transition to parliamentary democracy. These groups contributed to the erosion of the legitimacy of the Franco regime, although they never seriously represented a direct challenge to it. Rather, it was their moderation and acceptance of a strategy of *ruptura pactada* or negotiated break that allowed the regime to self destruct. The PSOE and PCE were faced with a serious dilemma: how to react to an authoritarian regime that was itself initiating and controlling a transition to parliamentary democracy (Share 1985, 88).

The moderation of the Left opposition was the result of several factors. Public opinion polls revealed that the Spanish electorate was moderate, located in the center-left of the political spectrum. Also, the Left opposition was firmly committed to the consolidation of parliamentary democracy as a precondition of the transition to democratic socialism. Events in Chile in 1973 had greatly influenced the strategy of Spanish Left opposition. And events in Spain at that time, such as the problem of terrorism, the rumblings of discontent within the military, and the economic crisis, all combined to produce an air of uncertainty. Thus the greatest fear of the Spanish Left opposition was a return to authoritarianism.

The leadership of the PCE believed that the struggle for democracy must be first waged within the ideological apparatuses of society and made to serve the interests of the popular classes. The influence of the PCE within the universities and publishing domain was very important for the establishment of a democratic hegemony.

At the end of the civil war, Spanish universities were organized to reflect the new character of the state—Fascist and clerical. In 1943 Franco promulgated the Law of University Organization formalizing joint control of the Catholic church and the movement on the universities. A state-controlled student union, the SEU, was formed, initially under Falangist domination. The 1953 Concordat between the Vatican and Franco established the monopoly of the Catholic church over Spanish education.

The beginnings of student unrest were during the mid-1950s. In October 1955 the death of philosopher José Ortega y Gasset provided the occasion for public expression of discontent. In February 1956 a manifesto demanding the democratization of the SEU and a National Congress of Students was submitted to the SEU president. Elections were held for representatives of the student body at the faculty level, but the government invalidated the elections, sparking student protest and violent confrontations with the police.

After 1956 opposition on university campuses took on a new character; there were several attempts to reorganize leftist parties on the campuses. Due to the efforts of Jorge Semprún and Simón Sánchez Montero, the PCE exercised considerable political influence in the universities well into the 1960s (Carr and Fusi 1979, 147). After 1962 student agitation became endemic. The Franco regime was unable to diffuse student unrest and resorted to a policy of repression and timid reform. The universities were a microcosm of Spanish society revealing the crisis of hegemony that was plaguing the Franco regime.

The educational system is an integral part of the ideological apparatus of the capitalist state. Traditionally in Franco's Spain the universities and educational centers were responsible for inculcating the dominant ideology. After 1955 the universities increasingly entered a period of crisis marked by the rejection of established norms. Knowledge and education of the lower and middle classes had revealed to them the conflict inherent in Spanish society and university life. The universities as part of the ideological apparatuses of the capitalist state were being "turned around," and made to serve the interests of the lower and middle classes from where the majority of students were recruited.

The communication media—television, radio, and the press—were very important components of the ideological apparatus of the state, and during Franco's era they were completely controlled by state censors with the exception of the church, which by virtue of the 1953 Concordat was free of state censors. After Vatican II, however, liberal Catholics began to take advantage of their privilege. In 1963 a group of young Christian Democrats, under the direction of Joaquín Ruíz Giménez, founded the monthly review *Cuadernos Para el Diálogo* as an arena for intellectual debate where leaders and intellectuals of the Marxist Left could publish articles providing a forum for contact between liberal Catholics and Communists and a vehicle for the circulation of democratic ideas.

## THE AUTONOMY MOVEMENTS IN THE OPPOSITION

Regionalism in Spain predates the creation of the Spanish state with the marriage of Ferdinand of Aragón and Isabel of Castile and the unity of two distinct kingdoms under a single but pluralistic monarchy respecting local customs, laws, privileges, and rights. A distinction, however, must be made between those contemporary autonomy movements in Spain that have their origin in language, culture, and customs and those that are based upon administrative or political criteria. In Catalonia, the Basque region, and Galicia, autonomy is based upon a distinct language, culture, and customs other than Spanish. The Catalan region in northeastern Spain comprises the provinces of Barcelona, Gerona, Lérida, and Tarragoña and is the second wealthiest area, ranking just behind the Basque country. There is a strong linguistic basis for Catalan nationalism. Catalan, the native language, is spoken by 97 percent of the native-born population and is also a literary language (unlike the Basque language Euskerra) with numerous scientific and literary works. The Spanish Basque country comprises four provinces: Álava, Guipúzcoa, Navarra, and Vizcaya. Basque nationalism tends to be more radical and violent than its Catalan counterpart. The linguistic base of Basque nationalism is weaker than that of Catalan nationalism because only 32 percent of the population in 1981 spoke Euskerra (Shabad and Gunther 1982, 446). After the civil war, immigration to the Basque country greatly accelerated due to industrialization. Between 1950 and 1970 the population increased by 62 percent. Basque nationalism found itself in a state of crisis, threatened with extinction. This led to the formation in 1959 of ETA (Euzkadi ta Askatasuna), which defined itself as a patriotic, democratic, and nonconfessional party. By 1962, however, ETA had moved ideologically to the left, embracing Marxism and calling for "revolutionary movement of national liberation." Eventually ETA became an underground separatist movement engaging in assassinations and bombings against the Spanish state. The climate of violence and terror created by ETA during the early 1970s threatened the transition to parliamentary democracy in Spain, and it was ETA that assassinated Franco's handpicked successor, Admiral Luis Carrero Blanco.

The movements for autonomy in Galicia and Andalucía, although important, are not regarded by most scholars as equal to those in Catalonia or the Basque country. The autonomy movements in Catalonia and the Basque country are different from those in Galicia and Andalucía, and many other European societies, in that the opposition challenging the central power did not emerge from an agriculturally and economically underdeveloped region. Catalonia and the Basque region are commercial and industrial centers. Catalan nationalism is a product of the commercial bourgeoisie and is used by this class as an instrument to pressure the Spanish government into making concessions favorable to the manufacturing interests. Basque nationalism has a strong populist component and the Basque financial and industrial bourgeoisie have never really been attracted to it and remain procentralist. They are satisfied to let Madrid make policy for the Basque country as long as that policy is not harmful to their economic interests. Basque nationalism is closely tied to the working class and to the changes in social structure concomitant with industrialization and consequent immigration (Linz 1973b, 80). Galicia is a region of immigrants, first to America and recently to Europe. The region is predomionantly rural with the majority of the population living on miniscule plots of land called *minifundios*. The region suffers from excessive population and an underdeveloped agricultural economy. The majority of the population speak Gallego, especially in the rural areas. Since the Middle Ages, Galicia has been integrated into the Castillian-Leonese monarchy. Unlike Catalonia and the Basque country, Galicia has never, since the beginning of the modern Spanish state, had political institutions of its own. Andalucía is similar to Galicia in many respects, although there is no linguistic basis to Andalucian nationalism—Spanish is the spoken language. It is also an underdeveloped region, but the majority of the population are landless laborers. Most of the good agricultural land is privately owned and held in large estates called *latifundios*. Andalucian nationalism dates back to the petty bourgeois intellectual, Blas Infante. Recently it has been revived by the urban middle classes under the leadership of Alejandro Rojas Marcos, a leader of the Andalucian Socialist party, or Partido Socialista Andaluz (PSA). The goal of the party is to achieve Andalucian autonomy and redress grievances against Madrid. Party rhetoric is Socialist and at times radical, even though party actions are very centrist, due in part to the party's urban middle class constituency. The PSA surprised observers by winning five seats in the 1979 general elections, but lost them in the general elections of 1982. Both Galician and Andalucian nationalist movements have their roots in the subordinate, dependent relationship with Madrid. Both regions suffer from high unemployment and underdevelopment. Intellectuals in both movements identify closely with Marxist ideas, and autonomy is seen as a panacea for their economic and social inferiority.

Regionalism in Spain sets it apart from the transition to parliamentary democracy in Portugal and Greece. This cleavage in Spanish politics adds a dimension of uncertainty. The army has always zealously guarded the territorial unity of Spain, and in both uprisings in the twentieth century has brutally crushed nationalist movements. So regional leaders must weigh their demands for autonomy against their demands for democracy. If they push too hard and too fast for autonomy, they might end up with neither. All four regions have regional governments, but the constitution distinguishes between "nationalities" and "regions." The Catalan and Basque regions have more power than in Galicia and Andalucía where transfer of power has been much slower (España 1981, 14–15). This is partly because the government in Madrid is centralist and cautious about the weakening of its own power.

After the passage of the Law of Political Reform on November 20, Suárez turned his attention to securing the support of the army. On September 8, 1976, he met with senior military officers and sought their support. Poulantzas tended to underplay the 'economic-corporate' interests of the military in seeking a normalization of the regime. There were many younger officers in favor of professionalizing and depoliticising the military, and many of them founded the clandestine Democratic Military Union, or Unión Militar Democrática (UMD), which supported the democratization of the regime (Caparros 1983; Fortes and Otero 1983, 26–38, 231–32). The army's cooperation with Suárez in supporting the Law of Political Reform was a crucial turning point in the transition and proved to strengthen the position of Suárez in leading the "reform from above."

Next, Suárez turned his attention to the democratic opposition forces. In contrast to his predecessor Arias Navarro, he decided, with the aim of isolating the Francoists, to open up a dialogue with opposition leaders. Suárez met with Felipe González, leader of the PSOE, and other leaders of the opposition in the ensuing months. He was successful in persuading them that his reforms would dismantle the Franco regime, and thus by the winter of 1976 and early 1977 the moderate opposition (Liberals, Christian Democrats, and Social Democrats) were willing to participate in "fair" elections. Under the leadership of the young González, the PSOE claimed 75,000 members (Carr and Fusi 1981, 224), and at their annual conference in December 1976 they agreed to participate in the constituent elections.

Suárez had successfully divided the opposition through his reform measures. The extreme Left refused to participate and the moderate opposition was skeptical about risking the democratization process over the question of the legalization and participation of the PCE. This left the PCE and its leadership with no alternative but to go on the offensive. On December 10, Carrillo appeared in Madrid and was promptly arrested. He was released within a couple of days because Suárez faced the possible defection of the moderate opposition, who considered repression of the PCE unacceptable. Negotiations between the government and the opposition began in the first months of 1977. The PCE was excluded from these negotiations, but the crucial question at this juncture was whether or not it would be excluded from legalization. The PCE still had bitter enemies within the government who opposed its legalization, such as Manuel Fraga Iribarne, not to mention the traditional hostility of the army. The PCE strategy was to make their legalization the central issue of the success or failure of the government, and in January 1977 the opposition announced the inclusion of Carrillo as representative of the PCE on the committee negotiating with Suárez. By February the climate of opinion was in favor of the legalization of the Communist party. The king and Suárez were still reluctant to legalize the PCE lest the army intervene.

Suárez came up with what he thought would release the government from this potentially dangerous decision. He announced a new law where political parties applying for legalization would be approved within 10 days or their case transferred to the supreme court. The court, however, refused to rule on the PCE application for legalization, declaring it a political question, and Suárez's maneuver failed. Nevertheless, in a bold move, he legalized the PCE on April 9, 1977. In a previous meeting on September 8, 1976, he had given the 29 highest ranking military officials assurances that he would not legalize the PCE. Rumors of a coup were everywhere and a general crisis took hold of the country. It was only through the intervention of the king in appeasing the army that a coup was averted. In addition, the relative moderation of the PCE, in accepting the monarchy and the national flag, played a significant role. Part of what motivated Suárez to legalize the PCE was an effort to split the Left electorate and weaken the PSOE in the upcoming general elections.

After this point the only questions that remained were the mode of elections. The government commission and the opposition decided on a method of proportional representation called the D'Hont system, which gave opportunities for some minority groups but advantages to the larger parties, so that splintering would not be a great problem. In addition, the movement, which was the only legal party of Franco loyalists, was to be dismantled, all parties given equal access to television during the campaign, and the general elections set for June 15, 1977. The elections closed an important chapter in the transition to parliamentary democracy in Spain. Suárez successfully used the institutional machinery of the Franco regime to gradually restore parliamentary democracy to Spain. The behavior of the opposition, especially the PCE and PSOE, in this first phase of the transition was crucial to the survival of the process. The majority of the opposition forces had agreed upon a gradual "negotiated" break or pacting as opposed to a rupture. The PCE, in particular, was forced to renounce some of its most cherished demands: "democratic rupture," a provisional government, and a referendum on the issue of monarchy versus republic. These compromises, however, proved important in the transformation of the Spanish regime from authoritarianism to parliamentary democracy because Francoists and the army were deprived of a pretext for intervention in the name of Francoism. Ironically, this moderation on the part of the Spanish Left may also preclude a transition to democratic socialism or a "sweeping transformation" of the Spanish state.

The electoral campaign officially began one month before election day. During the campaign political posters and handbills littered the streets of most cities and the election was held in an atmosphere of relative calm, marred by few incidents; 18 million people turned out to vote, 79 percent of the electorate. The PCE captured 9.3 percent of the national vote (1.7 million votes) and trailed well behind Suárez's UCD with 34.8 percent and González' PSOE with 29.4 percent. The electoral results for the PSOE were impressive and revealed that the party was still a major force in Spanish politics, even though two years previously it had lacked any organization in the country. In June 1977 it ranked as the second largest party and main opposition force in Spain, having won comfortably in every major city and most crucial industrial areas, including the Basque country. On the right the AP, composed mainly of Franco loyalists and leading figures of the last decade of the Franco regime, received only 8.5 percent of the vote. The big winners were the Suárez coalition, UCD, and PSOE. The PSOE captured 118 seats in the Congress of Deputies, whereas the UCD captured 165, just 11 short of an absolute majority of 176. The AP, headed by Fraga Iribarne, was able to secure only 16 seats, whereas the PCE garnered 20, most of them in Catalonia. The rest of the 31 seats were divided among regionalist and splinter parties.

The elections produced several important results. First, it confirmed the weakness of Francoism on the Right and the PCE on the Left, revealing the moderation of the Spanish electorate and its desire for democratization. Second, the major cleavages were formed by an ideologically polarized, class-based, Left-Right division, and a center-periphery, nationalism-centralism line of division (in Catalonia and the Basque country). Absent was the religious cleavage (clerical-anticlerical) and the institutional cleavage (monarchy-republic) (Maravall and Santamaría 1986, 85). Third, the results demonstrated an almost equal division between the Left and the Right, making a strategy of compromise and pact making a necessity.

Several authors (Lancaster and Prevost, eds. 1985) have focused on the factors that contributed to a climate of pact making or consociational techniques in the transition to parliamentary democracy in Spain. They focus on the composition of the decision-making coalition and the nature of the costs and benefits to the political participants. They are concerned with how the new regime institutionalizes particular patterns, processes, and structures of political recruitment, representation, and mediation. Their basic assumption is that a change in the decision-making coalition parallels a change in regime (Lancaster and Prevost 1985, 3–4). Others believe that the lesson learned from the experience of the Second Republic was to avoid block action and majoritarian principles in making basic decisions about political institutions (Maravall and Santamaría 1986, 86). The threat of army intervention also reinforced the tendency to compromise and avoid polarization.

The first tasks of the new parliament and Suárez's minority government were to write a new constitution, decide the issue of regional autonomy, and solve the worsening economic crisis. In addition, the post-1977 election period was marked by an upswing in political terrorism—aimed at destabilizing the young democracy.

The two most important issues for the new government were the economic crisis, reflected by rising unemployment, rampant inflation (above 30 percent), and the growing trade deficit; and the growing regional autonomy movements, particularly in Catalonia and the Basque country.

After the June 1977 elections, the PCE leadership realized the necessity of narrowing the gap between them and the PSOE in order not to become locked in a permanent position on the Left as a minor force. By the same token Suárez and the UCD were in need of electoral support, because they did not command an absolute majority. This unusual circumstance led the UCD and PCE to share a common interest, the prevention of the PSOE from acquiring more political power. By the summer of 1977 the PCE had begun its offensive against the PSOE. PCE leadership called for a "government of national concentration," which would include the participation of the UCD, the PSOE, Catalan and Basque nationalists, and the PCE.

The reaction of the PSOE leadership was lukewarm at best. Fresh from their electoral success in June, they were in no way willing to sacrifice their unity. They interpreted the call by the PCE as an effort to weaken them prior to the next election when they believed they would emerge as the majority party.

By September 1977 the economic situation had deteriorated to a near state of crisis. Inflation was out of control and Suárez seemed unable to come to an agreement with labor leaders over future wage increases. In addition, political terrorism was at a new height. The crisis of hegemony and threat to the fragile democracy led Suárez, on October 5, 1977, to ask the leaders of all the main political parties to join him in the Moncloa Palace for a two-day meeting to draw up an "emergency plan" and solve the "grave difficulties" facing Spain. Although initially there was much skepticism about his call for an "emergency plan," especially within the PSOE, all major parties attended. After much debate a general plan was outlined, and approved on October 25.

The Moncloa Pact was a big victory for the PCE and an explicit manifestation of the confluence of interests between it and the UCD. It further exacerbated tension between the PSOE and PCE. The PSOE had hesitantly signed the accords warning of possible complications. It was basically an austerity plan, which limited wage increases in 1978. Other measures included an increase in pensions and unemployment benefits, the establishment of trade union representation within companies, tax reform, a devaluation of the peseta, and a strict monetary policy. The Moncloa Pact included a number of concessions to the working class, in return for their support during this precarious transition period of economic crisis. It also served to demobilize the working class, at least temporarily, as economic conditions improved, inflation decreased to 16 percent in 1978 from 29 percent a year earlier, the balance of payments swiftly recovered, and exports increased 29 percent (Maravall 1982, 42).

The Moncloa Pact served as a major focal point during the trade union elections of 1978 and sharply divided the Socialist UGT and the PCE-dominated CCOO. The UGT criticized but eventually accepted the agreements, whereas the CCOO gave the agreements their wholehearted support. The UGT had made impressive gains since the Socialist electoral success in June 1977, coming back from virtual extinction to rival the CCOO within the labor movement. This was partly due to government aid, which was aimed at countering the predominance of the CCOO within the labor movement. In December 1977 the government decreed a law that established elections by workers of delegates to firm committees in the winter and spring of 1978. The CCOO won with 34.5 percent of the delegates; UGT was second with 21.6 percent; and USO a distant third with 3.7 percent. The CCOO was the clear but not overwhelming victor of the trade union elections, whereas the UGT did reasonably well considering their late start and previously limited geographically concentration in Asturias and the Basque country.

After the trade union elections, friction between the PCE and the PSOE continued unabated. The PCE gained some advantage from its privileged relationship with Suárez, largely at the cost of the PSOE. For example, the Communists insisted that the method of election for the mayors of the municipalities not be the head of the list with the most votes; rather they preferred a method that would include a second round if there was no clear majority. A plurality would then suffice. This forced the Socialists to turn to the PCE for support, and Suárez subsequently received Communist support during the constitutional debates on many key controversial provisions.

Drafting the constitution took slightly more than a year. Parliamentary debate was emotional but controlled, with the most intractable issue over regional autonomy. By mid-October a mixed commission of deputies and senators worked on the final draft, which was presented to the full Córtes for a vote on October 31. The new constitution was approved by both houses by a vote of 551 to 11, with 22 abstentions. On December 6, Spanish voters overwhelmingly approved the constitution by an 87.8 percent majority.

Shortly after the constitutional referendum, Suárez decided to call general elections for a number of reasons: terrorism was again on the rise; the military was showing signs of discontent, and a general mood of disenchantment had gripped the country. Suárez dissolved the Córtes and called for parliamentary elections for March 1979, to be followed by municipal elections in April. He was not going to repeat the mistake of Alfonso XIII in calling municipal elections first, and he was aware that the Left would be very strong in the municipal elections and did not want them to have momentum going into the general elections.

All major parties approached the general elections of March 1979 with the hope of greatly increasing their voting strength. It was generally believed that the electoral map had not yet crystallized (Maravall 1979, 304). The PSOE leadership believed that they would emerge as the number one party and form a government on their own. Suárez and the UCD believed the same. The PCE was not as ambitious; its strategy was to attract that portion of the electorate that had voted for the CCOO during the 1978 trade union elections and to prepare for the municipal elections the following month. Some 60 percent of the workers who had supported the Communist-dominated CCOO in the trade union elections voted for the PSOE in 1977 (Maravall 1979, 305). Thus the key element in the PCE strategy was to win the vote of the 3 million workers who had voted for the CCOO in 1978.

The campaign between the PCE and the PSOE became increasingly vitriolic as election day approached. The Communists were particularly harsh in their denunciation of the Socialists as Social Democrats fashioned after the West German example, thus not truly representative of the Left in Spain. The Socialists responded by arguing that a vote for the PSOE was a "useful" vote, which should not be wasted on a small political party (Maravall 1979, 350). Both parties were competing for what Maravall, utilizing Giovanni Sartori's party systems' model, refers to as strategic sections of the electorate; that is, the competition followed the model of polarized pluralism. Each party portrayed the other as the extremist. Thus the PSOE portrayed the UCD as a conservative Francoist party; the UCD portrayed the PSOE as a dangerous Marxist party; and the PSOE portrayed Fraga's new party, the CD, and PCE as extremist rightest and leftist parties, respectively.

There were two important aspects to the 1979 general elections: first, the advantage UCD derived from monopolizing state resources such as television and research institutes during the campaign; and second, the changed nature of the campaign to one more issue-oriented, where campaign rhetoric moved from the debate between dictatorship or democracy, to issues such as unemployment, divorce, abortion, and inflation (Maravall 1979, 360).

As election neared, pundits and pollsters erroneously predicted a Socialist victory on March 1. When Spanish voters returned to the polls for the fourth time in as many years, turnout was reduced by 316,839 votes due to an exceptionally high abstention rate (33.6 percent compared to 21.6 percent in 1977), even though the 1978 constitution gave 18-year-olds the right to vote (Maravall 1979, 307). Nevertheless, Spanish voters once again demonstrated their moderation and gradualism by returning the UCD to the Córtes as the major party with 168 seats. The UCD captured 35.5 percent of the vote for 168 seats; the PSOE 30.8 percent for 121 seats; the PCE 10.9 percent for 23 seats; and the CD (former AP) 5.8 percent for 9 seats. The rest of the vote (about 30 seats) was divided among other minor parties.

The PSOE and González regarded the elections as somewhat of a failure for them, for they did not attract enough of the centrist vote from the UCD and lost many votes to regional Socialist parties. The Right, represented by Fraga's new coalition CD, failed to produce their new majority; they fell from 16 seats to 9. The PCE leadership regarded the results as generally favorable; they had increased their vote in 41 of the 51 districts and increased their overall vote by approximately 300,000 (Mujal-León 1983, 184). The most significant features of this election were the high abstention rate (33.6 percent) and the success of the nationalist Left. Two parties in the Basque country, Herri Batasuna and Euzkadiko Ezkerra, captured four seats between them, and the Andalucian PSA captured five seats. The surprising performance of the nationalist parties, especially that of the PSA, probably reflected the dissatisfaction of the urban middle class in those regions with the progress of political and economic reform. Andalucía was one of the most unemployed and economically dependent regions in the country. The election of five PSA deputies to the Córtes reflected the electoral skepticism of Andalucian voters on the ability of the centralist-oriented PSOE to meet the needs of Andalucía.

Most scholars regard the adoption of the 1978 constitution and the general elections of 1979 as marking the end of transition to parliamentary democracy in Spain and the beginning of the consolidation phase. Both of these events led to a shift in the strategy of the opposition. The formation of a new UCD government signaled the beginning of a third phase of opposition and a new stage in the transition, characterized more by party opposition than by interparty cooperation (Maravall 1982, 159). Opposition from the PSOE and PCE was increasingly directed against the economic and social policies of the government. The PSOE specifically called for greater public investment, the creation of jobs, better and more extensive education, and unemployment benefits. The PCE demanded reform of the government-controlled RTVE (Spanish radio and television). These demands culminated in the failure of a PSOE-initiated motion of censure against the government in May 1980.

The bulk of left-wing opposition to the government was now represented by the Socialists and Communists. After the 1979 general elections both parties underwent a period of soul searching as they attempted to fit into the new democracy with organizational and ideological debate. After the 1979 elections, the PSOE intensified its attacks on the government, bitter over Suárez's last-minute attacks on its democratic credentials.

The failure of the PSOE to defeat the UCD in the legislative elections caused an internal debate around the issue of party alliance policies. The Communists and Socialists had been discussing for months the possibility of a municipal election alliance. The PCE favored such an alliance, hoping to gain local offices that would otherwise be denied due to their numbers. The PSOE was much more reluctant to enter into an electoral alliance and sacrifice their independence. The Socialists relented, however, when it became apparent that their candidates would probably need the support of the Communists. Political realism prompted the Socialist-Communist electoral pact.

The big winners of the April 3 municipal elections were the Left and the nationalist parties. Together the PCE and PSOE polled at least a million more votes than the UCD and won most of the major provincial capitals such as Madrid, Barcelona, and Valencia. Abstention was much higher than in the previous legislative elections, averaging more than 40 percent. In Andalucía the big winner was the Left, in particular the PSA, which held the swing vote in the formation of many local governments. The results of the municipal elections for the four major parties were as follows: the UCD captured 31.37 percent of the vote for 18,151 council seats; the PSOE 29.34 percent for 6,750 council seats; the PCE 13.20 percent for 2,231 seats; and the CD 2.96 percent for 1,355 seats. The rest of the seats were divided among nationalist parties.

After the municipal elections, the PCE believed that they could shift competition between themselves and the PSOE away from the political arena to the labor arena. Here Communist strength was much greater. The PCE pursued an activist, confrontational strategy during this third phase of opposition. The Socialist trade union, on the other hand, moved away from a strategy of confrontation to one of negotiation, whereas the party itself followed a strategy of firmer opposition to the UCD government, abandoning the politics of consensus (Maravall 1982, 160). The consolidation of the PCE and PSOE as responsible parties of the moderate Left during this third phase of opposition was a crucial step toward the consolidation of parliamentary democracy in Spain, but may have also precluded the possibility of a transition to democratic socialism. The right had no excuse for overthrowing the government as they had in July 1936, just five years after the advent of the republic.

During 1980 a series of electoral defeats for the UCD in regional parliamentary elections drew attention to the parties' future electoral prospects. In October 1981 the party suffered a stunning defeat in regional elections in Galicia, one of its electoral strongholds. This was followed in May 1982 by another serious defeat in regional parliamentary elections in Andalucía. These defeats sparked a crisis within the party between its various factions over the policies and future direction of the UCD.

The disintegration of the UCD was the result of its origins as a coalition of diverse political factions that had never completely solidified. This disintegration reached crisis proportions in the summer of 1982 when various factions broke away to form independent parties. It seemed certain that general elections were not far away and the different political groupings within the UCD began to jockey for position. This further hastened the decline of the party and led to its immobilization in governing the country and solving the economic problems facing the young democracy.

On August 28, 1982, President Leapoldo Calvo Sotelo dissolved the Córtes, calling for early general elections on October 28. He cited the ongoing crisis of the UCD and the creation of new parties dividing the government as obstacles to the opening of a new period of parliamentary sessions in stable and efficacious conditions. Quite simply, the ruling government party, the UCD, was disintegrating rapidly into its diverse elements of Liberals, Christian Democrats, and Social Democrats (López Pintor 1985, 301–5). Throughout September and October, the major parties began to prepare for the elections.

The Socialist party program was based upon five essential points, with a time frame of 10 years for its full implementation. First was the fight against the economic crisis and especially against unemployment, which in December 1982 was running about 17 percent; the PSOE program called for the creation of 800,000 jobs in the next four years. The second objective was the fight against inequality; González proclaimed that "education is the gravest instrument of social inequality" (*El Pais*, 9-17-82: 11) and the new government planned to renovate the educational system by making equal education available to all social classes. The third objective was the defense of individual civil liberties, including a system of public order that protects against terrorism and was seen as one of the biggest threats against the democracy. Also on the agenda was reform of the penal code, which prohibited abortions, permitting them in special cases. The fourth objective was a reorganization of the state bureaucracy to include improving state services and trimming unnecessary functionaires as well as reforming and reorganizing the repressive state apparatus. Also, the process of the transfer of power to the regional autonomies would be carried to its final conclusion. The fifth objective of the PSOE program was a reorientation of Spanish foreign policy, which the PSOE had indicated for its "lack of rationality." The main points of concern were Spanish membership in the North Atlantic Treaty Organization (NATO), which the PSOE wanted to submit to a national referendum, the return of Gibralter to Spanish sovereignty, and the expended role the government would play in relations with Arab neighbors and Latin America.

None of these objectives was revolutionary or threatened to radically alter capitalist relations of production. In fact, the PSOE program was rather conservative by comparison to other socialist parties of Europe. In the area of the economy the nature of the PSOE program was particularly revealing. The basic concern was the recuperation of private investment through the restructuring of official credit and savings. The program also called for the rescue of banks in crisis through state intervention, i.e., public money. The public sector was the principal instrument of economic development and would be used to rescue sectors in crisis. The PSOE program assigned a priority role to the public sector in cooperation with the private sector. The three areas where the public sector would play a major role were public services, energy, and businesses grouped under the INI. The PSOE program also called for modifications in the tax structure, such as fighting tax evasion and making taxes more equitable, but hardly called for any major reform that would threaten economic recovery by stifling capital accumulation.

The PSOE, PCE, and Suárez' newly formed center party, the Democratic and Social Center, or Centro Democrático y Social (CDS), all planned to run on an independent ticket. Anticipating victory, the Socialists were not about to share power with a second party. The Communists were hoping to increase their share of the vote, and Suárez's hastily formed party, the CDS, was as yet untested. The UCD, now headed by Landelino Lavilla, was considering entering into an electoral alliance with Fraga's right-wing party, the AP. This fell through when the executive committee of UCD overwhelmingly rejected an electoral coalition with the AP. Fraga's party did, however, enter into an electoral coalition with the party of Oscar Alzaga, the Popular Democratic Party, or Partido Democrático Popular (PDP).

The results of the October general elections ushered in a new era in Spanish politics. It was the first time that such legislative elections had produced an absolute majority; it was also the first time the Socialists had produced an absolute majority in the Córtes since its founding in 1879, and it ensured that the party would govern in a situation of democratic normalcy. In addition, there was a spectacular increase in participation from 68 percent in 1979 to 80 percent in 1982. This increase in voter participation seems to confirm the belief of many political observers that the 1982 general elections provided a major contribution to the legitimacy of the new democracy.

The most obvious result of the legislative elections was the spectacular advance of the PSOE and the right-wing AP at the expense of the center party UCD and the PCE. The PSOE won 46 percent of the vote for 201 seats, well above their 30.5 percent and 121 seats in 1979. The AP-PDP increased from 5.76 percent and 9 seats in 1979 to 25.3 percent and 106 seats in 1982. Both the PSOE and AP-PDP made considerable electoral gains since 1979. The UCD fell from 34.96 percent and 168 seats in 1979 to 7.2 percent and 12 seats, an incredible but not unexpected decline, and Calvo Sotelo did not even win a seat in the new Córtes. The PCE suffered a major defeat, falling from their 1979 high of 10.81 percent of the vote for 23 seats, to a dismal 3.8 percent good for only 5 seats. Suárez's party, the CDS, captured 2.8 percent of the vote for 2 seats, a rather disappointing show. The rest of the seats were divided among the various nationalist parties with the Basque and Catalan middle class parties capturing 20 seats between them.

The election of a Socialist majority to the Spanish Córtes in October 1982 exemplified a concrete case of class struggle and compromise on the road to parliamentary democracy, and it would be useful to analyze PSOE strategy and locate it within the historical and theoretical debate concerning the parliamentary road to socialism. Since the 1982 elections, the PSOE policies were closer to a social democratic model than a socialist one. The party program did not call for a transition to socialism, which would entail "the passing of state power to the working class, or a coalition of formerly exploited classes within which the working class plays a dominant role" (Bettelheim 1978, 21); or a transition to a socialist mode of production. Rather, their policies fostered capital accumulation and strengthened private capital. State power remained firmly in the hands of the bourgeoisie, and the capitalist mode of production was strengthened and rationalized, not weakened or challenged.

This change in PSOE strategy mirrored the transition of Spanish public opinion—from liberal to social democratic (McDonough 1986, 736–60). The PSOE attempted to implement a conservative version of social democracy, not socialism. The latter would entail overcoming the contradiction between socialized production and private ownership, an issue which the PSOE has so far side stepped. They did so, in my opinion, in the belief that the best way to overcome the current economic crisis facing Spain and obtain benefits for the workers is, as Mark Kesselman has suggested was the case for Sweden, a strategy of parliamentary reformism and compromise (Kesselman 1982, 397–438). One must keep in mind the history of the PSOE as an electoral party and its role in the breakdown of the Spanish Republic to fully understand its ambivalence toward a confrontational strategy and its rapid social democratization.

The debate over the proper path in the transition to socialism is an old one. Lenin was one of the first theorists to apply Marxist thought to the construction of socialism in concrete historical conditions. He believed that a dictatorship of the proletariat was necessary during the transition from capitalism to socialism because of the resistance of the bourgeoisie and the external/internal wars that socialist revolutions generate (Lenin 1976, 421). Lenin's ideas on the transition to socialism were challenged by other Marxists such as Karl Kautsky and Rosa Luxemburg. They differed with him regarding such issues as the pace of the transition process, the use of coercion in the process, the nature of the class struggle during this period, whether a dictatorial form of government was necessary, the importance of establishing political democracy in the transition, and the role of the revolutionary party during the transition period (Harris 1988, 10).

The Spanish Socialist party seems to have adopted the strategy of Karl Kautsky who argued that the transition from capitalism to socialism in advanced industrial societies could and should take place in a democratic manner following the electoral victory of a mass-based Socialist party. He believed that the parliamentary road to socialism would eventually culminate in a revolutionary break with capitalism and the rapid construction of socialism.

## SOCIALIST GOVERNMENT IN SPAIN

The PSOE governed Spain for more than three years before being reelected by a slightly smaller majority in the general elections of June 1986. The PSOE captured 44 percent of the vote and 184 seats, a decline of 4.4 percent of the vote, or 18 seats, still in absolute majority in the parliament. The PCE-dominated coalition United Left, or Izquierda Unida (IU), did surprisingly well in the 1986 elections, capturing 4.6 percent of the vote, and 7 seats, a big improvement over 1982. The other major parties of the center-Right remained relatively stable with Manuel Fraga's Popular Coalition, or Coalición Popular (CP), winning 26 percent of the vote, and 105 seats, a reduction of one from 1982; and Suárez's CDS party improving from 6.7 percent of the vote to 9.3 percent, a gain of 8 seats.

In 1989, Prime Minister González called for early general elections hoping positive economic growth rates since 1986 (4.6% a year) would help the socialist party retain its control of the parliament. González calculated that early elections would return a comfortable majority to parliament, while waiting another nine months might jeopardize the party's popularity due to tougher economic policies. He was correct, although his party almost came up short. The Socialists got 176 seats, the minimum necessary to govern without help from one of the opposition parties.

Since taking power in December 1982, The PSOE passed through a process of rapid social democratization (Share 1986b, 1–46). Winning a second term in office in June 1986 seems to have confirmed the electoral correctness of the party's ideological shift toward social democracy, which took place without the negative electoral consequences experienced by other European socialist parties. The PSOE came into power promising profound and radical change. The performance of the PSOE in its first term of office was a deep disappointment to those who expected profound changes in every aspect of Spanish society and a "true" transition to socialism.

The PSOE came into government promising to reduce unemployment by creating 800,000 new jobs, expanding public investment, reindustrializing the economy, democratizing the universities, reforming the bureaucracy and the military, holding a referendum on NATO membership, and joining the EEC. The program for change was referred to as "El Cambio" (the change). The most pressing problem faced by the new Socialist government was the economy. At the end of 1982, Spain's unemployment rate was approximately 16 percent of the active population, or over 2 million Spaniards (Share 1986b, 6). Nevertheless, the González government decided to reject its promise to create new jobs and expand the economy, and opted instead for an economic austerity program that involved limiting wages and government spending as well as immediate layoffs of over 60,000 workers. The government also devalued the peseta and raised the price of gasoline, electricity, and public transportation. Many observers believe the PSOE is the first government to institute a genuine economic stabilization program since 1957 (Share 1986b, 8).

On the foreign policy side, the PSOE reversed its earlier opposition to NATO membership. Spain had formally applied for membership in September 1981 under the leadership of the UCD, and the Córtes approved Spain's entry into NATO in October 1981. The PSOE and PCE originally voted against Spain's entry into NATO. Felipe González pledged to call for a referendum on the issue and promosed to campaign for Spain's exit from NATO. The PSOE's 29th Party Congress called for Spain's withdrawal from the alliance, but by late October 1984 the González government was willing to accept Spain's membership in NATO, although slightly over a majority of public opinion opposed NATO membership. The PSOE set March 12, 1986, for the NATO referendum and promised to campaign in favor of membership. The referendum passed with 52.53 percent voting in favor; 39.84 percent opposed; and 7.63 percent spoiled or blank. The most revealing result was the unusually high abstention rate of 40.26 percent, reflecting the public's disenchantment with the PSOE's shift in position over NATO membership.

The PSOE's radical departure from their previous position over entry into NATO was the result of several factors. First, acceptance of NATO by socialist and social-democratic parties in Europe was the norm not the exception, and the PSOE had close ties with many of these parties. Second, Spain's withdrawal from NATO would damage its image abroad and hurt its integration into the Common Market. And third, there existed within the military a very strong pro-NATO sentiment, and the Socialists were very reluctant to upset this sector. Integration into NATO also promised to modernize the military and occupy them with external defense rather than internal politics.

One of the most controversial reform measures implemented by the Socialist government was the social security system. In an effort to limit costs the government capped payments for injured, sick, and elderly, tied pension increases to cost of living adjustments, and increased the number of working years required to earn a pension from two to eight years (Share 1986b, 9). This reform bill split the PSOE and its trade union, the UGT, who complained that "the government wants to streamline the economy on the backs of the workers" (Share 1986b, 9). The split between the PSOE and its trade union, the UGT, reflected the class contradiction of the Socialist government's strategy of *pactismo,* or coming to agreement. Upon becoming a party in government, the PSOE ceased exclusively representing working class interests. The PSOE's austerity program was the result of the class contradictions inscribed in the very structure of the state. Poulantzas argued that as a relationship of forces between classes and class fractions, the state is riven with class divisions and the state's policy is the result of their functioning within the state (1980, 132).

Poulantzas explained how the state apparatuses consecrate and reproduce hegemony by bringing the power bloc and certain dominated classes into a game of provisional compromises (1980, 140). Throughout the transition to democracy, party and union leaders adopted "defensive positions" (Share 1986b, 6). As indicated earlier, the transition to democracy was a process controlled by the dominant classes whose primary concern was to consolidate the young democracy. Leaders of the opposition were similarly concerned with protecting the nascent democracy from those forces opposed to it. The result was a succession of government-sponsored political economic pacts starting with the Moncloa pacts of 1977, involving the state, the major political parties, the major trade unions, and business associations.

Victor Pérez Díaz (1987, 216–46) has examined the effects that social pacts and class compromise have had on the medium and long-term development of Spanish economic development. He argues that in Spain, where the western combination of liberalism and capitalism is just beginning, social pacts have made a very important contribution to the legitimation of the market economy.

After 1982 the Spanish state represented the hegemony within the power bloc of the monopoly fractions of the bourgeoisie. The austerity program implemented by the Socialist government was supported by these fractions of the bourgeoisie. As a result, class struggle between the dominated classes and the dominant class increased through strikes in 1984 by 30 percent (Share 1986a, 191). The austerity program favored the bourgeoisie by creating a favorable climate for foreign and domestic investment. This is supported by the subsequent boom in the Spanish stock markets and a marked increase in direct foreign investment. The Socialist government's decision to allocate scarce resources into the most technologically advanced and most competitive industries also favored those fractions of the bourgeoisie that are concentrated in these sectors.

## THE DEMOCRATIC ROAD TO SOCIALISM

Poulantzas' analysis of the transition to parliamentary democracy in Spain was largely concerned with the problems of class alliances and whether the transition should be coupled with an antimonopoly struggle and a strategy of democratic transition to democratic socialism. He commented on the decline of political democracy in the contemporary capitalist state and its implications for the rise of authoritarian-statism (Poulantzas 1980, 207–14). He pointed to the decline of democracy in civil as well as political society and to the development of a potentially fascistic, antipopular parallel state apparatus. This state operates to prevent any rise in popular struggles that would threaten bourgeois hegemony. To combat this trend toward authoritarian-statism, Poulantzas advocated a democractic struggle for democratic socialism. The important question for Poulantzas was: Under whose hegemony is the struggle for democratic socialism to be made (p. 60)?

In Spain the antidictatorial alliance within the dominant classes and with the popular classes was clearly under the leadership of the bourgeoisie, a process of reform from above. The popular classes played an important role in making demands from below but were clearly held in check by the oppositions' strategy of negotiated break, due to their fear that the repressive state apparatus, i.e., the army, would intervene to stop the process.

Poulantzas did not believe a transition to parliamentary democracy in Spain could be telescoped with a process of transition to socialism and national liberation because the world conjuncture and objective conditions in Spain excluded this possibility. It was also due to the failure of the working class and its organization to play a hegemonic role in the transition to parliamentary democracy (p. 60). In Spain the antidictatorial alliance was not an antimonopoly alliance. On the contrary, it was led by this fraction of the bourgeoisie. There was never an antimonopoly program, let alone a socialist one.

The Socialist rise to power in 1982 represented the political restructuring of the bourgeoisie on the basis of a new compromise between competing fractions of the bourgeoisie and between the bourgeoisie and the popular classes. The former compromise was a result of a crisis of hegemony, whereas the latter was necessitated because of a crisis of capital accumulation. The bourgeoisie involved the parties of the Left in the restructuring of capitalism. Thus they have achieved two goals: the legitimization of the democratic capitalist state under the control of a "workers" party, and a reorganized and rationalized process of capital accumulation.

Although Poulantzas did not believe that the transition to democratic socialism in Spain would take place under the hegemony of the bourgeoisie, he did believe that a transition from dictatorship to parliamentary democracy could be led by certain fractions of the bourgeoisie, or what he called the domestic bourgeoisie. But he was quick to point out that the forms of "democratic" regime that replace the dictatorships run the risk of remaining compromised by the way in which these regimes have been overthrown. This was particularly true in the Spanish case.

The transition to parliamentary democracy in Spain was a process of reform from above controlled by the bourgeoisie. Poulantzas provided a valuable analysis of the composition and politics of the ruling class, and its subsequent fragmentation and opposition to the dictatorship. He failed, however, to explain why the Spanish regime was transformed to parliamentary democracy without a serious rupture or break. This was due, as argued here, to his misunderstanding of the syncretic ideology of the Franco dictatorship and its ability to neutralize the popular classes and cement together the social formation. Poulantzas also neglected an analysis of the strategies and tactics of the major Left opposition parties—the Socialist PSOE and Communist PCE. This contributed to his misjudging the depth and rapidity of the transition to parliamentary democracy and subsequent rapid social democratization of the Spanish regime.

## References

Aramberri, J. R. 1979. The political transition in Spain. An interpretation. *The Socialist Register,* 172–203.

Arango, E. Ramón. 1978. *The Spanish Political System: Franco's Legacy,* Boulder, CO: Westview Press.

Ariza, Julián. 1976. *Comisiones obreras*. Barcelona: Ovance.

Balroya, Enrique (ed). 1987. *Comparing New Democracies: Dilemmas of Transition and Consolidation in Mediterranean Europe and the Southern Cone,* Boulder, CO: Westview Press.

Bermeo, Nancy. 1987. Redemocratization and transition elections: A comparison of Spain and Portugal. *Comparative Politics* 19 (12): 213–31.

Bettelheim, Charles. 1978. *The Transition to Socialist Economy*. Sussex: Harvester.

Biescas, José Antonio and Manuel Tuñon de Lara. 1980. *España bajo la dictadura* (1939–1975). Madrid: Labor.

Busquets, Julio. 1967. *El militar de carrera en España*. Barcelona: Ariel.

Cammack, Paul. 1986. Resurgent democracy: Threat and promise. *New Left Review* 157 (May–June): 121–28.

Caparrós, Francisco. 1983. *La UMD: militares rebeldes*. Barcelona: Argos Vergara.

Carr, Raymond, and Juan Pablo Fusi. 1979. *Spain: Dictatorship to Democracy*. London: Allen and Unwin.

Carrillo, Santiago. 1978. *Eurocommunism and The State*. Nan Green and A. M. Elliott, trans. Westport, CT: Lawrence Hills.

Claudín, Fernando (ed). 1980. *Crisis de los partidos políticos*. Madrid: Dédalo Ediciones.

Cooper, Norman B. 1975. *Catholicism and the Franco Regime,* Sage Research Papers in the Social Sciences, Contemporary European Studies. Beverly Hills: Sage.

Drake, Paul W., and Eduardo Silva (eds.). 1986. *Elections and Democratization in*

*Latin America, 1980–85*. San Diego: Center for Iberian and L.A. Studies, U.C. San Diego.

España, Rafael Acosta. 1981. Introduction in *La España de las autonomías*. Madrid: Espasa-Calpe.

Fernández, Carlos, 1982. *Los militares en la transición política*. Barcelona: Editorial Argos Vergara.

Fortes, José and Luís Otero. 1983. *Proceso a nueve militares demócratas: las fuerzas armadas y la U.M.D*. Barcelona: Editorial Argos Vergara.

Giner, Carlos. 1973. Metamórfosis de la iglesia en diez años, *Cuadernos Para el Diálogo* 30 VIII (38) (December).

Giner, S., and J. Salcedo. 1976. The ideological practice of Nicos Poulantzas. *Archives of European Sociology* 17: 344–65.

Giner, S. and E. Sevilla. 1980. From despotism to parliamentarism: Class domination and political order in the Spanish state. pp. 197–229 in Richard Scase, ed, *The State in Western Europe*. New York: St. Martins Press.

Gramsci, Antonio. 1980a *The Modern Prince and Other Writings*. New York: International Publishers.

———. 1980b. *Selections From the Prison Notebooks*. Quintin Moore and Geoffrey Nowell Smith, New York: International Publications.

Gunther, Richard, Giacomo Sani, and Goldie Shabad. 1986. *Spain After Franco: The Making of a Competitive Party System*. Berkeley: University of California Press.

Harris, Richard. 1988. Marxism and the transition to socialism in Latin America. *Latin American Perspectives* 15 (Winter): 7–54.

Herman, Edward S., and James Petras. 1985. Resurgent democracy: Rhetoric and reality. *New Left Review* No. 154 (November–December): 83–98.

*Informe sociológico sobre el cambio político en España 1975–1981*. 1981. Madrid: Euramérica.

Juaregui, Fernando and Pedro Vega. 1983. *Crónica del antifranquismo, Vol. I 1939–1962*, Barcelona: Argos Vergara.

———. 1984. *Los hombres que lucharon por devolver la democracia a España*, Vol. 2 *1963–1970: el nacimiento de una nueva clase política*. Barcelona: Argos Vergara.

Jessop, Bob. 1985. *Nicos Poulantzas: Marxist Theory and Political Strategy*. New York: St. Martins.

Kesselman, Mark. 1982. Prospects for democratic socialism in advanced capitalism: Class struggle and compromise in Sweden and France. *Politics & Society* 2 (4): 397–438.

Lancaster, Thomas D. 1984. Spanish public policy and financial power, in Lancaster and Prevost (eds.).

Lancaster, Thomas D. and Gary Prevost (eds.). 1985. *Politics and Change in Spain*. New York: Praeger.

Lenin, V. I. 1976. *Selected Works*. New York: International.

Liebermann, S. 1985. Spain's economy in the 1980s: The tragedy of stagnation in the young Spanish democracy, in Lancaster and Prevost (eds.), 168–201.

Linz, Juan J. 1973a. Early state-building and late peripheral nationalisms against the state: The case of Spain, in Eisenstadt and Rokkan (eds.): *Building States and Nations*. Beverly Hills: Sage, 32–116.

———. 1973b. Opposition in and under an authoritarian regime: The case of Spain, in Robert A. Dahl (ed.): *Regimes and Opposition,* Ch. 6. (New Haven: Yale University Press, 171–259.

———. 1975. Totalitarian and authoritarian regimes, in Greenstein and Polsby (eds.): *Handbook of Political Science: Macropolitical Theory,* Vol. 3. Reading, MA: Addison Wesley, 175–411.

López Pintor, Rafael. 1982. *La opinión pública Española del Franquismo a la democracia*. Madrid: CIS.

———. 1985. The October 1982 general election and the evolution of the Spanish party system, in Howard R. Penniman and Eusebio M. Mujal-León (eds.): *Spain at the Polls, 1977, 1979, and 1982: A Study of National Elections*. Durham, NC: Duke University Press.

McDonough, Peter, Samuel H. Barnes, and Antonio López Piña. 1986. The growth of democratic legitimacy in Spain. *American Political Science Review* 80 (3): 735–60.

Maravall, José María. 1978. *Dictatorship and Political Dissent: Workers and Students in Franco's Spain*. New York: St. Martin's.

———. 1979. Political cleavages in Spain and the 1979 general elections. *Government and Opposition* 14 (3): 299–317.

———. 1981. *La política de la transición, 1975–1980*. Madrid: Taurus Ediciones.

———. 1982. *The Transition to Democracy in Spain*. London: Croom Helm.

Maravall, José María, and Julián Santamaria. 1986. Political change in Spain and the prospects for democracy, in O'Donnell, Schmitter, Whitehead (eds.), 71–108.

Medhurst, Kenneth N. 1973. *Government in Spain: The Executive at Work*. New York: Pergamon Press.

Miguel, Amando de, and Benjamin Oltra. 1978. Bonapartismo y catolicismo: Una hipótesis sobre los orígenes ideológicos del franquismo, in *Papers: Revista de Sociología,* No. 8. Barcelona: Universidad Autónoma de Barcelona, 53–102.

Mujal-León, Eusebio. 1983. *Communism and Political Change in Spain*. Bloomington: Indiana University Press.

Needler, Martin. 1980. The military withdrawal from power in South America. *Armed Forces and Society,* 6 (Summer): 14–624.

———. 1987. *The Problem of Democracy in Latin America*. Lexington, MA: Lexington Books.

Nef, Jorge. 1986. Redemocratization in Latin America, or the modernization of the status quo? *Canadian Journal of Latin American and Caribbean Studies* 11 (21): 43–55.

O'Donnell, Guillermo. 1973. *Modernization and Bureaucratic-Authoritarianism: Studies in South American Politics*. Berkeley: Institute of International Studies.

O'Donnell, Guillermo, Philippe Schmitter, and Laurence Whitehead (eds.). 1986. *Transitions from Authoritarian Rule*. Baltimore: John Hopkins University Press.

Payne, Stanley. 1984. *Spanish Catholicism: An Historical Overview*. Madison: University of Wisconsin Press.

Pérez Díaz, Victor. 1987. Economic policies and social pacts in Spain during the transition, in Schmitter and Streck (eds.): *Political Stability and Neo-Corporatism: Corporatist Integration and Societal Cleavages in Western Europe*. Beverly Hills: Sage, 216–46.

Poulantzas, Nicos. 1976. *The Crisis of the Dictatorships: Portugal, Greece, Spain*, London: New Left Books.

———. 1978. *Political Power and Social Classes*. London: New Left Books, Verso ed.

———. 1979. *Fascism and Dictatorship: The Crisis of the Third International*, London: New Left Books, Verso ed.

———. 1980. *State, Power, Socialism*. London: New Left Books, Verso ed.

Preston, Paul. 1986. *The Triumph of Democracy in Spain*. London: Methuen.

Przeworski, Adam. 1986. Some problems in the study of the transition to democracy, in O'Donnell et al. (eds), 47–63.

Richards, Gordon. 1985. The rise and decline of military authoritarianism in Latin America: The role of stabilization policy. *SAIS Review* 5 (Summer-Fall): 155–71.

———. 1986. Stabilization crisis and the breakdown of military authoritarianism in Latin America. *Comparative Political Studies* 18 (January): 449–85.

Roca, Jordi. 1987. Neo-corporatism in post-Franco Spain, in Schmitter and Streck (eds.): *Political Stability and Neo-Corporatism: Corporatist Integration and Societal Cleavages in Western Europe*. Beverly Hills: Sage.

Ruíz Rico, Juan José. 1936–71. *El papel político de la iglesia católica en la España de Franco (1936–1971)*. Madrid: Editorial Tecnos.

San Miguel, Luís García. 1981. *Teoría de la transición: Un análisis del modelo español, 1973–1978*. Madrid: Editora Nacional.

Servicio de Estudios del Banco Urquijo. 1980. *La economía española en la década de los 80*. Madrid: Alianza Universidad.

Shabad, Goldie, and Richard Gunther. 1982. Language, nationalism, and political conflict in Spain. *Comparative Politics,* 14 (14): 443:77.

Share, Donald. 1985. Two transitions: Democratization and the evolution of the Spanish Socialist Left. *West European Politics* 1 (January): 82–103.

———. 1986a. *The Making of Spanish Democracy*. New York: Praeger.

———. 1986b. Four years of Socialist Government in Spain: Tensions and Successes in the Consolidation of Party and Regime. Chicago, Paper delivered at the 1986 annual Meeting of the American Political Science Association.

Tusell, Xavier. 1977. *La oposición democrática al franquismo 1399–1962*. Barcelona: Editorial Planeta.

Vilar, Sergio. 1971. *Protagonistas de la España democrática: la oposición a la dictadura 1939–1969*. Madrid: Librería Española Ediciones Sociales.

———. 1977. *La naturaleza del franquismo*. Barcelona: Ediciones Peninsula.

———. 1984. *Historia del anti-franquismo 1939–1975*. Barcelona: Plaza y James Editores.

Weber, Max. 1958. From *Max Weber: Essays in Sociology*. Gerthe and C. Wright Mills, eds. and trans. New York: Oxford University Press.

Wright, A. 1977. *The Spanish Economy: 1959–1976*. New York: Holmes & Meier.

# Chapter 3

# Classes, Hegemony, and Portuguese Democratization

*Daniel Nataf and Elizabeth Sammis*

On April 25, 1974, a military coup d'etat ended Europe's oldest dictatorship, the Portuguese Estado Novo. Popular mobilization followed. Rather than a mere change in regime, the coup d'etat ushered in the "Revolution of Carnations." The ensuing social upheaval substantially transformed the Portuguese social structure. Southern agricultural workers occupied the large landed estates and thereby eliminated the economically and politically powerful latifundists; urban workers occupied many industries; and eventually the nationalization of the banks and major industries dismantled the "monopolistic groups" that had controlled finance, basic industries, and a large share of Portuguese social capital.

The scope of working class mobilization, the multitude of revolutionary organizations, the appearance of independent trade unions as well as councils of workers and residents, coupled with specific governmental acts such as nationalization, implied that the dominant class had lost control of the democratization process that followed the rise to power of the Movimento das Forças Armadas (Armed Forces Movement, MFA) in 1974. However, the "revolutionary gains" did not deepen with the consolidation of parliamentary democracy in 1976. Both the revolutionary interlude (roughly 1974–75) as well as the deradicalization process associated with the development of parliamentary democracy need to be explained. To what extent did the dominant class really experience a loss of power during the revolutionary period? What accounts for the apparent erosion of economic gains and political influence by the popular masses? How was socialism, once on the historical agenda, displaced by "bourgeois democracy"?

In *The Crisis of the Dictatorships,* Nicos Poulantzas (1976)* provided an analytical framework for examining these issues. He drew attention to the relationship between changes in the structure of the dominant class and the overthrow of the dictatorship. He maintained that historically the most influential segments of the dominant class were the comprador bourgeoisie, who acted merely as conduits for foreign capital and perpetuated Portuguese underdevelopment and colonialism, and the latifundists (large southern landowners) who also kept the country economically backward. Poulantzas identified a new segment, the domestic bourgeoisie, as a nationally based element that benefited from foreign investment and the European export market. He recognized that the entire dominant class supported the Portuguese dictatorship. Nonetheless, he asserted that the dictatorship favored the political and economic dominance of the comprador bourgeoisie and the latifundists. Consequently, as its economic importance increased, the domestic bourgeoisie sought political liberalization to acquire greater political power and influence over government policy. Unable to wrestle control from the comprador bourgeoisie and the latifundists under the dictatorship, the domestic bourgeoisie elicited the support of the popular masses in its program of instituting a competitive party system, civil liberties, and a negotiated "solution" to the colonial wars. Whereas the democratization process was to entail some popular participation, it largely remained a means of resolving antagonisms within the dominant class.

Poulantzas did not envision that the dominant class would lose control over the democratization process. He emphasized that the break with the military dictatorships could not "skip over a specific stage of democratization" and "be simply telescoped together with a transition to socialism." He argued that a socialist transition could not occur because "this process was taking place . . . under the hegemony of the domestic bourgeoisie" (p. 135). However, he also recognized that the direction and scope of democratization was strongly disputed, with the domestic bourgeoisie and the popular masses at times locked in combat, but he believed that the popular masses held only momentary control over the democratization process, and thus socialism, despite the rhetoric about it, was never really on the agenda. For Poulantzas, the erosion of economic gains and the political influence of the popular masses was an inevitable part of the bourgeoisie's ultimate control over the transition from dictatorship to parliamentary democracy.

Poulantzas assumed that the domestic bourgeoisie remained hegemonic throughout the revolutionary period and that a socialist transition necessitated a condition of dual power. We contend that the first assumption is not

*Unless noted otherwise, all page numbers in parentheses in this chapter refer to Poulantzas 1976 (see References).

strongly supported by the evidence, and that Poulantzas misidentified the domestic bourgeoisie and mistakenly maintained that the monopolistic groups comprised the comprador bourgeoisie. Our examination of the stock holdings of these groups suggests that whereas some groups comprised the comprador bourgeoisie, others constituted a *monopoly* domestic bourgeoisie. This had important political ramifications for the monopoly domestic bourgeoisie had little incentive to join with the popular masses who sought immediate decolonization and the nationalization of the groups. Furthermore, it is unlikely that the monopoly domestic bourgeoisie sought to dismantle a political regime that desired to balance its contradictory economic and political interests. This analysis leads to a conclusion distinctly opposed to that offered by Poulantzas: the domestic bourgeoisie did not take a leading role in the overthrow of the dictatorship, and who would succeed in controlling the democratization process was hardly apparent at the time of the coup and in the months that followed.

The assumption that hegemony was retained by the domestic bourgeoisie, a segment of capital distinct from the main dominant class segments supporting the dictatorship, led Poulantzas both to underestimate the strength of antimonopolist sentiment among the popular masses in general, but more importantly, to undervalue the association between the monopolistic groups and the domestic bourgeoisie. Broadly speaking, the masses saw little distinction between the dictatorship and the "monopolistic groups," irrespective of the latter's comprador, landed, or "domestic" underpinnings. This sentiment forestalled the possible emergence of a political alliance between the domestic bourgeoisie and the popular masses. Instead, at least for a time, the most "advanced" sections of the popular masses challenged the economic basis of the political power of the monopoly domestic bourgeoisie, the comprador bourgeoisie, and the latifundists by openly supporting land reform, nationalization, workers' control, and other radial changes.

Antimonopolist sentiment put socialism on the agenda, although the possible route to socialism was not envisioned by Poulantzas at the time of his writing. Rather than dual power, democratic socialism was at stake in the revolutionary period. It was the failure of the Left to agree on a common project, and not the hegemony of the domestic bourgeoisie, that undermined chances for a telescoping of democratization and socialism.

The Left's failure to agree on a common program helped ensure an ongoing reconsolidation of capitalist power and institutions, a process that accelerated with the ebbing of mass mobilization and the institution of parliamentary democracy. Should the Left's failure to establish a clear agenda for democratic socialism necessarily imply that the domestic bourgeoisie reasserted political and economic hegemony, momentarily lost in the heat of battle? We maintain that to a significant extent, the re-establishment of capitalism has occurred in an incremental and only partly conclusive manner.

In many ways, during the decade following the revolution (1976–86) Portuguese politics can be better classified as *dishegemonic,* with neither the popular masses nor the domestic bourgeoisie clearly ascendant in terms of political leadership. Both continued to examine new political formulas and alliances in pursuit of a more lasting basis for pursuing their interests. As the domestic bourgeoisie and popular masses struggled to find a hegemonic destiny, this left the country increasingly open to policy agendas favored especially by international lending agencies and foreign capital. In the end, neither of the two primary contestants for hegemony during the revolutionary period proved victorious.

In the following sections, we discuss the analysis and argument offered by Poulantzas in more detail and provide the evidence for our own position. The first part discusses the structural characteristics of the Portuguese dominant class prior to 1974 as well as the political struggles that took place within the dictatorship. The second section looks at the democratization process and the implications it has had for Portuguese politics in the years since the coup d'etat.

## THE PORTUGUESE DOMINANT CLASS

Poulantzas believed that the fall of the dictatorships in Spain, Portugal, and Greece and the return to democracy required a shift in dominant class interests, the by-product of a new form of industrial development that emphasized European export markets and foreign capital investment. We examine his contention that this new form of industrial development allowed the domestic bourgeoisie to emerge as a distinct segment of the Portuguese dominant class. First we present his description of the Portuguese dominant class, then examine the structure and interests of this dominant class in order to evaluate his categories.

In the capitalist world economy, according to Poulantzas, Spain, Portugal, and Greece are hybrids and exhibit characteristics associated with both developed and dependent countries. Like the developed countries, they were characterized by "an old-established primitive accumulation of capital" (p. 10) obtained from colonial exploitation. Yet, despite this primitive accumulation of capital, "the blockage . . . of an endogenous accumulation of capital at the right time" places them "alongside other countries dependent on the imperialist metropolises" (p. 11).

Although he recognized the unique position of the Southern European countries, Poulantzas concluded that the structure of the dominant class was similar to that found in dependent and "underdeveloped" countries: an oligarchy, composed of landed proprietors and a comprador big bourgeoisie, dominated and blocked industrialization. This comprador bourgeoisie had a weak economic base in the country and "functioned chiefly as a commercial and financial intermediary for the penetration of foreign imperialist capital, being closely controlled by this foreign capital" (p. 12). In Portugal, Poulantzas identified the oligarchy as the southern landowners and the monopolistic groups.

Dependent industrialization, Poulantzas maintained, transformed the structure of the dominant class. Although the comprador bourgeoisie continued to function "as a kind of staging-post and direct intermediary for the implantation and reproduction of foreign capital" (p. 42), it no longer remained confined to speculative activities and began to invest in the industrial sector. Despite its industrial investments, the comprador bourgeoisie remained closely allied to foreign capital in the African colonies and in the metropole.

At the same time, a new segment emerged: the domestic bourgeoisie, which had "a chiefly industrial character" (p. 41) but was also involved in commerce and tourism. Unlike the comprador bourgeoisie, it had "significant contradictions" with foreign capital and was "interested in an industrial development less polarized towards the exploitation of the country by foreign capital, and in a state intervention which would guarantee it its protected markets at home, while also making it more competitive vis-a-vis foreign capital." Most importantly, it sought "an extension and development of the home market by a certain increase in the purchasing power and consumption of the masses" (p. 43). Poulantzas suggested that "'the autochthonous capitals of the Lisbon/Setúbal/Porto industrial belt" comprised the domestic bourgeoisie (p. 42).

How did the changes in the dominant class undermine the dictatorship? According to Poulantzas, the dictatorship represented the economic and political interests of the comprador bourgeoisie and the latifundists. As its economic power increased, the domestic bourgeoisie sought greater political influence within the dictatorship and hoped to break the alliance between the comprador bourgeoisie and the latifundists. The domestic bourgeoisie favored a reorganization of the power bloc to exclude the latifundists. This proved impossible under the dictatorship for largely institutional reasons, and the domestic bourgeoisie "distanced" itself from the military dictatorship, whereas the comprador bourgeoisie "supported these regimes till the end" (pp. 46–47). Poulantzas suggests that the domestic bourgeoisie elicited support from the working class to bring about a return to bourgeois democracy.

Using Poulantzas' description, the differences between the Portuguese domestic and comprador bourgeoisie can be summarized in Table 3.1.

Structurally, then, two types of economic investments differentiate the comprador and domestic bourgeoisie: colonial investments and direct association with foreign capital (i.e., common ownership of firms). These in-

**Table 3.1**
**Poulantzas description of the Portuguese bourgeoisie's investments and political and economic positions**

| | Comprador Bourgeoisie | Domestic Bourgeoisie |
|---|---|---|
| ECONOMIC INVESTMENTS | | |
| Industry | Yes | Yes |
| Finance | Yes | Yes |
| Commerce | Yes | Yes |
| Colonies | Yes | No |
| With Foreign Capital | Yes | No |
| POSITION ON ECONOMIC DEVELOPMENT | | |
| Industrial Development with Minimal Foreign Direct Investment | No | Yes |
| Export-oriented Development | Yes | No |
| Protectionism | No | Yes |
| State Aid | No | Yes |
| Wages | Low | High |
| POSITION ON POLITICAL OPTIONS | | |
| Democratization | No | Yes |
| European Integration | Yes | No |
| Colonial Empire | Yes | No |

vestment differences, Poulantzas suggests, account for the different policy positions.

Three questions may be asked to evaluate Poulantzas' argument. Did a comprador bourgeoisie exist and did the groups he identified conform to his description of a comprador bourgeoisie? How was the economy transformed during the 1960s and what impact did this have on the structure of the dominant class? What political options were articulated during the 1970s and who supported each?

The Portuguese dictatorship from 1926 to the 1960s pursued policies to sever the ties between domestic and foreign capital, particularly in metropolitan Portugal. Under António Salazar's leadership, the government emphasized autarchic development. Salazar believed that foreign investment would jeopardize Portuguese independence if "key economic activities belonged to foreign, and not national, capital" (Matos 1973, 39). The cornerstones of his economic policy were the Wheat Campaign, the Colonial Act, protectionism, and the condicionamento industrial.[1] These policies stimulated *national* production in order to guarantee Portuguese independence. Salazar's government restricted foreign investment. Governmental approval was needed before a national firm could be sold to a foreign firm. Special laws were adopted to ensure national control over insurance, fishing, and shipping. In 1943 the government declared that foreign capital could not control firms involved in public service, defense, or activities fundamental to the Portuguese economy. Exchange policy restricted the inflow of foreign capital so that foreign capital investment in metropolitan Portugal remained insignificant until the 1960s (Matos 1973, 94–97).

These policies were not particularly suited to a comprador bourgeoisie seeking to act simply as a conduit for foreign capital. Yet, it is possible that an analysis of the investment patterns of the groups might reveal a structural basis for the comprador bourgeoisie.

Directly or indirectly, key families controlled the most important commercial, industrial, and financial assets. Much of this control was exercised through the banks that owned stock and provided capital to firms under the group's control.

The source of family wealth that launched each of the Portuguese groups varied. Some families derived their wealth from commercial activities: Espírito Santo (Banco Espírito Santo e Comercial de Lisboa) from colonial commerce and Miranda (Banco Português do Atlantico) from wine commerce. Other families had industrial origins: Mello (Companhia da União Fabril, CUF, and Banco Totta e Açores) from the chemical industry, Champalimaud (Banco Pinto e Sotto Mayor) from cement. Only one group derived much of its capital from foreign sources: Banco Burnay was partly owned by Belgium capital.[2]

Until the 1960s, Banco Espírito Santo, Banco Burnay, and Banco Nacional Ultramarino were "nonindustrial" banks, i.e., less than 10 pecent of their stock portfolio was invested in industrial firms.[3] These three banks invested primarily in colonial firms. Banco Espírito Santo controlled Companhia Açucar de Angola, Sociedade Agrícola do Cassequel, and Companhia de Moçambique. The colonial estates operated by these companies produced sugar and coffee destined primarily for the export market and were associated with foreign capital. Banco Burnay controlled the lucrative Companhia do Diamantes, Angola's diamond mining company. Banco Nacional Ultramarino served as the national bank of the Portuguese colonies and its investments followed the same pattern as that of Banco Espírito Santo and Banco Burnay. These groups exhibited many of the characteristics of a "comprador bourgeoisie" because they were centered in agriculture and mining activities whose products were destined for the export market and associated with foreign capital in the colonies.

In contrast, Banco Português do Atlantico, CUF, Banco Pinto e Sotto Mayor, and Banco Borges e Irmão historically held a significant part of their investments in the industrial sector. These industries produced for the domestic market and had no association with foreign capital. Although they also had colonial investments, their colonial firms produced raw materials needed for Portuguese industries (e.g., cotton, jute, oil seeds). These groups did not meet the description of a "comprador" bourgeoisie.

This analysis indicates that important divisions existed within the groups that Poulantzas identified as part of a "comprador" bourgeoisie. This suggests that the dictatorship was already balancing contradictory interests among the groups and had a far more dynamic relationship with the dominant class than Poulantzas envisioned. The dependent industrialization of the 1960s does not alter what for Poulantzas was already a homogeneous comprador bourgeoisie, but only adds a growing split between this segment and a domestic bourgeoisie. By contrast, we argue that new investment patterns weakened the historic divisions within the groups. Rather than further polarizing a split between a comprador and domestic bourgeoisie, new investment patterns created a considerable overlap between comprador and domestic interests.

The presence of foreign capital increased considerably in the 1960s. Between 1943 and 1960 foreign capital investment was only 2 million escudos, increasing to 20 million escudos between 1961 and 1967. In 1971 alone, foreign capital investment was three times as high as the entire period from 1943 to 1960 (Matos 1973, 99). Foreign capital investment contributed only 0.8 percent to the formation of social capital in 1959 but increased to 21 percent by 1971. Foreign capital was particularly important in the industrial sector and represented 19.1 percent of the social capital formed in industry in 1962, 52.2 percent in 1968, and decreasing to 30.8 percent in 1971 (Matos 1973, 120–24).

During the same period, Portuguese exports shifted from Africa to Europe. In 1960, 26 percent of all exports were bound for the colonies and 21 percent to the European Free Trade Association (EFTA), whereas by 1970 the colonial share had decreased to 14 percent and the EFTA rose to 41 percent (Bracia and Branco 1979, 49). Moreover, exports contributed a larger share to the gross national product (GNP), accounting for 30 percent of the GNP in 1950, 39 percent in 1960, and to 43 percent in 1969. The type of goods exported abroad also changed. Traditional exports included textiles, wood, cork, resin, and wine. Of these, only textiles continued to play an important role as these exports were replaced by tomato concentrate, chemicals, wood pulp, machinery, and nonmetallic minerals. Bound for Europe, the new products accounted for 39 percent of the growth among all exports (Fernandes and Alvares 1972, 36).

New market opportunities stimulated and transformed Portuguese industry. Industry employed 32 percent of the active population in 1970, up from 27.8 percent in 1960, and contributed 36.6 percent to the GNP in 1960 and 45.9 percent by 1970. Small industrial firms were gradually displaced by medium and large firms; in 1959, 93.7 percent of all industrial firms employed less than 20 workers, decreasing to 88 percent in 1971. More importantly, the percentage of the industrial work force employed in these small firms decreased from 34.3 percent to 20.6 percent during the same period (da Costa 1979, 222). Finally, the importance of various industries changed: mining, food, textiles, wood, and glass lost importance; paper, chemicals, metallic products, and diverse industries gained importance (Moura 1974, 155). These modern industries were the primary beneficiaries of the European export market. Those that would benefit the most from European integration were the most concentrated: six chemical firms received 63 percent of the income generated in this sector, two glass manufacturers held 53 percent of the capital and employed 39 percent of the work force, one naval repair yard held 75 percent of the capital and employed 50 percent of the work force, and six machine construction firms controlled 42 percent of the capital. In contrast, traditional industries remained largely dispersed: among 571 textile firms, the top five controlled only 9.8 percent of the capital (Martins 1975, 105–106). Foreign capital investment was the highest in the industries that would benefit the most from European integration, including over 40 percent of the social capital in chemicals, ceramics, metallurgical products, and electric machinery, and less than 15 percent in textiles, food and drink, or cork (Matos 1974).

Despite the growing importance of foreign capital, the groups did not become mere conduits for external interests. There are four important points with regard to this issue. First, whereas the division between industrial and nonindustrial groups remained, industrial groups invested more in the colonies and the nonindustrial groups invested more in Portuguese industries. Second, there was no greater association between the groups and foreign capital than between nongroups and foreign capital. Third, the industrial firms controlled by the groups were a significant part of the Portuguese economy. Fourth, firms outside the groups often had interests in policies connoted with the comprador bourgeoisie, specifically retention of the African colonies. This suggests that the industrial groups featured many of the characteristics of Poulantzas' domestic bourgeoisie and constituted the monopoly domestic bourgeoisie. As seen later, this monopoly domestic bourgeoisie was more likely to directly benefit from European integration than its nonmonopoly counterpart.

By 1974 only Banco Nacional Ultramarino had less than 10 percent of its stock in industrial firms. The previously nonindustrial banks, Banco Espírito Santo and Banco Fonsecas e Burnay, increased their industrial holdings (to 16.1 percent and 32 percent, respectively). Also, the banks that had shown little interest in the colonies, Banco Borges e Irmão and Banco Pinto e Sotto Mayor, began to diversify some of their stock holdings to firms operating in the colonies. Whereas the percentage of Banco Pinto e Sotto Mayor's stock holdings in colonial firms remained small (16.9 percent), it expressed an increased interest in the colonies in its 1973 annual report: "With regard to our stock portfolio, the significant movement to our colonial stock, whose value reflects their interdependence with representative stock from metropolitan activities, should be noted." The industrial banks continued to hold the bulk of their stock portfolio in industry: Banco Totta Aliança (controlled by CUF) 51.7 percent in 1974, Banco Pinto e Sotto Mayor 76 percent in 1972, Banco Português do Atlantico 68.1 percent in 1974. By the end of the 1960s, the groups held an interest in both domestic industry and in the colonial economies, but it was not clear that they had, in fact, become a comprador bourgeoisie.

In metropolitan Portugal, the groups did not differ significantly from others in their association with foreign capital. Maria Belmeira Martins (1975) compiled a list of nearly 600 industrial, commercial, and other firms and noted their association with foreign capital. Among industrial firms, 55 were partially owned by foreign capital and Portuguese interests with no association with the groups, whereas 49 firms were controlled by both foreign capital and the groups. Only 17 percent of the firms controlled by the groups were also partially owned by foreign capital. This negates the characterization of these groups as simply conduits for foreign capital.

The industrial holdings of the groups were not insignificant in the Portuguese economy. Of the top 100 industrial firms in 1973, 43.9 percent were controlled by the groups, 18.7 percent by foreign capital, and 37.4 percent by domestic nongroups (Instituto Nacional de Estatística 1975). The groups controlled oil refining, chemicals, steel, ship building, paper, cement, and tobacco, and thus encompassed firms among the dynamic industries that supplied raw materials needed in other sectors (metallurgy, textiles) and provided spinoffs for other industrial firms.

The industrial investments of the groups differed in one important respect from other Portuguese industrialists: the groups had more to gain from European integration. Of the top 100 firms in sectors that would benefit from European integration, 45.8 percent were associated with the groups, 33.3 percent with foreign capital, and 20.8 percent with the nongroups.

The groups associated with foreign capital in the colonies. CUF, together with the Anglo-American Corporation, launched two colonial banks: Banco Totta-Standard de Moçambique and Banco Standard-Totta de Angola. Banco Espírito Santo held an interest in Sociedade Agrícola de Cassequel that was also partially owned by British capital. Banco Pinto e Sotto Mayor, together with Bank of America, introduced credit card operations in Portugal, Mozambique, and Angola. But it was questionable that the groups alone had an economic interest in the colonies.

Although industrialists unassociated with the groups had not directly invested in the colonies, this did not mean that they had no interest in the traditional economic relationship between Portugal and Africa that the groups and foreign capital seemingly promoted. In particular, textile manufacturers historically had depended on colonial raw materials and markets, a pattern that continued well into the 1970s.[4] Clothing exports to Angola, for example, grew 26.8 percent between 1960 and 1970. Moreover, in his analysis of the transference of technology to Portugal, Rolo found that 41 percent of the contracts restricted the market to Portugal and its colonies (1977, 113). Thus for many firms that received technology from abroad, the market for their goods extended to the colonies.

Portuguese industrialists, associated and unassociated with the groups, shared an economic interest in the colonies and had a similar degree of direct association with foreign capital. The industrial firms controlled by the groups were more likely to benefit *directly* from European integration.

The groups are not easily classified as comprador or domestic. The historically nonindustrial groups seem to have undergone the transformation that Poulantzas envisioned by moving from speculative activities to industry as the emphasis in foreign capital investment changed. And these nonindustrial groups continued to emphasize mining and agricultural activities in their colonial portfolio.

In contrast, the historically industrial groups conform more to Poulantzas description of the domestic bourgeoisie—the groups largely controlled the "autochthonous" industrial capital around Lisbon and Setúbal. Although the groups had some association with foreign capital in the 1960s, they also had a strong and continuing interest in domestic industrial production. These industrial groups invested indigenous capital and developed Portuguese basic industries (e.g., cement, chemicals, steel). Even their colonial holdings featured a notable industrial component. Champalimaud, for example, began producing cement in Angola and Mozambique. The involvement in colonial industrial development did not conform to a traditional comprador activity.

The groups and other industrialists held an interest in the development of the Portuguese industrial sector, had the same degree of direct association with foreign capital in the industrial sector, and had an interest in the colonial market. What distinguished the groups from other industrialists was their association with foreign capital in the colonies.

We do not agree with several aspects of Poulantzas' characterization of the division between comprador and domestic bourgeoisies. Whereas the nonindustrial groups had comprador elements, these were eroding somewhat during the 1960s. The industrial groups constituted a kind of "monopolist domestic bourgeoisie" as they remained a vital part of Portuguese industrial development during that time. Although they did stand to benefit more from closer ties with Europe than nonmonopoly counterparts and had some colonial investments as well, this did not warrant their inclusion within the comprador bourgeoisie.

Given our analysis of the domestic bourgeoisie, Poulantzas incorrectly identified the domestic bourgeoisie's position on economic development. Whereas some (textile manufacturers) may have held the position that Poulantzas described, it is clear that important segments of the domestic bourgeoisie (the industrial groups or the monopoly domestic bourgeoisie) would have favored export-oriented industrialization and stood opposed to protectionism. As shown in the next section, an economic interest in European integration and an ability to develop industrial firms in the colonies had far different political consequences than Poulantzas envisioned.

## ECONOMIC AND POLITICAL LIBERALIZATION OR THE STATUS QUO?

Among government supporters two factions emerged, the Europeanists and the colonialists, who articulated different political and economic options for Portugal. The colonialists favored the continuation of the status quo. Economically, they supported limited market competition, a restriction on foreign capital investment, isolation from the European market, and continued economic integration with the African colonies. Whether Portugal should emphasize industrialization remained a matter of debate. Politically, the colonialists opposed any liberalization efforts such as free trade unions, greater political participation, recognition of individual rights, and other civil liberties. The colonialists stood for the political and economic principles pursued by Salazar since the 1930s.

The Europeanists looked abroad for a new economic and political orientation that would allow Portugal to join the more developed European countries. The Europeanists advocated export-oriented industrialization, the concentration of industrial firms, relaxation of restrictions on foreign capital investment, the use of state funds for projects to stimulate industry, and an end to the colonial war. Politically, they favored liberalization and, after a long evolutionary process, eventual democratization.

These two factions became clearly visible after Salazar was forced to abandon the government due to illness in 1968. His successor, Marcello Caetano, attempted to reconcile these two factions and hoped to merge the political and economic options advocated by each through "renovation in continuity." Between 1969 and 1971, during the so-called *primavera* (literally springtime, a term used by journalists to describe the first years of Caetano's rule), it seemed as if Caetano might accomplish this goal: efforts were made to liberalize the economy and to extend political debate and participation. Throughout the primavera, the technocrats who occupied various government ministries, the liberal wing in the parliament, and a newly recognized interest group, the Sociedade para o Desenvolvimento Económico e Social (Society for Social and Economic Development, known as SEDES), were the spokesmen for the Europeanist position. The antagonism (and differences) between the Europeanists and the colonialists was most visible in the National Assembly. Caetano encouraged the entrance of new men into the National Union—the only "political" party recognized by the dictatorship—during the 1969 elections. Caetano pledged that those who ran for office would not be bound to support the government's position. Consequently, a number of liberals, dubbed the "ala liberal," ran for office on the party ticket. Once in the National Assembly, they sought to liberalize Portuguese political institutions and initiate a slow, evolutionary return to democracy. They proposed sweeping constitutional reforms, introduced legislation (something that deputies had never done) on a number of social and political issues, and openly debated the wisdom of government-proposed legislation.

Initially, ala-liberal members Pinto Leite and Oliveira Dias challenged the economic views of others in the National Assembly, arguing in favor of the liberalization of the condicionamento industrial, for the concentration of firms, increasing exports (particularly to Europe), and autonomous economic development for Portugal and its colonies. Deputies who supported traditional economic policies raised objections to autonomous economic development. Franco Noqueira, for example, argued that Portugal and its colonies provided the market needed for industrial development and that it would be absurd to abandon the colonies and enter the European Economic Community. With the death of Pinto Leite in July 1970, the liberal deputies shifted their concern from the economic sphere to other issues such as freedom of the press, modernization of the university system, and political autonomy for the colonies, whereas economic issues fell to the government technocrats: Rogério Martins, Xavier Pintado, Vasco Leonidas, and João Salgueiro.

Rogério Martins authored the Law of Industrial Development. This law modified the condicionamento industrial so that some sectors would still be subject to government approval to establish new firms or expand their capacity (basic industries), whereas others would no longer be subject to any regulation. The law established a development fund to provide financial support for the "creation of new firms, and the expansion, conversion, or modernization of existing ones" (Martins 1970, 99).

In 1971 the government revised the system of interterritorial payments by placing a tax on Portuguese exports to the colonies. The change was designed to promote colonial industrialization.

The government also began to take a more active role in directing industrial development. It planned and found investors for the SINES project that included a new oil refinery and port. SINES provided the raw material petrochemical firms needed to produce synthetic fibers for the textile industry.

The secretary of agriculture, Vasco Leonidas, called for a "competitive agriculture." Leonidas argued that landowners could no longer remain mere suppliers of raw materials but had to produce consumer goods as well. A more competitive agriculture, he noted, required larger farms that utilized modern equipment.

The emphasis of the liberalization period was to prepare Portugal for greater competition as the country became more economically integrated with Europe. Over time, this would reduce the economic importance of the colonies and decrease the necessity of political interdependence. The reaction of industrialists and landowners to these new policies indicated that some industrialists supported this new economic orientation while others did not, and that landowners generally resisted the Europeanist move.

The annual reports of the groups indicated a marked contrast between the economic views of the industrial and the nonindustrial groups. Banco Espírto Santo e Comercial de Lisboa and Banco Nacional Ultramarino often lauded the military's efforts to defeat the African liberation movements. These banks, together with Banco Borges e Irmào, were the most likely to discuss the system of interterritorial payments and to advocate a change in this system that would facilitate trade between Portugal and the colonies. On the other hand, Banco Português do Atlantico, Banco Totta Açores, and Banco Pinto e Sotto Mayor never referred to the war effort. Instead, their annual reports discussed policies that were needed to stimulate industrial development: more competition, policies to facilitate exports, and an end to the condicionamento industrial.

Textile firms (Companhia Nacional de Fiação e Tecidos de Torres Novas and Quintas e Quintas) lamented the problems of obtaining raw materials. They sought an improvement in trade between the colonies and Portugal to correct this situation.

Small and medium industrialists raised objections to the Law of Industrial Development. For example, the National Federation of Millers favored the condicionamento industrial and maintained that it was necessary for national economic development. Small and medium industrialists maintained that "excessive change in the economic direction of the Portuguese economy generates insecurity for industrialists" (*Jornal do Comércio,* January 10, 1971).

In general, it was large firms, among the modern industries, that supported policies advocated by the Europeanists. The *Jornal do Comércio* reported that Sorefame, Plessey Automática Eléctrica, and Fábrica de Tintas de Sacavém (all industrial firms owned in part by foreign capital) publicly supported the Law of Industrial Development. Cel-Cat, Metalúrgica Duarte Ferreira, F. Ramada, Fosforeira Portuguesa, and Phillips seemed to support the government's efforts to promote industrial development in the colonies.

The Associação Central de Agricultura Portuguesa (Portuguese Central Association of Agriculture, ACAP) called for development and integration between Portugal and its African colonies. Nunes Mexia, a leader of ACAP and a deputy in the National Assembly, vociferously defended the Portuguese empire. Others claimed that the colonies were essential for wine growers and that Europe could not make up for any loss in this market.

The liberalization period was short-lived. By 1972 two important liberal leaders, Sá Carneiro and Miller Guerra, had resigned from the National Assembly, and the government technocrats, Rogério Martins, João Dias Rosas, and Xavier Pintado, also departed.

It was not altogether clear that the liberals had failed. They successfully introduced economic reforms, and although the condicionamento industrial was not dismantled, significant inroads were made to give economic autonomy to the colonies and to integrate economically with Europe. The government signed an agreement with the European Economic Community that would facilitate exports into this market. The government advanced policies that met with the interests of the entire dominant class: limits on internal competition that satisfied small and medium industrialists and traditional industrialists (textile manufacturers), new trade agreements with Europe that met the approval of the monopoly domestic bourgeoisie, and continued economic relations with the colonies that were in keeping with the interests of all industrialists and landowners. By the end of the primavera, the government was preparing to join Europe and yet hold on to the colonies. Through this policy course, the dictatorship balanced the contradictory interests of the dominant class.

The liberals failed, however, to carry out their political reforms. Whereas political debate was enhanced in the short-term, by the end of the primavera it was clear that the government was not going to oversee a gradual return to democracy. Poulantzas infers that this signaled the inclusion of the domestic bourgeoisie. It is unclear that the domestic bourgeoisie supported extensive political reform and it may have been satisfied with the compromise offered by the regime. Political liberalization meant expanded political participation beyond those loyal to the dictatorship, including the extraregime opposition. The extraregime opposition called for immediate decolonization, nationalization of the monopolistic groups, recognition of individual rights, and free trade unions.[5] Many Portuguese industrialists already lamented the "excessive" demands of the workers and argued that wages could be increased only as productivity increased. The present dictatorship was best equipped to contain "unreasonable" workers' demands.

Moreover, open debate on the colonial issue might have led to immediate decolonization, as the opposition demanded. The dominant class had little to gain from the complete severance of ties to the colonies. The government provided the hope that, over time, Portuguese industrialists could increase their direct colonial investments and maintain a neocolonial relationship once political independence was accorded. Clearly, the monopoly domestic bourgeoisie had little to gain from nationalizations. As the target of such actions, the groups would lose their economic base and power.

Although the monopoly domestic bourgeoisie favored economic liberalization, against the immediate interests of the latifundists, the comprador bourgeoisie and the nonmonopoly domestic bourgeoisie, it had little to gain from political liberalization. The fear of political liberalization kept the monopoly domestic bourgeoisie within the regime. Whereas Poulantzas asserts that the domestic bourgeoisie elicited the support of the popular masses to bring about democratization, we conclude that the domestic bourgeoisie opposed democratization and did not seek a fundamental shift in political regime.

If the regime continued to follow policies that appealed to the Portuguese dominant class, why was it overthrown? The military situation deteriorated throughout the 1970s. As defeat seemed imminent in Guinea-Bissau and Mozambique, the time needed to create favorable conditions for a neocolonial solution was running out and the military grew increasingly frustrated with the dictatorship. As the colonial wars required more and more men, the military underwent significant transformation. In particular, officers were no longer recruited solely from wealthy, established families. Until the early 1970s the traditional officers and those recruited specifically for the war did not have the same rights and privileges. Caetano announced that commissioned and noncommissioned officers would be given equal status, which meant that the noncommissioned officers could overtake commissioned officers on the promotion list. Commissioned officers began to meet to discuss how best to prevent this action and from their meetings the MFA was born (Harsgor 1976; Rodriques, Borga, and Cardoso 1979). Finally, many in the military came to the conclusion that the colonial wars could not be won. A nonmilitary solution to the colonial question had to be found. A no-win situation combined with specific grievances formed a consensus within the MFA that the dictatorship had to be overthrown.[6]

Poulantzas argued that the MFA represented a previously marginalized domestic bourgeoisie. Much of the evidence suggests that the officers aligned to the "Europeanists" (e.g., Spínola) did not directly participate in the formulation and execution of the coup d'etat. Spínola joined with the MFA only after the coup had taken place and after he received instructions from Caetano (Blackburn 1974, 16). Rather, the officers who spawned the MFA were more closely aligned to the extraregime opposition.

Spínola's tenuous alliance with the MFA did not, however, represent the catapulting of the domestic bourgeoisie into a hegemonic position within the democratization process. Rather, it symbolized the historic reticence of the monopoly domestic bourgeoisie to accept a broad change in regime and policy. The nonmonopoly sector of the dominant class, which Poulantzas generally sees as at the heart of the process, was in fact unwilling to lead it and not obviously positively affected by it. Without the initiatives of more radical forces within the MFA, there was a very low probability of an abrupt regime change based largely on underlying tensions and antagonisms with the dominant class.

We turn now to the democratization process in Portugal and the remaining two questions: why the dominant class lost control over the democratization process and why the popular masses were unable to sustain the revolutionary gains.

## DEMOCRATIZATION: TWO PHASES

Poulantzas' *The Crisis of the Dictatorships* (1976) is divided into two parts, the first ending around February 1975 and the postscript taking the analysis to the end of that year. In the Portuguese case, this results in a curious parallel to a decisive sequencing of events, and ultimately to much of the trouble in Poulantzas' own work. Specifically, we argue that Poulantzas in tracing a singular flow from the initial coup on April 25, 1974, to the events of November 25, 1975, fails to appreciate important aspects of a dynamic situation. The period concerning the bulk of his book was one in which the conflict over the democratization process was marked by contradictions within the dominant class and between the dominant class and the popular masses. However, the period from March until at least November 1975 was much more focused upon conflicts within the popular masses and their political representatives. Thus the democratization process is not marked by as much continuity as Poulantzas suggests, but rather encounters a break that he does not anticipate when writing about the period prior to March 1975.

Our difference with Poulantzas hinge on three general issues: whether he correctly interpreted the nature of the dominant class, its internal contradictions, and the relative ascendancy of one segment over another; to what extent he took into account *both* the prospects for radicalization among the popular masses, as well as the actual and potential limits to such radicalization; and in what measure his conception of socialism shaped the interpretation of events. Poulantzas argued that the democratization process could not be telescoped together with socialism and that "socialism was never really on the agenda" (p. 144), but this depended in part upon a specific concept of the "transition to socialism." We suggest that what Poulantzas characterized as a process based on the continuing "hegemony of the domestic bourgeoisie" could be quite compatible with a transition to socialism, although perhaps not the transitional conception held by Poulantzas at that time. As already suggested in our discussion of the precoup period, the domestic bourgeoisie's "hegemony" was extremely problematic, leading to the possibility for a transition to democratic socialism.

We also stress the importance of alternative conceptions of a transition to socialism in terms of their effects upon the strategies and alliances of major actors such as the political parties and the MFA, who initially overthrew the dictatorship. These alternative conceptions played a decisive role in forestalling the emergence of a clear popular base for socialism. The opportunity arose for a major movement in a socialist direction, but the inability of the diverse parties on the Left to agree upon a common minimalist program and strategy led to internecine warfare among the parties and augmented the divisions among the popular masses. This party warfare and splintering of the popular masses, more than the predestined hegemonic pretensions of the domestic bourgeoisie, placed the most outstanding barriers to the erection and consolidation of a socialist regime.

Our assessment of these points begins by considering whether the events and actors associated with the period April 25, 1974, to the middle of March 1975 are effectively described and understood using the terms or concepts introduced by Poulantzas. We have addressed his view of the dominant class by investigating his dissection of the dominant class and its interests as these existed prior to the coup. Despite the significant popular actions (for example, the September 28, 1974, anti-Spínola mobilization; confrontations with residues of the secret police and other Salazarist elements; extensive strike activity; large-scale public demonstrations, parades, etc.), during the first year after the coup, the ultimate impact of these popular actions still depended considerably upon the alliances and strategic choices made by the contending segments of the dominant class. The question of the unity of the dominant class becomes central to the analysis of the prospects for the radicalization of the democratization process.

The period from March 11, 1975 (the date of the abortive Spínola coup), to the end of November 1975 (when the most radical elements in the military were removed from power) signaled a disjuncture in many ways from the preceding period, and we consider it separately. The effects of the nationalizations, land reform, struggles over civil liberties, and the strategies of the major Left political parties were fundamental in this period because they not only opened new political opportunities but also revealed the limits on the scope and direction of change. Specifically, we argue that these events strained further the competing conceptions of socialism, the social basis of support for these conceptions, and ultimately the ability of Left organizations to agree on a coherent model for the transition to socialism. Finally, we investigate the enduring political consequences of this democratization process. We demonstrate that in the intervening years the Left remained in disarray as did the Portuguese dominant class. Rather than democratization resulting in the hegemony of the domestic bourgeoisie or the popular masses, the political situation was marked by dishegemony.

## Phase One: April 25, 1974–March 11, 1975

The first phase opened with the swift overthrow of the Caetano government, followed by efforts at re-establishing state authority by the MFA. A Junta da Salvação Nacional (Council of National Salvation) was organized, General Spínola was chosen as the new president, and Aníbal Palma Carlos was appointed prime minister. For Poulantzas, the political interests represented by Spínola and Palma Carlos correspond to the growing contradiction between two important segments of the Portuguese dominant classes: the domestic and the comprador bourgeoisies, each contending for a larger share of the spoils resulting from the economic development induced by foreign investment.

From our previous discussion of dominant class divisions, it should be clear that the interests at stake were not necessarily those that Poulantzas has identified, given our differences in the identification of structural components of the dominant class. Poulantzas also was unclear as to exactly which dominant class elements were best represented in the new government. In part this stemmed from his confusing analysis of the interests of the domestic bourgeoisie and its love-hate relationship with the other segments of capital. The contradictions associated with this relationship appeared, on the one hand, just strong enough to push the domestic bourgeoisie into the liberal opposition, but, on the other, remained based upon a mere "rearrangement of the relationship between the domestic bourgeoisie, foreign capital and the comprador bourgeoisie." The domestic bourgeoisie never seriously challenged the hegemony of the comprador bourgeoisie, but rather sought only a "renegotiated hegemony of the comprador bourgeoisie" (p. 51). Poulantzas thus would have it both ways: the comprador bourgeoisie had conflicting structural interests with the domestic bourgeoisie, yet these were not sufficiently severe to question the whole hierarchy within the power bloc.

Poulantzas implied that Spínola's entrance was indicative of the growing strength of the domestic bourgeoisie, the "hegemonic" fraction of capital during this time. However, it is clear that the duality between the growing dominant class "contradictions . . . [which] soon burst into the open" (p. 52) and the generalized subordination of the domestic bourgeoisie seeking only to "renegotiate" the hegemony of comprador capital leads to an empirical muddle.

First, we find that it was not *necessarily* the domestic bourgeoisie that sought an end to the ancient regime as he argued that "only in Portugal, with the failure of the colonial war and its sequels, did certain sectors of the big comprador bourgeoisie start to seek an escape route from the existing regime (Spínola)" (p. 52). Further, he mentioned that "even sectors of big comprador bourgeoisie (the Champalimaud group for example), including big international firms, supported Spínola" (p. 61). Thus in support of Spínola, we find a discontented "big comprador" element, rather than the expected domestic bourgeoisie. Yet, things are not quite so simple, since "it was the monopoly sectors of the domestic bourgeoisie that took the lead . . . This was clearest of all at the beginning of the Portuguese events (Spínola)" (p. 57); by contrast, "Other sectors, however, such as the Espírito Santo group, strongly rooted in Angola, maintained their policy of support for the colonial war" (p. 61).

This interpretation suggests that a sizable portion of the Portuguese dominant class found expression in some way through Spínola. The difficulty lies in pinning down which segments were excluded. Rather than a drive to hegemony by the domestic bourgeoisie, the big comprador elements may have sought refuge in Spínola as well. This leaves us with the question of identifying these big comprador elements and how they differed from the monopoly domestic bourgeoisie.

Poulantzas could not provide an unequivocal answer to this question. For example, he cites a key event that occurred during the Spínola presidency that was meant to illustrate the empirical agents involved in supporting that government by saying "the representatives of the big comprador bourgeoisie, including José Manuel de Melo, the major shareholder in the CUF, Manuel Ricardo Espírito Santo, and António Champalimaud paid a visit to Gonçalves and presented him with their five-year plan for a 'modern, developed and progressive capitalism' " (p. 62). What is unclear in all this is, again, the excluded segment of capital: Espírito Santo had previously been linked to the colonies, and presumably faced the sharpest contradiction with non- or neocolonial fractions; CUF and Champalimaud are seen as part of the "big comprador bourgeoisie"; only the "monopoly domestic bourgeoisie" appears left out, despite the fact that "it was the monopoly sectors of the domestic bourgeoisie that took the lead" (p. 57). We have argued that the Champalimaud and Mello holdings placed them in the monopoly domestic bourgeoisie. Espírito Santo, by contrast, was part of the comprador bourgeoisie. What Espírito Santo's and Champalimaud's visit to Gonçalves symbolized was a *compromise* between the monopoly domestic bourgeoisie (CUF, Champalimaud) and the comprador bourgeoisie (Espírito Santo).

This compromise had several political implications. It was one example of the basic development of the overall political situation: rather than a badly split bourgeoisie, it demonstrated a continuing ability to unite and present a common front. As under the dictatorship, the bourgeoisie sought to reconcile its divergent interests, only now without the facilitating role of the old regime. As before, this unity prevented a rapid end to the colonial wars as indicated by the uncertain future for the colonies charted by Spínola, with the pace of decolonization and the transitional regime poorly defined.

This strategy failed to address the demands of the MFA for a clear break with the colonial past. Moreover, the Left feared that the regrouping of the dominant class under Spínola would resurrect the policies of the previous regime with its limits on political liberties and popular participation. As illustrated by Spínola's frustrated effort to mobilize support during the rally of the silent majority on September 28, 1974, a large portion of the population shared the fears of the MFA and the Left. Increasingly, the anti-Fascist dimension could now be tied to the antimonopolist one: if the dictatorship's dominant class support was reorganizing after the coup, who could be sure that the "liberal" tendency would prove ascendent over the traditional comprador-colonialist one? In this sense, the basis for coupling the widely felt anti-Fascist sentiment with an antimonopolist one was present and indeed used with considerable success by various Left organizations during this time.

Poulantzas emphasized that the "antimonopolist" dimension of the democratization process was secondary, always following the lead of the domestic bourgeoisie. He failed to appreciate the implications of the fact that the leading element of the domestic bourgeoisie was precisely the "monopoly" segment. The real ascendency of the domestic bourgeoisie around October 1974 or "after the departure of Spínola" cannot be separated from the dominant role that the monopolies played within the domestic bourgeoisie. The latter hardly followed the lead of the relatively few heavy industrialists and dispersed (and often reactionary) light industrialists outside of monopoly control: these elements simply could not compete with the concentrated financial and industrial strength of the monopolies. Thus the period from September to March was primarily one in which the major monopolies, leading the domestic bourgeoisie and allied with colonial comprador elements, attempted to stave off the rise of antimonopolist sentiments within the MFA and certain sections of the popular masses.

The failure of this strategy became obvious, as illustrated by Spínola's efforts to create an army in exile (the Exército de Libertação de Portugal, or Liberation Army of Portugal), which would re-establish the hegemony of the monopoly domestic bourgeoisie within the repressive structures of the state. Ultimately, the frustrations of the Spínola effort gave rise to the abortive coup of March 11, 1975. As the first period drew to a close, the monopoly domestic bourgeoisie was unable to forge a broad hegemonic consensus around its continued rule. It had lost ground both within the military and among the masses. Both Spínola and Palma Carlos were long gone, but the exact direction of political events remained uncertain. The marginalization of Spínola and his allies within the government and the MFA meant that an opportunity had been created for a distinct leftward turn. Increasingly, the problem became whether the popular masses and the political organizations claiming to represent them could take advantage of this opportunity. Poulantzas acknowledged the growing importance of the radicalization of the situation, insofar as this shifts attention to the struggle for popular leadership over the democratization process. He appeared more conscious of this in his postscript, where he emphasized the tenuousness of the domestic bourgeoisie's hegemony and the role of the popular masses in greater detail. Yet our argument stands, for his ambiguity in assessing the dominant class predisposes him to underestimate the rising importance of the antimonopolist sentiment such that he does not prepare us for the events that follow in phase two.

## Phase Two: March–November 1975

The start of the revolutionary second phase began after the failed Spínola coup. The MFA, broadly supported by the major Left organizations, proceeded with an anti-Fascist, antimonopolist strategy, concretized by the nationalization of the monopolistic groups. The nationalization of the groups was largely unanticipated by Poulantzas who argued that "this process was taking place (or would take place) under the hegemony of the domestic bourgeoisie" and featured the "absence of an antimonopoly policy and alliance during this stage" (p. 135). In the postscript, Poulantzas attempts to clarify his position after the nationalizations had taken place where he argues that "the hegemony and leadership of this democratization process by the popular masses" was at stake (p. 136). The nationalizations under Prime Minister Vasco Gonçalves were one instance in which the popular masses appeared to win this leadership, but subsequently lost again to the domestic bourgeoisie.

There are several difficulties with this position. Whereas Poulantzas qualifies much of his discussion about the type and extent of control exerted by the various parts of the capitalist class, it is clear that we could not have anticipated the Gonçalves initiatives from Poulantzas' work. Poulantzas emphasized that the domestic bourgeoisie would not lose control over the process of democratization at any point. The Left organizations were inappropriate and bitterly divided, and "even the most politicized part of the Portuguese masses lacked the historical experience of open class struggle" (p. 138). How can the unexpected dethroning of the domestic bourgeoisie be explained in light of the shortcomings among the popular masses?

The answer lies in part in Poulantzas' failure to understand the nature of the Portuguese dominant class. As we argued previously, the monopoly domestic bourgeoisie had an alliance with the comprador elements and did not have an acceptable hegemonic project. Poulantzas might have argued that the MFA increasingly functioned as a "political organization of the dominant classes" in an instance in which "the dominant classes are more often than not unable to raise themselves by their own efforts to a hegemonic level vis-a-vis the dominated classes" (Poulantzas 1978, 287). This interpretation emphasizes the relative autonomy of the state, which he admitted was "a relative autonomy which I myself tended to neglect in this book" (p. 143). But this view would make sense only by modifying the assumption that the domestic bourgeoisie was leading the democratization process.

The idea of "relative state autonomy" seems most applicable to the period between the resignation of Spínola and the failed March coup attempt. The Emergency Economic Plan of the MFA elaborated in February 1975 did not envision any rapid nor comprehensive nationalizations. It was largely a project that tried to assuage working class demands, control the impact of decolonization upon the economy, and simultaneously provide an atmosphere conducive to private accumulation. However, it should not be assumed that this corresponded to the direct "hegemony" of the domestic bourgeoisie, especially after Spínola's ouster when the MFA became increasingly susceptible to popular demands. In this sense, the "relative autonomy" of the MFA was rather feeble, touched constantly by the difficulties of sustaining a dominant class coalition that included comprador elements, at the same time meeting the economic and political demands of the dominated classes. After the March coup, the argument for "relative autonomy" seems even weaker because the nationalizations simply cannot be seen as somehow satisfying the interests of the domestic bourgeoisie unless these are understood in obscure and probably teleological ways. Poulantzas' failure to attribute sufficient relative autonomy to the state may ultimately stem from his insistence that state power is reducible to the hegemony of a dominant faction, thus granting largely by analytical presupposition more coherence and importance to the bourgeoisie than can be discovered empirically.

The nationalizations moved virtually the entire Portuguese holdings of the monopoly domestic bourgeoisie and comprador bourgeoisie into the state's hands and could be seen as the initial step toward socialism. This created the potential for a decisive state role in orienting production, and in combination with other measures such as land reform and growing workers' control in factories, might have provided decisive first steps in a transition to some form of socialism. Even assuming that a considerable share of production would be left to private capital, the major "commanding heights" of the economy were no longer held by the monopolies, effectively minimizing the strength of the most potent and resource-laden element within the dominant class. This point was even recognized by the Partido Socialista (Socialist party, or PS), which argued:

> among the hesitations and partial measures [conducted by the Gonçalves government], one fundamental step was taken and will constitute without a doubt a great moment in the history of Portugal: the absolute power of a reduced number of capitalist groups was destroyed, having nationalized a decisive part of the productive apparatus. In this way is gained [by the state] means for exercising economic power (Partido Socialista 1975, 7).

The inability of the popular masses to consolidate leadership positions and proceed to a transition to socialism requires a closer examination of the issues dividing the Left. Of particular importance are the conceptions of democratization and socialism held by the various leftist organizations. For Poulantzas, on the one hand, these organizations were flawed due to their failure to agree on a "democratization program with clearly defined objectives" that minimized the chances for the popular masses to maintain their hegemony over the democratization process (p.145). On the other hand, the organizations of the Left were altogether inappropriate for conducting a socialist revolution, as Poulantzas stated: "the first striking factor here is the absence of a mass revolutionary party with a consistent and well-adapted line for the transition to socialism in a European country such as Portugal, an essential condition for such a transition to take place" (p. 142). Poulantzas seemed to imply that his conception of such a transition was based on the Russian experience and, in particular Lenin's conception of dual power, because "at no time [could we find] the characteristic situation of dual power that results from the organization of a centralized popular power parallel and exterior to the official state apparatus, a major condition for the transition to socialism" (p. 142). For Poulantzas, the state could not be whittled down bit by bit, but rather had to be "smashed" in the transition to socialism.[7] Unfortunately, there was no effective "mass revolutionary party with a consistent and well adapted line for the transition to socialism . . ., (p. 142)" and the MFA itself could not function as a surrogate for a revolutionary party because it only served the radicalized petty bourgeoisie and the alliance between the petty bourgeoisie and domestic bourgeoisie. The MFA could not go beyond a certain political vacillation and corporate professionalism. Thus "socialism was never really on the agenda" (p. 144).

Poulantzas attributed serious strategic and political failings to the major Left organizations, which he criticized for not sharing his view of the transition to socialism. He also focused on the plentitude of conceptions about socialism that divided the popular masses and prevented them from maintaining a hegemony over the democratization process.

The main strategy evidently favored by Poulantzas and much of the revolutionary Left (i.e., left of the Partido Communista Português, Portuguese Communist party, or PCP) was some version of armed struggle/dual power. The major components of such a strategy included: a clear break between the popular masses and the various segments of the bourgeoisie; the creation of a grassroots network of workers', residents' and soldiers' councils, which appeared for varying periods during late 1974 and 1975; the mobilization of leftist elements in the military for a conclusive assault on other less progressive groups; and the final establishment of a "democratic dictatorship of the proletariat," either with or without a single-party format.

As this option forced a direct "frontal" confrontation with capitalism and impelled vacillating elements to polarize to one side or other of the revolution, it is clear that the costs of this project would have been enormous: The existing polarization between the north and south of the country would have resulted in civil war; the peasantry—ideally a class that could be won over to the side of the revolution but under the existing conditions concentrated in the north with little sympathy for socialist appeals—would have been much more inclined to resist violently; much of the working class would have joined the revolution, but a significant part (especially in parts of the mid and northern regions) would have abstained from or even opposed it; the strength of the Left within the military would have been severely tested, with no assurance of victory given the emerging balance of forces within the MFA. In short, this would have been an all-or-nothing strategy, in which the capitalist state would have been "smashed" or, conversely, the Left exposed to a long-lasting defeat as a broad coalition of national and international capital, most of the peasantry, important segments of the urban petty bourgeoisie, and even parts of the industrial working class itself rallied against the prospect of a "new dictatorship of the Left." These costs must certainly have been in the minds of many "socialists" during the events of November 25, 1975 (when the "ultra-Left" military uprising failed).

It is only in light of this strategy for the transition to socialism that Poulantzas' ideas start to make sense. It is obvious to Poulantzas himself that the conditions likely to sustain the armed struggle/dual power strategy did not exist: the lack of a centralized coordinating mechanism, the fragmentary and embryonic nature of the various forms of popular power, and the limits of the MFA demonstrated that this strategy for the transition to socialism was not on the agenda and ultimately bound for failure. However, this did not necessarily mean that another strategy could not place socialism on the agenda, only with fewer immediate costs and with prospects for greater popular adhesion.

Three other strategies were possible. The first was the overtaking of bureaucratic positions in an effort to grab portions of state power bit by bit. As with the practice of the PCP, this involved the insertion of loyalists into the state apparatus who sought to control certain branches of the existing state and ultimately set up a network within the state from which to take complete control. The PCP sought to maintain an alliance with leftist sympathizers within the MFA in the form of the Povo (People)-MFA alliance.

The PCP felt that in the context of a discredited and poorly organized right wing, it could rise to power by offering to subdue certain popular demands in exchange for MFA backing. In the long run, the PCP hoped to control bureaucratic and political centers of power, and thereby use them to leverage its demands against those of others.

The long-term objectives for the PCP remained dim, because it is not clear that it sought inevitably to monopolize political power. The PCP supported the institutionalization of the MFA within any new governing arrangement. The party saw the MFA as the main guarantor of gains already made. The far Left argued, much like Poulantzas, that the MFA could not be more than the expression of a radicalized petty bourgeoisie; the only guarantee for the revolution would exist not by maintaining the coherence of the MFA, but by elimination of the vertical military structure altogether and linking soldiers and workers directly. The PCP clearly did not want the dismantlement of the vertical structure of the MFA, but instead wanted to cement ties with those officers sympathetic to its cause. In this sense, the PCP was a brake upon the armed struggle/dual power strategy of revolution. However, Poulantzas was correct in arguing that the PCP had little consistency during this period, swinging from a general acceptance of elections and parliamentary democracy to an insistence upon the Povo-MFA alliance as a means of preserving revolutionary gains despite the election outcomes. One PCP leader, Octávio Pato, insisted *prior* to the April 25, 1975, elections that "communists, defend the most ample liberties and the free existence of political parties" (Pato 1975, 174). This suggested a willingness to abide by the results of elections. By October, Pato was arguing that

> revolutionary practice has demonstrated that the electoralist proportions [i.e., those resulting from the April elections, which the PPD and PS sought to use to determine the allocation of ministries in government] are in opposition to the necessities of the revolutionary process. The opposition of the PPD, and also of the PS, to popular forms of organization and election (workers and resident commissions, etc.) is one example that effectively demonstrates the contradictions of those who intend to subordinate everything to voting percentages (1975, 185).

This points to the extraordinary difficulty of resolving the direct democracy/representative democracy contradiction during a transition to socialism, even assuming that the PCP favored either in the end.

To a large extent, the eventual shortcomings of this strategy were similar to those associated with the previous one: at no point was there a clear prospect for winning over the MFA as a whole to this line, nor were the broad bases of popular support likely to rally to that which would be readily perceived as a Communist coup, imposing a new dictatorship, etc. Poulantzas was acutely aware that this option was flawed both in conception and in practice.

A third conception of the transition to socialism was the purely reformist one and a strategy that Poulantzas tacitly endorsed. Since there was no prospect for the overthrow of the capitalist state by frontal assault, the reformist strategy emphasizing social democratic reform, electoral and parliamentary processes, party competition, etc. was the only viable option left. Ultimately, this must have been what Poulantzas meant in arguing that socialism could not be telescoped with the democratization process. Given the terms of his argument, Poulantzas would insist that the reformist process would not lead to socialism, or at least his variant, but only to the continued hegemony of the domestic bourgeoisie. This can be seen in his remarks about the strategy of the reformist Socialist party whose policy "was never more than that of a democratization process under the hegemony of the domestic bourgeoisie, and as the process accelerated, it progressively showed itself a privileged representative of that class" (p. 145). That Poulantzas did not perceive the Socialists in terms of a kind of "democratic socialist" strategy indicates the extent to which he continued to depict the situation as one defined by the hegemony of the domestic bourgeoisie, rather than a struggle over strategies for a socialist transition. Whereas it is certainly true that the PS did not believe in any strategy that ultimately marginalized the role of competitive elections and a multiparty system, it gave much verbal attention to the possible contribution of cooperatives and self-management to the realization of socialism. For example, the PS argued that with the nationalized sector it was possible "to already promote progressive forms of control [of production] by the workers" (p. 34). The seriousness of these proposals is open to question. Even after the parliamentary elections of 1976 in which the PS and PCP together held a majority of seats in the assembly, the PS was unwilling to entertain a PS-PCP alliance, which under the circumstances might have reinforced some of the incipient forms of direct democracy. However, unless a simple identification between the Socialists' desire to stabilize parliamentary democracy and the political interests of the domestic bourgeoisie is made, it is likely that the PS resisted the PCP due to the latter's equivocation regarding the parliamentary format, not merely because the PS acted as an agent of the domestic bourgeoisie. Mário Soares has argued that the PS had proposed in the aftermath of the 1974 coup a "Common Program of the Left," which might have conceivably aided a dual-track strategy reinforcing representative and direct democracy. According to Soares, the PCP undermined all prospects for reaching such an agreement by "privileging its alliance with the MFA, linking itself to pseudo-unitary movements like the MDP/CDE, seeking to expel socialists from the union movement" (Soares 1979, 14).

The reformist strategy increased prospects for attaining social democracy, but the benefits were relatively few compared to the dual-power strategy: capitalist exploitation was not ended, the capitalist state went on only mildly encumbered by the demands of the popular masses.[8] Yet, it was obvious that this strategy had certain advantages as well: it limited the dislocations and hardship of civil war; it forestalled the intervention of foreign governments and pressures from national and international capital; it set the stage for a broader popular alliance (including some peasants, parts of the urban petty bourgeoisie and working class) for "progressive" reforms.

Poulantzas' tacit acceptance of reformism under the conditions found in Portugal seems paradoxical: the only country undergoing considerable working class mobilization, with nationalizations, land reform, popular councils, and the emergence of civil liberties would be destined to adopt a regime and state not significantly shaped by revolutionary components of the democratization process. Rather than emphasize what was unique to the Portuguese experience, Poulantzas' analysis placed Portugal closer to the other Mediterranean democratizing experiences, and aloof from the Portuguese popular masses and their strong antimonopolist/anti-Fascist sentiments.

Ironically, Poulantzas in *State, Power, Socialism* offered an alternative strategy for the transition to socialism, which seems absent in *The Crisis of the Dictatorships*. In his discussion of democratic socialism, he asked

> how is it possible radically to transform the State in such a manner that the extension and deepening of political freedoms and the institutions of representative democracy are combined with the unfurling of forms of direct democracy and the mushrooming of self-management bodies? (Poulantzas 1978, 256)

Portuguese democratization offered an ideal setting for the blending of these two tracks: representative democracy and direct democracy. The "telescoping" of democratization and socialism seems entirely plausible if it is taken into account that the "democratic road to socialism is a long process" that concentrates on "the internal contradictions of the State" (Poulantzas 1978, 257). This strategy would avoid the excessive reformism of social democracy, which seeks incrementally to capture "the state machinery piece by piece." Indeed, the nationalizations, land reform, and popular councils would appear to offer a "stage of real breaks" climaxed by a new "relationship of forces within the State [which] touches its apparatuses and mechanisms as a whole" rather than simply Parliament or other "ideological state apparatuses." The Portuguese experience showed that "these apparatuses are themselves traversed by the struggles of the popular masses" (Poulantzas 1978, 259). These observations suggest that Poulantzas had not fully realized the implications of the Portuguese case at the time he was writing *The Crisis of the Dictatorships*. Had more attention been placed on the extent to which the domestic bourgeoisie had lost power, a better emphasis upon the "real break" during the Portuguese transition would have resulted.

More importance could have been placed on the strategic implications of the April 1975 elections for the constituent assembly. Whereas Poulantzas insisted that the "radicalization of the popular masses in Portugal remained the radicalization of a minority" (p. 138) this was true mainly in terms of an armed struggle/dual-power strategy. As the data on Table 3.2 suggests, there remained between April 1975 and April 1976 a broad base of support for some leftist program. Poulantzas accurately stated that the *radicalization* remained valid only for a minority and that disenchantment with the process was "particularly the case with broad sections of the rural petty bourgeoisie in the north of the country, but it also affected the middle peasant in all areas" (p. 138). However, it is likely that the peasantry never felt much enthusiasm toward democratization. He also argued that service sector support fell dramatically during this time as "sizable fractions of the urban petty bourgeoisie came to detach themselves from the process that was underway (viz. among other things the rise of the PPD and the Socialist party)" (p. 139). Yet this suggested that the urban petty bourgeoisie had somehow been "attached" to an ongoing process that included continued radicalization. Moreover, it may have been deceptive to lump the PSD[9] and PS together, because despite certain similarities in political positions, they had very different historic origins and social bases. For example, the PCP continued to refer to the Socialists as a "democratic" party, a label it never foisted on the PPD or the Centro Democrático Social (Center Social Democratic, CDS). As Poulantzas himself notes, whereas parts of the PS leadership had strong

**Table 3.2**
**National election results in Portugal 1975–76 (in percentages)**

| | PCP | PS | PPD/PSD | CDS | Other Left |
|---|---|---|---|---|---|
| 1975 | 12.5 | 37.9 | 26.4 | 7.6 | 7.3 |
| 1976 | 14.6 | 35.0 | 24.0 | 15.9 | 3.4 |
| | PCP + PS | WITH OTHER LEFT (FSP, LCI, MDP, MES, UDP)[a] | | | |
| 1975 | 50.4 | 57.7 | | | |
| 1976 | 49.6 | 53.0 | | | |

[a] The MDP did not run in 1976. For numerous subsequent elections, it ran as part of an alliance with the PCP. Some revolutionary Left parties called for a blank vote during 1975 as a protest against the development of parliamentary institutions, deradicalization, etc. The total blank or null ballots was 6.9 percent of all votes cast in 1975, although the share constituting a political message as opposed to unfamiliarity with voting procedures is impossible to judge. *Source: Eleição para A Assembleia da República—1976,* Lisbon: Instituto Nacional de Estatísticas, 1976.

ties to a conservative strand of social democracy, the popular base of the party was often more leftist. As he puts it, "If it [the PS] rallied to the anti-monopoly measures taken by the Gonçalves governments, this was only in self defense, and under pressure from its base" (p. 146). The same cannot be said for the PPD or CDS, which never "rallied to the antimonopoly measures" and, during the subsequent period of parliamentary rule, actively pressed for the denationalization of firms and the opening up of sectors closed to private capital. Although the PS displayed a certain willingness to go along with the Right, it resisted drastic changes in the constitution during its revision in 1982.

The data in Table 3.2 reveal that the size of the combined PCP and PS vote did not change much over the year: the Communist vote increased slightly, whereas the Socialists saw their percentage descend somewhat. If the vote for the União Democrática Popular (Popular Democratic Union, a major revolutionary Left party) is compared, it shows a slight increase from 1975 to 1976 (1.8 to 2.3 percent). Otelo de Saraiva de Carvalho, as a candidate for the non-PCP revolutionary Left, received 16.5 percent of the vote in the 1976 presidential elections. This suggests that, even if the PCP candidate's (Octávio Pato) total of 7.6 percent is added, the truly radicalized minority was perhaps no greater than 25 percent of the electorate. Still, this is a rather impressive number considering the popular masses had "no experience in open class struggle." In sum, the electoral results indicated a sizable basis of popular support for some combination of socialist policies.[10]

Table 3.3 provides estimates of smallholder votes for each party based upon an ecological regression estimating technique.[11] It shows that over 50 percent of the conservative CDS 1976 vote came from smallholders. The Right (combining the CDS and PSD votes) was conclusively chosen by the smallholders as their favorite political tendency.

These trends suggest that the smallholders, as a consistent basis of right wing electoral support, constituted a support class for the policies offered by the Right: private ownership of the means of production, a more market-

**Table 3.3**
**Estimates of smallholders party vote**

| | 1975 | 1976 | 1979 | 1980 |
|---|---|---|---|---|
| PCP | −27.0 | −36.4 | −36.6 | −32.6 |
| PS | −16.0 | −3.4 | 15.7 | 7.7 |
| PSD | 92.6 | 70.2 | — | — |
| CDS | 26.3 | 50.3 | — | — |
| LEFT (PCP + PS) | −42.5 | −39.0 | −21.4 | −48.0 |
| RIGHT (CDS + PSD ± PPM) | 118.9 | 120.5 | 106.5 | 113.2 |

**Source:** Census data supplied by the Instituto Nacional de Estatísticas in 1981.

oriented economy, enhancement of church authority, etc.[12] Because smallholders did not comprise an electoral majority, the Right had to forge broader alliances with parts of the urban petty bourgeoisie. This created a number of contradictory pressures within the Right, because some technocratic modernizers favored the rationalization of agriculture (lowering food prices and subsidies to agriculture), thereby jeopardizing the strength of rural electoral support. In this sense, the popular base for the Right presents obstacles for the effective representation of dominant class interests.

Analysis of the electoral support given by industrial workers presents contradictory results. It is clear from Table 3.4 that the PCP and PS captured a consistent 60 to 70 percent of working class votes, even during the heyday of the Right's Aliança Democrática (Democratic Alliance, AD, comprised of the CDS, PSD, and a small monarchical party). However, although the Left generally retained the bulk of working class votes, a closer look at the individual party data reveals the problems with telescoping democratization with armed struggle/dual-power socialism because the Socialists received much greater support than the Communists, due largely to PCP weakness in northern urban centers such as Porto and Braga. Only a policy that coupled the specific appeals of each party into a general outlook on the transition to socialism might have succeeded. The possibility for such a coupling depended on the stands of the PS and PCP. Although pinpointing the specific appeals of each party involves much conjecture, it is clear that the Socialists compaigned strongly in favor of fusing liberal democracy with elements of a socialist program; the Communists were more concerned with accelerating the socialist transition itself, albeit largely when such an acceleration did not threaten their own positions. What remains unclear is whether the Socialists would have lost electoral support after 1976 had they offered conces-

**Table 3.4**
**Estimates of industrial workers party vote, 1975–80**

| | 1975 | 1976 | 1979 | 1980 |
|---|---|---|---|---|
| PCP[a] | 18.3 | 18.0 | 24.9 | 15.1 |
| PS | 52.5 | 51.1 | 41.1 | 43.1 |
| PSD | 17.2 | 17.7 | — | — |
| CDS | 5.6 | 8.3 | — | — |
| LEFT (PCP + PS) | 70.7 | 69.2 | 66.1 | 58.6 |
| RIGHT (PSD + CDS) | 23.2 | 25.6 | 28.9 | 34.5 |

[a] The parties to the left of the PCP were too inchoate and electorally insignificant to allow effective estimates of class participation in their votes (see Nataf 1987, chapters 2 and 3 for regional breakdowns of each social category).

*Source:* Census data supplied by the Instituto Nacional de Estatísticas in 1981 (for 1975–1979) and 1988 (for 1980).

sions to the PCP on matters of vital importance to it, such as the land reform. On the other hand, the Communists have fairly consistently sought a "majority of the Left." This implies that the PCP would have been willing to make certain concessions if the Socialists had genuinely been interested in making a bargain. Moreover, the Communist party's voters were frequently forced to "swallow live toads" in subsequent elections, such as the presidential elections of 1980 (when told to vote for the formerly "Fascist" candidate Ramalho Eanes) and 1986 (when the largest toad of all, PS leader Mario Soares, was reluctantly endorsed as the lesser evil by the PCP). All in all, the PCP and its voters showed that—by force of circumstances—they would be willing to be partners with the Socialists. It was the Socialists who, for diverse reasons, were unwilling to pursue relations with the PCP. Electorally, the PCP strongholds in the nationalized heavy industries could have been potentially coupled with the PS support in light industries and in less radicalized regions. This might have been compatible with the "dual-track" option for a transition to socialism.

The estimates for the service sector (see Table 3.5) suggest that Poulantzas misjudged the extent of urban petty bourgeoisie deradicalization during this period.[13] It was true that the Socialists experienced a decline in their support, with some of this going to the PPD and CDS. Nonetheless, the Communists obtained consistently high levels of support from this sector. This shows both sustained political commitment to some anticapitalist positions, as well as signs of rightward movement.[14] In general, it can be said the urban classes did support the two largest left parties by backing the measures that attacked the monopoly domestic bourgeoisie.

The broad support for some form of socialist transition is increased further when the rural pattern is examined. This is especially true for the agricultural workers (and especially those in the south, where the latifundia exist). Table

**Table 3.5**
**Estimates of service sector employee party voting, 1975–80**

| | 1975 | 1976 | 1979 | 1980 |
|---|---|---|---|---|
| PCP | 32.4 | 34.1 | 38.2 | 33.3 |
| PS | 60.3 | 48.9 | 27.0 | 29.0 |
| PSD | −1.6 | 4.6 | — | — |
| CDS | 1.5 | 7.5 | — | — |
| LEFT (PCP + PS) | 93.0 | 80.3 | 63.7 | 65.4 |
| RIGHT (PSD + CDS) | .3 | 11.6 | 30.2 | 30.2 |
| Change in PS vote | — | −11.4 | −20.1 | +2.0 |

*Source:* Census data supplied by the Instituto Nacional de Estatística in 1981.

**Table 3.6**
**Estimates of Agricultural Workers Party Vote**

| | 1975 | 1976 | 1979 | 1980 |
|---|---|---|---|---|
| PCP | 26.4 | 21.8 | 26.2 | 25.8 |
| PS | 24.5 | 23.2 | 20.0 | 18.6 |
| PSD | 24.7 | 22.7 | — | — |
| CDS | 11.1 | 17.3 | — | — |
| LEFT | 51.0 | 44.1 | 46.2 | 50.7 |
| RIGHT | 30.1 | 37.4 | 41.0 | 44.0 |

*Source:* Census data supplied by the Instituto Nacional de Estatísticas in 1981.

3.6 shows that a large percentage of this sector supported the PCP or PS, despite some losses by the latter in 1976. The direct democracy aspect of the "dual-track" option for the transition to socialism would have been strengthened among the southern agricultural workers given the extensive land reform started during the Gonçalves period. Naturally, this land reform process also facilitated the Right's insertion among the smallholders, fearful of expropriation.

The prospects for a successful transition to democratic socialism might have been significantly increased if some agreement between the Socialists and Communists had been possible. It is clear that for most social sectors, had combined electoral support for these two parties been translated into collaboration and a leftist government emerged, such a government would have enjoyed a broad legitimacy.[15] Exactly how broad is difficult to say, since it involves a counterfactual. For instance, to what extent would the Socialists have retained their support had they expressed the intention of collaborating with the Communists? Naturally, we might assume that *given the Communists policy of subordinating party collaboration in favor of the "Povo-MFA" strategy,* the Socialists would have indeed seen a sizeable portion of its support erode. However, as later elections have shown, even when the immediate "Communist threat" was over, the Socialists retained around a quarter or more of the total vote. This suggests that most of the Socialist support during that time was not simply a visceral anti-Communist reaction, but also to a significant degree of pro-Socialist preference. Moreover, the Communist electorate would surely have benefited from a policy of greater openness to the Socialists *during the Gonçalves period,* because it would have conceivably reduced pressures upon the PS from the Right. As mentioned earlier, the PCP electorate proved enormously flexible, going so far as to massively support archenemy PS leader Mário Soares in the second round of the 1986 presidential elections. This suggests that had the basis for a dual-track representative/direct democracy strategy been laid during the

Gonçalves period, the social support would probably have been there to sustain a broad leftist government.

Poulantzas was correct in pointing to the problem of Left collaboration as tied to the contradictory strategies of these two parties, the PCP and PS. To a large extent, the revolutionary period showed that the PS and PCP had very distinct conceptions of the transitions to socialism, despite momentary connections on certain issues like the nationalizations. What Poulantzas overemphasized, however, was the extent to which the Socialists' attitudes and behaviors during the process (and subsequently) could be reduced to its role as servant of the domestic bourgeoisie. As Poulantzas put it, in reaction to the PCP,

> the Socialist Party was able to use its democratic cover to conceal the real alternative that it represented—not merely a realistic process of democratization as against an unrealistic transition to socialism, but rather a process of democratization under bourgeoisie leadership and hegemony (p. 146).

This perspective trivialized the problems of the transition to socialism by asserting that the PS could not stand for anything other than "bourgeois leadership and hegemony." We are left again at the precipice: either the armed struggle/dual-power strategy successfully overthrows the capitalist state, or the domestic bourgeoisie (or perhaps the bourgeoisie as a whole) remains ascendent. Conceptualized in this way, the consolidation of representative democracy is simply another means for representing the bourgeoisie, not a part of a strategy for the transition to socialism as he himself seems later to suggest.

## POSTREVOLUTIONARY PORTUGAL: CAPITALIST RESTORATION OR A SOCIALIST "MIXED ECONOMY"

The period from 1976 to the present offers a complicated picture of class and state interactions. For the most part, the tensions and divisions continued among the popular masses and their organizations. The political divisions between the Left parties generally did not heal, and the prospects for a transition to socialism further eroded. Moreover, the nature of the capitalist class in Portugal significantly altered with the consolidation of capitalist social relations.

The political deadlock on the Left was not fundamentally altered. What were incipient tendencies in the revolutionary period crystallized into definite patterns of competitive and typically antagonistic relations between the Socialist and Communist parties. This was seen in the pattern of governing coalitions that formed after 1976 and the start of the constitutional period.

The PS and PCP never joined together in government and only voted in favor of two of the 11 governments that formed. In the first case, the PCP supported the minority PS government headed by Mário Soares in 1976; in the second, the PCP lent its votes to a temporary caretaker government headed by Maria Lourdes de Pintasilgo. In neither case was there any evidence of enduring ties between the parties. In the 1986 presidential elections, the Communists followed a pattern first established during the presidential elections of 1980 when they supported the candidate favored by the PS. In 1980 it was Ramalho Eanes; in 1986 they supported PS leader Mário Soares in the second round. This points to the underlying relationship between the two parties, with the PCP reluctantly following PS initiatives in a "lesser of two evils" mode in which the Socialists gain Communist votes without needing to offer much in exchange.

The presence of a broad Left government would not in itself guarantee that Socialist policies would be carried out. Indeed, the obstacles to a Socialist outcome in a country with considerable external dependencies such as Portugal would be multiple in any case. In the absence of a Left government, a Socialist transition would be even more unlikely. Further, the legal framework for a Socialist transition was well established in the 1976 constitution, which meant that in the event of a Left government, the coalition in power could claim to be legitimately following the priorities and legal constraints established within the constitution.[16] The failure to implement many of these Socialist features in supportive policies was a consequence of Socialist concessions to the Right, partly understood by the entrenched hostility between the PS and PCP. Thus our analysis underlines the importance of the PCP-PS split as a political contradiction inspired as much by a dissensus over the nature of the transition to socialism as by an intrinsic Socialist representation of a hegemonic domestic bourgeoisie.

The nature of the interests that came to be represented by the first Socialist and later governments in the postrevolutionary period can be broken down into two basic types of policies: those essentially meant to stabilize the overall nature of capitalist productive relations; and those intended to improve the "investment climate" for private accumulation.

Policies defining the role of capitalist enterprise in Portugal were linked to delimiting the private and public sectors, including the return of previously nationalized or other collectivized property to old owners or its sale to new (including foreign) owners; and to the identification of the respective roles of markets and plans for each sector. These policies contributed more to the framework of the accumulation process, rather than to the specific managerial rights and concrete economic benefits accruing to classes within the framework, despite obvious overlaps. Policies improving the investment climate were regarded as stimulating capitalist production within an "accepted" delimitation of public and private sectors and would include policies related to social security, wages, employment, and the rights of workers' organizations (e.g., trade unions and workers' committees), the conditions placed upon foreign investment, etc. Whereas both of these types of policies were related, the constriction of workers' wages and benefits might have occurred independently of the resurrection of much capitalist production given the objective possibilities of the Portuguese economy, its foreign dependencies, level of productivity and competitiveness on the world market, and growth of the labor pool.

Policies defining the respective roles of the private and public sectors, as well as domestic versus foreign capital, were introduced soon after the 1976 legislative elections by the Socialist minority government (1976–78). These laws signaled both a turn to the right in Portuguese politics as well as an attempt by the PS to retain some of the most notable "revolutionary gains." Most notable were a series of laws defining the public and private sectors and establishing the agricultural land and resources that were available for expropriation as well as the foreign investment code. The first decree attempted to distinguish those sectors and industries where either private companies could coexist with nationalized ones, or where one or the other would hold a monopoly. The nationalizations under the Vasco Gonçalves administration had been broad, branching into numerous sectors and industries. Banking remained closed to private enterprise, although para-bank agencies (such as "investment societies" or "societies for regional development") were not.[17] Infrastructure, such as electricity, natural gas, water, sewers, most transportation and ports, were largely to remain under state control. Important industries such as armaments, petroleum refining, petrochemicals, steel, and cement were also to be largely monopolized by the state, despite instances in which private capital could become "associated" with the state. However, the state could hire private managers for state enterprises, conceivably opening the door for the reconsolidation of real control by old management over nationalized firms. In 47 industries, private capital faced no direct restrictions, such as in fishing, textiles, cork, wood products, synthetic fibers, pharmaceutical products, construction, tourism, and much of the assembly of metal goods.

The Socialists sought to limit the direct prospects for a resurrection of the monopoly domestic and comprador/colonial segments of the dominant class while also making overtures to small and medium capital. In this sense, the PS was inclined to represent non-monopoly sectors within a stabilized capitalist (but clearly with "mixed" components of both private and public enterprises) sphere of operations. To what extent this could be characterized as an attempt to institutionalize the hegemony of the domestic bourgeoisie is debateable; more obvious was the Socialist reluctance to support either monopoly segments of capital, whether of domestic or comprador origins, or forms of state intervention advocated especially by the PCP.[18]

The agricultural legislation was particularly concerned with three overriding objectives: negate the influence of the PCP in the southern land reform areas; attempt to assuage the fears of smallholders regarding possible expropriation; and improve agricultural productivity and output while reducing government subsidies. A fourth aim, the conversion of the latifundia form of enterprise to smaller, more easily managed cooperatives, was more apparent during legislation passed when a progressive Socialist, Lopes Cardoso, was minister of agriculture in 1976.[19] The 1977 "lei Barreto" named after the PS minister of agriculture was predominantly concerned with the first three goals as the government sought to consolidate ownership patterns, largely by establishing more exact criteria regarding the type of holdings that could be legitimately taken over. The legislation aimed especially to undermine the PCP's social basis of support in the south, where it received nearly 50 percent or more of the vote in many electoral districts. The land reform spawned in the Vasco Gonçalves period had created numerous collective and cooperative farms; the PCP was the only major party enthusiastic about the process and directly involved in the management of most of the farms.[20]

The PS and succeeding governments engaged in a systematic policy of returning lands that had been taken over by the agricultural workers to old owners (or sometimes new smallholders). This policy failed in several ways. It did not do much to improve agricultural productivity, which suffered in part from poor weather. It may have contributed to some increases in unemployment, as land parcels were returned to old owners who, in perpetuation of traditional patterns and given the lingering instability of property relations, left much land uncultivated and neglected. Furthermore, it did very little to erode the PCP's overt political influence in the south, where the Communist party maintained control over many municipal governments. Last, it did not lead to new experiments in innovative farm organization, but rather left the collective farms under constant financial stress.

The Socialist government was faced with a very difficult set of contradictory pressures during that time. On the one hand, agricultural cooperatives, nationalized industries, and other sectors wanted additional subsidized funds to maintain their investment plans and pay off previous debt. On the other hand, the government was faced with increasing balance of trade deficits and assumed that only by lowering domestic demand could a better balance be struck. The PS government had to choose between the perils of prolonged international indebtedness, with the possibility of losing its creditworthiness, and the social and economic consequences of restricted credit. This choice, coupled with Socialist vacillation on land reform and, to a lesser extent, the nationalized industries, helped structure the outcome: sharp cuts in domestic credit and an attempt to encourage private investors to provide capital. This meant that the resurrection of Portuguese capital was closely connected with the external dependency faced by the government, rather than a special desire to represent a hegemonic domestic fraction of capital. In sum, the PS policies had many roots in external dependency and party antagonism, coupled with distinct popular bases and alternative conceptions of the breadth of the social coalitions meant to sustain a reformist government in a postrevolutionary setting.

The foreign investment code passed by the Socialist government was particularly important from the point of view of the analysis of the representation of segments of capital. If Poulantzas was correct, the PS would have adopted a restrictive code meant to facilitate the expansion of the domestic bourgeoisie rather than to invite foreign capital. However, it follows from what has already been said that the PS (and subsequent governments) generally relied on traditional instruments of intervention to control the outstanding problems of inflation, unemployment, and balance of payments. One traditional instrument for solving a balance of payments crisis was the encouragement of foreign investment. From 1978 private medium and long-term capital started a spectacular rise (calculated in U.S. dollars): 1977, $19 million; 1978, $249 million; 1979, $462 million; 1980, $1,000 million; 1981, $1,357 million; 1982, $1,885 million. This was encouraged in part by the liberalization of the Foreign Investment Code under the PS government. The previous more restrictive code had been devised under the Sixth Provisional Government in 1975. The major change imposed by the Socialist government greatly facilitated the repatriation of profits by abandoning the limit of 20 percent of invested capital per year. Also liberalized was the ability of foreign capital to enter into all the sectors not specifically prohibited to private capital. For some industries, such as armaments, petroleum refining, steel, and fertilizers, the government reserved for itself the possibility of entering into joint partnerships, with the state retaining majority control. Thus the PS accepted the presence of private capital, both domestic and foreign, as long as the prospects for the remonopolization of the economy could be kept at bay.[21]

The Socialist government as well as ensuing governments clearly did not envision a model of socialism that would result in a rapid elimination of capitalism. Within the mixed economy, the state sector could conceivably be a major part of a gradualist socialist transition, for, as the Socialists had argued at one time, state enterprises could serve as a laboratory for experiments in workers' control and planning. Unfortunately, the purpose and functioning of the state sector in Portugal were traversed by the political instability of frequent changes in government with no clear role emerging. At times the nationalized firms were expected to function like capitalist enterprises, their performance judged largely on profit criteria. Critics of the state-sector frequently pointed to the failures of many public firms on these grounds. However, the state-owned firms were also to have a social function. Many of the public enterprises were compelled to accept excess labor, as with the banks that hired many *retornados* (returning emigrants) who had held banking positions in the former colonies. Moreover, these firms acted as a further buffer against unemployment by closely adhering to labor laws as well as by further expansion. The OECD stated that "labor legislation on job protection was certainly applied more rigidly than in the private sector," implying that the public firms could not simply fire redundant workers. In addition, its report mentioned that "public enterprises have had to contend with growing investment costs and a steep rise in labor and financial costs, and some of them have been required by the government to limit increases in their prices" (OECD 1984b, 29).

Such adherence to labor codes and employment practices could not be internally financed given the poor economic conditions of the late 1970s and the capital intensive character of a substantial number of these firms (see Bruneau 1985). The nationalized enterprises were therefore obliged to borrow enormous amounts in order to meet their conflicting objectives. By the end of 1982, the foreign debt alone for the public enterprises was a staggering $8 billion, or 56 percent of Portugal's total external debt. As the debt increased, these firms saw a growing share of their revenues disappear in interest payments instead of investments. Rather than a motor for development, the state sector was increasingly perceived as the culprit for economic hard times. As a constant drain upon public resources, it was in competition with other government priorities for limited funds. As a drain upon the economy as a whole, it was resented not only by other segments of capital, which preferred to have investment funds flowing to their own projects, but also by parts of the working class and petty bourgeoisie who paid taxes or envied the relative privileges and working conditions found in the state sector.

The weak financial condition and lack of clear orientation of the nationalized sector were part of the ambiguous results of the revolutionary period. The desire of some Socialists and Communists to emphasize the importance of a strategic state sector as the motor of a transitional socialist economy was awkwardly combined with other social objectives such as maintaining employment and resuscitating private accumulation. Given the lack of a stable Left governing coalition, the nationalized sector was subject to continual buffeting between a divided Left and an obviously pro-capitalist Right, which sought to blame many of the country's ills on the state sector. The political divisions on the Left-facilitated the emergence of a new, if precarious, hegemonic principle, an antistatist belief in free markets and a less interventionist state. This was the theme of the AD during the 1980 campaign. Although the acceptance of this principle was still problematic, the reconstruction of the class interests of at least some segments of the capitalist class (especially large domestic and foreign capital) was hastened by the emergence of a new legitimating idea.

Implicit in the examination of these policies was the notion that certain segments of the capitalist class saw their political and economic interests represented in the postrevolutionary period. Whereas these policies variably represented small, medium, and to some extent foreign capital (largely during the PS period), or sought to reconstitute capitalism as a whole and favored large capital (the AD and the Cavaco Silva PSD governments), they also had important effects upon the bread and butter economic gains made by the popular masses.

The unemployment situation, for example, presented a mixed picture. On the one hand, it was clear that despite the rapid expansion of the work force due to the demobilization of the military and the influx of *retornados*, unemployment rates were not as high as might have been expected. Table 3.7 reveals that Portugal had an unemployment rate much below that of Spain, for example. This may be due in part to different ways of calculating the rate, although given the colonial refugees and returning soldiers combined with the depressive effects of sharp oil price increases, the OECD figures probably understated the Portuguese situation. The priority of maintaining employment in the face of circumstances beyond direct government control would indicate that the popular masses had dislodged to some extent the hegemony of capitalist segments that would have preferred more flexible firing laws, lower wages by increased competition among workers, etc. The Silva PSD government's efforts to introduce a more liberal code against union resistence expressed an attempt to consolidate the hegemony of capital.

It is tempting to conclude that the employment policies, especially prior to the Silva government, were an effort at maintaining the political interests of the dominant class by a relatively autonomous capitalist state. Moreover, to the extent that underemployment was hidden in state sector enterprises,

**Table 3.7**
**Comparison of unemployment rates—1973–82**

| | 1973–76 | 1977–79 | 1980–82 |
|---|---|---|---|
| Portugal | 4.1 | 7.8 | 7.7 |
| Spain | 3.7 | 7.6 | 14.8 |
| Greece | 2.1 | 1.8 | 4.2 |
| Ireland | 6.4 | 6.9 | 8.6 |
| OECD Europe | 6.0 | 4.4 | 8.3 |

*Source: OECD Economic Survey of Portugal—1983–84.*

with possible delegitimizing effects such a strategy entails, the political interests of the dominant class seem further served. Yet, this assumes that the Portuguese state is (or was) a capitalist state, rather than a transitional one with a complex mixture of capitalist and socialist elements. Surely Socialists have insisted upon the social functions of enterprises and would have thereby insisted on using state enterprises in this way. It is wiser to interpret the employment and state sector enterprise issues as subject to intense class conflict, rather than simply a devious attempt by a capitalist state to secure the political interests of the whole capitalist class.

On the other hand, the decline of real wages over the period 1976 to 1983 revealed the relative weakness of the popular masses after the revolutionary period. Average gross annual real wages dropped steadily from 1976 to 1979 (1974, +9.1 percent; 1975, +13.5 percent; 1976, −.1 percent; 1977, −7.2 percent; 1978, −3 percent; 1979, −2.5 percent; 1980, +3.7 percent) (Rosa 1982, 315). In 1979 the AD attempted to gain prolonged control over the government by engineering a period of artificial prosperity. Using a technique mastered in other capitalist democracies, the alliance expanded internal demand by 6.2 percent, lowered inflation from 24 to 16 percent, and increased real wages by nearly 4 percent. This was done by preventing the further slide of the escudo while maintaining or increasing subsidies and borrowing. This strategy succeeded brilliantly in securing victory in the 1980 legislative elections. Unfortunately, the electoral victory also forced the AD to govern in face of the burgeoning balance of payments deficits which these economic policies also produced. The deficit nearly tripled from $1.251 bil lion in 1980 to $3,245 billion in 1982. The external debt doubled from 1979 to 1981, finally reaching $14.2 billion in 1983 or 13 percent of GDP.

By the 1983 elections the AD broke apart. Real wages under the PS led government in 1983 to 1985 declined sharply as austerity policies took effect. By 1985 and especially 1986, the PSD minority government (1985–87) was able to capitalize upon more favorable external conditions and domestic economy, represented by an increase in the national product, in real internal demand, lower unemployment and rising real wages. This coupled with public anticipation regarding the entry of Portugal into the European Economic Community and dissatisfaction with the lack of a credible left alternative prepared the ground for the PSD's electoral success in 1987.

The erosion of living conditions was seen also in the shrinking share of wages in the national income. Wages went up dramatically during the height of the revolution, from 51.6 percent in 1973 to 68.9 percent in 1976, only to sink back to a level nearly equal to 1973 by 1979 (52.9 percent). These economic downturns were indicative of power losses experienced by the popular masses. The decline in wages could be seen as an intrinsic part of a strategy made possible by the divided Left and PS concessions to the Right, which re-established an atmosphere conducive to private accumulation.

However, these wage losses were also attributable to factors beyond the immediate control of any government, given the external dependencies and structural weakness of the Portuguese economy. With the country's historical productive shortcomings, it ran chronic deficits in its commodity trade. The deficit in its balance of trade was partly compensated by the inflow of tourists and emigrant remittances, which together helped balance its payments. The post-revolutionary period was shaped by the need to deal with escalating deficits.

The actions of the various governments in the post-revolutionary period had minimal impact on correcting the pattern of imbalance in commodity imports and exports as the trade deficit increased consistently from 1975 to 1981. Yet, despite excessive reliance upon imports, insufficient emphasis was placed upon changing the structure of production and adopting policies emphasizing import substitution and incentives for exportation. The trend was to follow International Monetary Fund recommendations: increase taxes, limit government expenditures, raise interest rates, institute sharp limits on the growth of the money supply, hold down wage increases, raise prices, and devalue the currency . These policies, first enacted in earnest by the PS/CDS government in 1978, were intended to reduce aggregate domestic demand and thereby reduce the inflow of imports, but failed in this respect, although they did, however, lead indirectly to balancing the current balance of payments accounts. From a peak deficit of $1.495 million in 1977, there was a sizable drop to $826 million in 1978, and finally to only $52 million in 1979, largely the consequence of increases in tourism, emigrant remittances, as well as private and official capital transfers.[22] The governments were singularly ineffectual in reversing the deficiencies in Portugal's productive capacities, but they were quite successful in convincing austerity-oriented international lenders, budget-minded tourists, and high interest-seeking, stability-minded emigrants that the Portuguese economy was being corrected of its "excesses" from the short-lived Vasco Gonçalves era. By 1983, the 'politics of stabilization' meant that the socialists would again bear the burden of dealing with the balance of payments disequilibrium by overseeing the decline in demand, falling real wages and diminishing growth rates. Socialists, inclined to correct averse business cycle effects upon the popular masses through reflation, were instead to oversee the bottoming out of the Portuguese economy. The PSD was to be the real beneficiary of social democratic reflation—carrying it through to its electoral victory in 1987.

From the analysis above, it is hard to see how the policies of the Socialists were especially beneficial to the domestic bourgeoisie. Austerity policies undermined the standard of living for workers, but they also did little to favor the domestic bourgeoisie which needed a growth in the internal market. An editorial in *Empresa Privada* (representative of some interests associated with the domestic bourgeoisie) commented on all governments prior to 1980:

> . . . burdened by high taxes, paying salaries which are already relatively high, confronted by the fall of the escudo and a constant increase in the cost of raw materials, prevented from going to the Bank as much by the low loan ceilings as by the astronomical interest rates . . . and not being able to count on the state when one intends to guide production towards exports, the entrepreneur, who feels the reduction in national buying power, feels isolated.

The depiction of the Portuguese entrepreneur as orphaned by the state hardly seems compatible with the 'narrow' or more instrumentalist conception of the domestic bourgeoisie as represented in state policies. The bulk of the economic policies followed by virtually all governments was similar and involved policies oriented to reestablishing capitalism to some degree, but unlikely to assuage the interests of domestically based capitalists, including: the reduction of domestic demand through administered controls on wages coupled with the decontrol or removal of subsidies from commodities; reductions in government services; lessening support for the nationalized sector; and credit restrictions. These were hardly the contents of a program specifically favoring the domestic bourgeoisie.

The electorally inspired reinflation of the economy during 1979–80 conveyed a sense in which the AD may have represented the domestic bourgeoisie. However, to the extent that this was true, this was not the relatively autonomous state looking after the political interests of the hegemonic fraction of the bourgeoisie: rather, it was an ill-fated attempt to satisfy immediate political demands. The irrationality of this attempt in terms of the long-term political interests of the bourgeoisie was striking: record balance of payment deficits, a redoubling of austerity policies, the dissolution of the AD, the failure of the right wing strategy of political bipolarization and total isolation of the PCP, and so on. The Silva governments were blessed by a more opportune conjuncture, but still faced sharp contradictions as with the policies of privatization and the indemnification of old owners, economically weak firms unable to pay worker salaries, and labor agitation.[23] Indeed, the Silva governments' efforts to assuage the interests of organized labor and employers only resulted in greater polarization and more unity between Socialists and Communists both at the party and union levels.

Although policies undertaken by governments of varying political complexions tended to reveal an anti-socialist dimension based on the diminution of the state sector and a decline in working class conditions, they did not necessarily suggest a strongly resurrected capitalist hegemony either. The political outcome could be conceived as "dishegemonic": a situation in which neither the popular masses nor the domestic bourgeoisie attained a clear ascendancy in terms of political leadership. Both were better characterized as eclipsed by events and forces which they poorly controlled. While certain measures such as the formation of the neo-corporatist Permanent Council of Social Concertation appeared to establishs one basis for class collaboration, its functioning did not lead, at least in the short-term, to much greater class harmony.

The entry of Portugal into the European Community has provided a renewed vigor to the attempts to use the model of capitalist democracy found elsewhere in Western Europe for Portugal: perhaps as the linkages between European political institutions, capital, labor organizations and their Portuguese counterparts grow in a context of declining East-West conflict, the positive language of 'modernization' and 'Europeanization' will form the basis for a renewed capitalist class hegemony as the atrophy of alternative hegemonic projects for the left establishes the foundations for class-conflict *within* the confines of a market-based, mixed but largely capitalist national economy integrated within a liberal world trading regime.

In the case of Portugal, we would speculate that the "dishegemonic interlude" after the revolutionary period and perhaps ending in the late 1980s was strongly tied to the inadequacies of a Portuguese domestic bourgeoisie which proved inept at providing political leadership because of its historic subordination to the monopolies. With the monopolies nationalized, the Portuguese bourgeoisie was a headless horseman, which for years sought comfort in negative themes (anti-communism, anti-statism, anti-MFA, anti-constitutional) but unable to provide a broadly acceptable alternative. One test of the resurgence of Portuguese capitalism will lie in the eventual reconstitution of the private monopolies, which in the context of Europeanization, will not be likely to have the "domestic" character possessed under the Estado Novo should they reappear at all.[24]

## PROSPECTS FOR CHANGE

Have recent political events signalled a change in this situation? Five interrelated aspects of the historically dishegemonic Portuguese context are clearly connected to the extent and direction of change: the political deadlock on the Left; the strength and unity of the Right; the institutional developments seeking to create an umbrella for renewed hegemony; the changing economic conjuncture; and the impact of entry into the European Economic Community.

The political deadlock on the Left has shown some signs of change. The 1985 legislative elections brought forth a new party, the Partido Renovador Democrático (Democratic Renewal Party, PRD) into the Portuguese political arena. Its electoral performance exceeded all expectations as it obtained about 18 percent of the vote. The party seemed to indicate a change in the form in which the Left's constitutencies found political expression given that the PRD's votes came largely from the PS and, to a lesser extent, the PCP. As it did not suffer from the historical antagonisms separating the PS and PCP, it might serve as the missing link required to forge a broad coalition of the Left. However, this scenario was improbable as the party was supported largely by followers of former President Eanes and included parts of the rural and urban petty bourgeoisie and represented somewhat the interests of small and medium capital. Ideologically heterogeneous, neither its electoral base nor its policy objectives were likely to be very compatible with the formation of a broad alliance of left parties including the PCP. Moreover, the hostility and competition between the PRD and PS as political organizations with similar clienteles also undermined any remote opportunity for a broadly based Left government. In fact, the appearance and rapid decline in 1987 of the PRD also reinforced our basic argument that the situation was still quite dishegemonic, as the bourgeoisie and popular masses both grasped at new "political formulas" without clear direction.

Within the Socialist party, a leadership change brought in Jorge Sampaio, who managed to energize the party and open up its alliance strategy somewhat. As the PRD declined and the PSD rose, the PS moved more clearly into the opposition. Its assessment of the main political challenge changed and efforts focused more on the erosion of the Social Democratic strength. Collaboration at the trade union level between Communists and Socialists—for example, among the bank workers' union in 1988—was directed against the PSD-led tendencies within the UGT to the extent that they sided with the PSD government's proposed labor code revision. There was talk of the formation of a third labor confederation, composed of white collar unions. This inspired the UGT, particularly threatened in its base among service sector workers, to state:

> although a defender of pluralism, [we consider this initiative to be] another attempt by Social Democratic Workers-TSD, with a base in imaginary, non-existent unions, to try to construct a third confederation whose only objective is to divide and weaken the Portuguese union movement and put at the Government's disposition a subservient and attentive errand-boy (mandarete) (*O Jornal,* 2-9-90).

Like the CGTP in the period after the coup (1974–77), the originally PS-PSD inspired UGT reacted defensively to the prospects of further dilution of union representative structures. For all their historic differences, the UGT and CGTP came to similar positions on this issue. Since the labor movement had been sharply politicized since the revolution, the transformation of the scene from one of PS-PSD common action in opposition to the Communists to one of PCP-PS common action against the Social Democrats may have a profound impact upon the patterns of political polarization to the degree that it continues over time.

Not only has PC-PS collaboration occurred at the trade union level, but party to party relations have improved. The election of Mário Soares brought together an ample spectrum, ranging from the center to the far Left. His narrow victory over rightist rival Freitas de Amaral required the delivery of votes from all parties to the left of the PSD. Combined with the majority election of the PSD in 1987, this fostered an ambience in which Left/Right bipolarization rather than Left/Center/Right tripolarization was ascendent. By 1989, the Socialists and Communists joined in their first explicit electoral coalition since the revolution as the "Por Lisboa" slate ran against the Right in the Lisbon municipal elections. The success of that effort may signal a significant if incremental decline in the long-standing ravine which has separated the Communists and Socialists.

The other question which, in 1990, must be posed in this regard is "which Communists" will the Socialists be facing in the next few years. António Barreto, a Socialist leader, declared in February 1990 that after the next legislative elections (anticipated in 1991) "the PS shouldn't form a government with the PCP until the Communists have changed from top to bottom. The PCP always copied that which was bad among its congener in the East. Now when there is something positive to copy, Dr. Alvaro Cunhal and the party have ignored the situation . . ." (*O Journal,* 2-16-90).

The PCP faces an imminent leadership change, both due to Cunhal's advancing age (76 years old) but also from tensions arising due to his association with the increasingly discredited pre-Gorbachev Soviet leadership and party line.[25] Within the party, several groups and personalities have arisen to question the party's program, internal functioning and international orientation. Vital Moreira, the noted Communist constitutionalist and Coimbra professor, has led one drive to democratize the party and remove its Stalinist residues. The formation of the National Institute for Social Studies (INES), with the adhesion of hundreds of PCP members as well as members of other Left parties, has been one offshoot of that tendency. Another group, Terceira Via (Third Way) has also suggested a set of needed reforms. Zita Seabra, a longtime ranking party member, has been outspoken in her denunciations of elements of Leninism, earning her a formal expulsion from the PCP. At the time of this writing, the internal situation within the Communist party remained highly uncertain. Thus, just at a time when relations between the PCP and the PS might be on the mend, the once all-too-predictable Communists showed signs of instability and transition. In the long run, however, "glasnost" within the PCP would only enhance its attraction as a Left partner for the Socialists and possibly lead to a Left government within the next few years.[26]

Given the ideological uncertainty of the period, it also remained to be seen how the Communists would define their platform and establish their distinctiveness vis-a-vis the Socialists. The PCP has long campaigned in favor of the 1976 Constitution and the retention of its socialist elements. The latest (1988) revision of the Constitution reduced much of the Left imprint from the revolution. The PCP may seek to reverse some of these changes as part of an alliance with the Socialists. This might include renewing government support for land reform, as the PSD has returned much expropriated land to old owners; reserving a larger role for nationalized industry; and further expanding worker and union rights. Nevertheless, while these aspects might form the basis of compromise with the Socialists, it will be harder than ever for the Communists to define the overarching contours of an accumulation model in a manner which sharply reverses the privatizing and internationalizing processes which the previous governments have set into motion. As the Eastern European centralized economies undergo a purge of their statist components, the legitimacy of statist socialism throughout Europe will lessen further and the Communists will be forced to fundamentally reassess their options. Whether "economism," "utopian socialism," a proecology, antinuclear and antiauthoritarian "postmaterialism" or some other creative attempt to tap the positive components of the Portuguese revolution without ignoring the political, ideological and economimc impact of European integration will take form in the PCP and the Left more broadly is part of the challenge the left now faces.

Within the Right, the PSD has seen its popularity decline since its unparalleled election victory of July 1987. Its vote count went down substantially in the 1989 European Parliament elections (32.7 percent) from the 1987 European vote (37.4 percent) and its 1987 legislative vote (50.1 percent). In the major politicized race in the 1989 municipal elections, the Right lost to the PC-PS coalition in Lisbon. The CDS has expressed frustration at its marginal role on the Right and sought to dissociate itself from the PSD somewhat. There is some question regarding the prospects of a rightist candidate for the coming presidential elections: the CDS has argued that it would not support a PSD candidate. The PSD has speculated about giving its support to incumbent Mário Soares. Internal dissent within the PSD after the remodeling of the Silva government following the loss in the municipal elections has also led to internal disarray. The PSD has generally taken advantage of a proEuropean, privatizing and modernization line which has appealed to young people as well as elements of the petty bourgeoisie and export-oriented parts of the bougeoisie. This line will probably not be subject to much change, despite some of the tensions it has caused between different sections of its social base—for example, among small and medium capitalists and smallholders who fear the effects of EEC integration and competition.

In sum, there are important signs of fluidity in the Portuguese party system and labor movement. This fluidity may forestall somewhat the emerging hegemony around the "Euro" modelled market-based, but neo-corporatist supplemented capitalism which the PSD and Socialists have tended to support when the spectrum was completely tripolarized, with the Communists in isolation and the "bloco central" (center block composed of PS and PSD) the only alternative to the rightist AD or PSD alone. Yet, the Left itself remains uncertain with regards to the global character of the alternative it represents. The "class" character of the socialist alternative to capitalism may be reduced to the narrowly redistributional and regulatory form taken by social democracy, thereby minimizing the exceptional character of Portuguese democratization within the framework of a homogenized Euro-model. While that model is certainly not without its own contradictions, its growth mechanism remains private accumulation and the hegemony of capital, however controlled and mitigated by the state in response to pressures from the popular masses.

From an institutional point of view, the emergence of the Permanent Council for Social Concertation (CPCS) in 1984 has been a key part of the importation of the Euro-model, neo-corporatism favored by the PS and PSD. Since both the CGTP and UGT have now generally accomodated themselves to participation within the council, the replacement of the "class struggle" perspective traditionally held by the CGTP by a "pluralist" orientation may signal a growing general acceptance of or resignation to a hegemonic model of private accumulation. As Stoleroff (1989: 15) has noted, however, even for the CGTP the strategic change emphasizing a more pragmatic approach was based on an acknowledgement of the difficulties posed by European integration, the increasing liberalization of the economy, the permanance and growth of the UGT and the important role that reformists from the PCP played in the national union leadership. While the labor movement may attempt to expand the scope of discussion within the council beyond prices and wages, branching into the labor code and even the role of state and private sectors, the involvement of the CGTP symbolizes the accomodation of the Left to at least some of the basic elements of the Euro-model.

More broadly, the integration of the Portuguese economy within the EEC has diminished the exceptional character of the democratization process by providing incentives for conformity to the general orientation of other European countries. The heavy dependence upon exports to Europe as well as the growing reliance upon foreign capital have greatly limited the options in Portugal. A "stable" political economy is also more likely to be rewarded by EEC structural funds for helping weaker sectors modernize, building infrastructure and more advanced worker training. By 1992, free capital flows are to be allowed across EEC borders: industrial trade will be opened up, with agriculture to follow by 1995. Increasingly, as protectionist barriers are lifted, pressures will continue to mount forcing the accumulation model to conform to the parameters dictated by the international economy. The homogenization of national legislation by virtue of the growing influence of the European Community's political institutions implies a declining ability for the specific circumstances of the Portuguese revolution to impact the long-term development of the political economy.

The economic conjuncture continues to reinforce some of the measures taken by the PSD government. The privatization of a beer company, a bank and two insurance companies in 1989 was a success in the sense that demand drove up share prices beyond most expectations. The Constitution was amended in 1989 to permit fuller denationalization than the 49 percent which had been previously allowed: the Privatization Act passed by parliament in February 1990 promises to facilitate the process even more. The readiness of foreign capital to enter into the Portuguese market to take advantage of privatizations and the general opening up of sectors—such as banking—has helped the country's balance of payment situation and its total foreign debt, which declined from 85 percent of GDP in 1982 to 40 percent in 1989. Portugal's net foreign assets are strongly positive; the country continues to repay its foreign obligations in advance.

The economic conjuncture has been equally rosy with regards to the unemployment picture, with the rate in the third quarter of 1989 falling to only 4.9 percent, with a growth rate of 5.5 percent. Partly due to the sharply increased flows of foreign assets into the economy, inflation has been hovering around 12 percent. Moreover, certain sectors are still problematic: chemicals, steel and to some extent shipbuilding (especially Setanave). While traditional industries have been holding their own, the most rapidly expanding areas have been in services such as banking, insurance, and real estate as well as metal works, electronic assembly, public works, beer and food. Lastly, the stock market, which was strongly negatively impacted by the October 1987 crash, has only partly recovered.

The current success of the Portuguese economy implies that the process of reconsolidating some form of capitalist hegemony will continue. As long as the PSD government remains in office and offers domestic and international capital the guarantee of political stability, that party will be able to exercise its ideological preferences in those areas in which discretion exists. The pace and scope of privatization is one such area. The favorable external conjuncture allows the government to fear the effects of privatization less, since with a low general unemployment, the social functions of the nationalized enterprises become less critical to maintaining political stability and legitimacy. The cohesion of the capitalist class is aided by the macroeconomic environment; the contradictions of representing both traditional and modern, light and heavy industries as well as small and large, domestic and foreign capital are more easily blunted.

Since 1974, some of the old antagonisms within the bourgeoisie which tore apart the dictatorship were liquidated if not forgotten, as the colonial option for capitalist development was foreclosed and only the European, free market, pro-foreign capital option remained to compete with the domestically oriented, protectionist one. The Right still faced the dilemmas of capitalist accumulation within a small, weak and vulnerable social formation as it had to reconcile the demands of the international lenders and foreign capital with those of domestic capital, while attempting to legitimate capitalism to the popular masses. With Portuguese integration into the European Economic Community, in 1986, the Right was threatened with further divisions since much of Portuguese industry was weak and likely to seek government protection from competition, rather than be entertained by lectures about antistatism. Similarly, with a particularly inefficient agriculture, the right also faced a crisis in reconciling its commitment to the EEC with its domestic electoral support from smallholders. The election of the Silva government in 1987 under particularly favorable economic conditions, followed by large infusions of European Community funding, managed to deaccentuate conflicts within the Right and give the appearance of revitalized Right hegemony. However, while the period of obvious "dishegemony" seems to be at an end, it is too soon to forecast the long-term stability, strength and endurance of the model of capitalism pursued by the Right. The importance of party/electoral outcomes for shaping the reconstruction of bourgeois hegemony points to the continuing importance of the state in structuring capitalism, which points to at least some degree of uncertainty. A reformed Communist party might stimulate greater Left/Right bipolarization and involve the popular masses more in shaping the emerging hegemonic model. With the state still a critical factor in determining that model, fortuitous outcomes in the party and political sphere remain for the Right a vital corrective to the "dishegemonic" residues of the revolution.

## CONCLUSION

We close by stressing that the revolutionary period caused a major reordering of the relations both within and between the main classes. The dominant class saw its historically leading element rapidly displaced through nationalization and decolonization. Its members faced the task of reconstituting bourgeoisie hegemony in the absence of its historically ascendent segment and with the unprecedented recent need to take into account the demands of the popular masses. Suddenly shakened from its dependence upon dictatorial repression, it was singularly unprepared for the task: the Portuguese democratic transition was therefore much less incremental and elitist than that observed in Spain and instead coupled a large measure of state autonomy with the initiatives of the popular masses. Since 1976, the dominant class continued to rely heavily upon state actions to reconstitute capitalism, under conditions where the "natural beneficence" of capitalism often could not be assumed by virtue of prevailing bourgeoisie hegemony.

The popular masses also faced mounting difficulties. As the anti-Fascist dimension of democratization became insufficient to carry through common actions, the particular interests of the peasants, agricultural and industrial workers, white collar employees surfaced repeatedly and merged with regional and religious differences. This was found in the antagonisms between the major parties (PS and PCP), the question of representative democracy versus dictatorship of the proletariat, the protection of "pluralism" and civil liberties, the role of the nationalized industries, the scope and nature of the land reform, and the divisions within the labor movement.

While the collapse of the leading segment of the historically dominant class, the monopolistic domestic bourgeoisie, led to a unique opportunity to engage in actions which could have shifted state power more decisively in favor of the popular masses, after many months of popular contestation, the incremental reconstruction of a "mixed economy" type of capitalism resulted instead. The failure or inability of either the capitalist class or the popular masses to assume a convincing leading position in this process left a key role for the gradual reconsolidation of capitalism to international capital in concert with the elected politicians.

We have shown that Poulantzas overestimated the extent of control exerted by the domestic bourgeoisie both during and after the revolutionary period and underestimated the possibility for a transition to some version of socialism. He did, however, point to several difficulties encountered in attempting to reconcile divisions within the popular masses and their representative organizations even if he rejected the prospect that any alternative to capitalism was on the agenda.

## Notes

1. These policies were enacted in the 1930S. The Wheat Campaign guaranteed wheat prices, provided subsidies for fertilizers and machinery, and limited the importation of wheat. The Colonial Act restricted colonial development to that required to meet the needs of metropolitan Portugal. The condicionamento industrial limited internal competition by requiring government approval before a firm could be formed, new technology introduced, or production increased. The condicionamento industrial aided the survival of small and medium industrial firms.

2. Over the course of the dictatorship, the banks controlled by each family changed due to the acquisitions and mergers. The link between the family and the bank noted here corresponds to the situation in the early 1970S.

3. Each year, the banks were required by law to submit an annual report, which included a list of the firms and the dollar value of the stock that each bank owned. The bank did not have to report all of its stock ownership. The bank listed its major stock holdings in these reports. The percentage of the stock held in industry, agriculture, colonial firms, and other activities between 1926 and 1974 has been calculated from this listing for each bank. For further documentation, see Elizabeth Sammis, "Limits of State Adaptability: The Formation, Consolidation, and Breakdown of the Portuguese Estado Novo (1926–1974)," PhD dissertation, University of California, Los Angeles, 1988.

4. In its yearly report, the textile firm Quintas e Quintas noted its dependence on colonial sisal. Companhia Nacional de Fiação e Tecidos de Torres Novas decried its inability to obtain raw materials at acceptable prices as colonial cotton began to match world market prices. Fábricas Lufap blamed its commercial difficulties on colonial export restrictions.

5. For a thorough compilation of the democratic opposition writings prior to and after the coup, see Ronald H. Chilcote, *The Portuguese Revolution of 25 April 1974* (Coimbra: Centro de Documentação 25 de Abril, 1987).

6. To a limited extent we agree with Phillippe Schmitter (1975) and Kenneth Maxwell (1986) that conflict between institutional elites led to the overthrow of the dictatorship. We would emphasize that the dictatorship's efforts to achieve the political unity of the dominant class undermined the government's relationship to the military.

7. We examine the "later Poulantzas" below. Poulantzas made himself clearer in the last major work prior to his death, *State, Power, Socialism.*

8. Przeworski and Wallerstein (1985, 72) have dubbed this accommodation between liberal democracy and capitalism a "compromise" in which "those who do not own instruments of production consent to the institution of private ownership of capitalist stock while those who own productive instruments consent to political institutions that permit other groups to effectively press their claims to the allocation of resources and distribution of output." They argue that Keynesianism provided the "foundation r class compromise by supplying those political parties representing workers with a justification for holding office within capitalist societies." Thus reformism would cost capitalists only that which could be sustained within the framework of private accumulation, with the assumption that the fatal contradictions of the capitalist mode of production can ultimately be controlled (or postponed) by macroeconomic demand management. Przeworski and Wallerstein assess the strengths and limits of this reformist compromise, although they make no attempt to directly link it to the experiences of Portugal.

9. The PPD has run in national elections as the PSD since 1979; PPD or PSD are used here interchangeably.

10. The only party that saw a doubling of its votes was the right wing CDS, not a surprising result since it was prevented from actively campaigning in 1975 and

derived a disproportionate part of its vote from the smallholder and semiproletarianized north and center of the country. The regional characteristics of the vote are analyzed in Nataf (1987). As a simple illustration of the strength of the CDS in the center and north, the party gained 80.9 percent over its previous 1975 total in 11 such districts (Vila Real, Bragança, Viana do Castelo, Porto, Braga, Aveiro, Coimbra, Viseu, Guarda, Castelo Branco, and Leiria), which corresponded to 67 percent of its total vote.

11. This technique has its limitations. Because both the electoral and socioeconomic census data are organized on the basis of common administrative and statistical geographic units, attributing electoral behavior to various subgroups can make the unwitting analyst a prey of the "ecological fallacy"; that is, the improper making of inferences across levels. However, ecological regression can be effectively used to make such inferences, even when certain cell entries feature results beyond the logical 0 to 100 percent range as with the smallholder vote for the PCP (see Kousser 1973). We have chosen to use ecological data in part due to the relative lack of reliable survey data that cover the same periods of time and provide similar types of information. The 274 concelhos of continental Portugal used in data for 1970 was not available at the frequesia level. 1970 Census were the unit of analysis for the ecological analysis. Unfortunately, it was not possible to acquire the frequesia level, which would have afforded a much higher N. The election data was taken from official government publications produced for each election and published by the Instituto Nacional de Estatística.

12. There was little change in the pattern of smallholder support for the right in subsequent elections: it remained quite high. See (Nataf, 1989).

13. The equivalence between the aggregate percentages of tertiary workers and Poulantzas' "new petty bourgeoisie" (the term he used to refer to urban service sector workers) was certainly not one-to-one. Given the nature of aggregation, the "service sector" necessarily includes a large number of heterogeneous occupations, some of which are managerial/professional, whereas others are low status positions (domestics, janitorial, clerks, sales, etc.). As argued elsewhere (Nataf 1987, chapter 3), the very heterogeneity of this statistical category probably explains its electoral radicalism (in support of the PCP) as well as its vacillation (elections in 1979 and 1987 showed a marked shift to the right, usually away from the PS rather than the PCP, whereas the PS vote blossomed again in 1983; in 1985 this sector moved in favor of the Democratic Renewal party as reported in Nataf, 1989). In short, the service sector has been a support for a variety of political positions. This suggests that unlike Poulantzas' characterization of the service sector as the "new petty bourgeoisie," at least in Portugal this sector is politically heterogeneous, showing only a few signs of "classlike" behavior.

14. This sector was vital to the PSD's victory in July 1987 when that party nearly doubled its 1985 electoral percentage, jumping from 29.8 to 50.1 percent. See (Nataf, 1989) for estimates of the lower service sector vote from 1980 to 1987 using 1980 census data.

15. As analyzed later, the success of the 'Por Lisboa' coalition composed of the PS and PCP in the December 17, 1989, municipal elections in Lisbon showed that the mere fear of Communist involvement in governance was not enough to dele-

gitimate a left coalition with an effective program and campaign as a credible alternative to the right. Naturally, these election were not for national offices, making inferences about the transference of these results to a country-wide level quite speculative.

16. Many of the Socialist "gains of the revolution" were enshrined into the 1976 constitution. The Constitution obligates the state to eliminate and impede the formation of monopolies, makes the nationalizations irreversible, calls for agrarian reform, and calls upon the state to stimulate working class economic and political participation. The original document (revised in 1982) could be regarded as a kind of model for a dual-track "democratic socialism" with its extensive provisions guaranteeing the social and economic rights of the workers coupled with its respect for procedural safeguards meant to secure the rights of individual citizens.

17. Later, under the PS-PSD coalition government, the banking was further opened to the private sector in 1984. The Cavaco e Silva PSD governments started the process of privatization of nationalized banks and generally sought to shrink the public sector during its years in power.

18. José Martins Barrata (1982) has argued that starting with the initial Socialist government and continuing since, governments engaged in economic policies that relied largely on fiscal and monetary adjustments to deal with inflation, unemployment, and the balance of payments problems. He suggested that whereas these mechanisms proved unable to correct the deficiencies in these ares, governments clung to them because the alternative—the use of government planning and more direct controls over investment—would have jeopardized the entire system of private accumulation that the governments sought to preserve. Thus the choice of government instruments for intervention could be seen in terms of the kind of class interests that the governments represented. Nevertheless, it should be kept in mind that Barrata relies essentially on an unprovable counterfactual: that the use of planning and more direct controls would have provided better strictly economic results than those obtained with the instruments used.

19. Law No. 236/76 attempted to deal with the conversion from latifundia to cooperatives.

20. PS leader Mário Soares characterized the Socialist position regarding the land reform by saying, "we don't agree with the collective farms, directed by the rural unions and "telecomandados" [commanded from above] by the PCP . . . [although] the return of the old landowners has been always out of question . . ." Soares said that nationalizations "won't be put to question." (1979, 19) This reflects the PS position in favor of policies that helped neither the old dominant class monopolists nor the PCP.

21. Eugenio Rosa (1978) has made much of the vagaries in the law that allow 'non-residents' rather than 'foreigners' to make investments in Portugal, claiming that this would allow members of the former monopoly segment to reemerge as important actors. Moreover, he suggested that they could even use the indemnities received as payment for the nationalization to do this. While this may be a valid concern, as long as the state maintains the great bulk of the old monopolies' holdings, it was unlikely that the true reconstruction of the groups will occur. This is

not to suggest, however, that the stipulation of 'non-resident' rather than 'foreigner' was incidental, since it was a change introduced from the former, more restrictive code. In this sense, it is a concession to the right made by the minority Socialist government. The Silva PSD government was less concerned about the resurrection of a private monopoly segment to the extent that it was eager to engage in the privatization of major banks, insurance and manufacturing firms especially after the state was no longer obligated to withhold a majority share. However, the low indemnities paid to former owners meant that the reconstruction of the capitalist class would take place with new capitalists as much or more than old monopolists. In this sense, the PSD did not represent the traditional Portuguese bourgeoisie, but rather sought to enhance both 'entrepreneurial' domestic capital as well as foreign capital. In addition, as the reprivatization thus far has been limited with regards to the percentage of shares available to foreigners, there has been speculation in the press that Portuguese citizens have acted as middlemen for foreign capital—resurrecting an element of the 'comprador' role for the Portuguese bourgeoisie which Poulantzas insisted was typical of the pre-revolutionary situation.

22. According to the OECD (1984a), capital flowed into the country in the following quantities: 1976, $26 mn; 1977, $95 mn; 1978, $758; 1979, $813; 1980, $1,853 mn. A large loan ($750 mn) accompanied the IMF's much smaller loans in 1978. The contribution of other transfers, especially emigrant remittances, can be seen in these figures: 1976, $964 mn; 1977, $964 mn; 1978, $1,635 mn; 1979, $2,476 mn; 1980, $3,000 mn.

23. The PS-PSD government tried to deal with the austerity period by proposing a neo-corporatist format of interest representation as a means of institutionalizing conflict between labor and capital. The receptivity of labor to this format was variable, with the reformist UGT (General Workers' Union) accepting it in principle and the PCP-oriented CGTP (General Confederation of Portuguese Workers) rejecting it. However, the failure of the CGTP in its enterprise strategy—based upon a politicization of strikes and labor actions combined with the growth in UGT strength caused it to relect accept participation in the Permanent Council for Social Concertation (the tripartite chamber). However, demonstrating the weak hegemony of capital, the agreement over wages and prices in the Council on January 18, 1988 *excluded* the CGTP *and* the CIP (the employer's Confederation of Portuguese Industry). The debate over the revision of the labor code combined with other continuing struggles to result in the first general strike involving both the UGT and CGTP on March 28, 1988. As Stoleroff point outs, even the CIP decried the labor code revision proposal offered by the PSD government—the target of emnity by both labor confederations—to be a major concession to the unions and significantly worse than the proposals offered by the PS-PSD governments (see Stoleroff, 1989).

24. The sale of nationalized banks does not in itself mean that the old monopolies will be resurrected. The bank holdings were removed from bank control and placed under the guidance of the state Participations Institute (Instituto das Participações do Estado, E.P.) which became Investimentos e Participações do Estado, S.A.R.L. or IPE in 1982. Although the later is expected to be 'an active instrument of the government's economic policies geared towards cooperation with the private sector' (IPE, 1986) this does not necessarily mean that it will facilitate the recomposition

of private groups. Again, this seems like an area of political discretion in which the composition of governments will strongly affect the 'objective function' of this institute. Moreover, the banks insurance companies and other firms being privatized are being sold as individual firms, not as groups. However, this would not prevent the eventual grouping of capital through the purchase of each firm's shares by a new holding company.

25. It is interesting to note that Cunhal has argued that the PCP's line in Portugal was distinctive from the Eastern European model of socialism precisely insofar as it involved a critical assessment of negative aspects of that model. As he put it, "our critical examination [of that model] . . . was taken into account in our own Program, our democratic and socialist objectives for Portugal and in our party life . . .. We were, however, overconfident in the possibilities for positive evolution and correction in those countries. Events suggest that it will be necessary to better inform the party [in the future]" (*O Jornal,* 1-5-90). Thus, Cunhal's error was not one of excessive admiration for Eastern European regimes, but one of insufficiently publicizing criticisms which he and the PCP had held all along.

26. At this writing, no short list of candidates to replace Cunhal has been determined. The press has reported a series of names including prominent trade unionists as well as long-standing deputies to the parliament. One source said that "it was quite possible that some elements from critical sectors will be integrated into an eventual renovated leadership" although within Cunhal's distinctions between the "good" and the "bad" critics. See (*O Jornal,* 1-5-90).

## References

Anonymous 1980. Commentary. *Empresa Privada,* 1 (January): 4.

Bracia, Paulo, and António Branco. 1979. Evolução do comércio entre Portugal e os novos estados africanos (I). *Economia e Socialismo.* 34 (January): 48–58.

Blackburn, Robin. 1974. Lisbon—The fall of fascism. *New Left Review.* 87/88 (September–December): 5–48.

Bruneau, Thomas C., and Alex Macleod. 1986. *Politics in Contemporary Portugal.* Boulder, CO: Lynne Reinner.

Chilcote, Ronald H. 1987. *The Portuguese Revolution of 25 April 1974: Annotated Bibliography on the Antecedents and Aftermath.* Coimbra: Centro de Documentaçao 25 de Abril.

da Costa, Ramiro. 1979. *Elementos para a história do movimento operário em Portugal.* Lisbon: Assírio e Alvim.

Fernandes, Carlos, and Roma Pedro Alvares. 1972. *Portugal e o Mercado Común.* Lisbon: Moràes Editores.

Harsgor, Michael. 1976. *Portugal in Revolution.* Beverly Hills: Sage.

Instituto Nacional de Estatística. 1975. *Principais Sociedades.* Lisbon: INE.

———. 1976. *Eleições para a Assembleia da República.* Lisbon: INE.

IPE. 1986. *IPE—The Holding and the Group.* Lisbon: IPE.

Kousser, Martin J. 1973. Ecological Regression and the Analysis of Past Politics. *Journal of Interdisciplinary History*, 4: 232–62.

Martins, Maria Belmeira. 1975. *As multinacionais em Portugal*. Lisbon: Estampa.

Martins, Rogério. 1970. *Caminho de país novo*. Lisbon: Gris Impressores, SARL. 1973. *Tempo imperfeito*. Viseu: Author's edition.

Matos, Luís Salgado de. 1973. *Investimentos estrangeiros em Portugal*. Lisbon: Seara Nova.

Maxwell, Kenneth. 1986. Regime overthrow and the prospects for democratic transition, in Guillermo O'Donnell, Phillippe Schmitter, and Laurence Whitehead (eds.): *Transitions from Authoritarian Rule: Southern Europe*. Baltimore: Johns Hopkins University Press.

Moura, Francisco Pereira de. 1974. *Por onde vai a economia portuguesa?* Lisbon: Seara Nova.

Nataf, Daniel D. 1987. Social Cleavages and Regime Formation in Contemporary Portugal, Ph.D. Dissertation, University of California, Los Angeles.

———. 1989. "Social Ecology of Recent Legislative Elections: Continuity and Change." Paper presented to the IV International Meeting on Modern Portugal, University of New Hampshire, Sept. 1989.

OECD. 1984a. *Balances of Payments of OECD Countries, 1963–1982*. Paris: OECD.

———. 1984b. *OECD Economic Survey of Portugal—1983–84*. Paris: OECD.

Partido Socialista. 1975. *Política económica de transição*. Lisbon: PS.

Pato, Octávio. 1976. *Pela democracia, pelo socialismo*. Lisbon: Ediçótes Avante!.

Poulantzas, Nicos. 1968/1978. *Political Power and Social Classes*. London: Verso.

———. 1976. *The Crisis of the Dictatorships*: Portugal, Greece, Spain. London: New Left Books.

———. 1978. *State, Power, Socialism*. London: New Left Book.

Przeworsk, Adam, and Michael Wallerstein. 1985. Democratic capitalism at the crossroads, in Norman Vig and Steven E. Schier (eds.): *Political Economy in Western Democracies*. New York: Holmes and Meier.

Rodrigues, Avelino, Cesário Borga, and Mário Cardoso. 1979. *Abril nos quarteis do Novembro*. Lisbon: Livraria Bertrand.

Rolo, José Manuel. 1977. *Capitalismo, technologia e dependência em Portugal*. Lisbon: Presença.

Rosa, Eugénio. 1975. *A economia Portuguesa em números*. Lisbon: Moraes.

———. 1978. *O fracasso da política de direita*. Lisbon: Seara Nova.

———. 1982. *O fracasso dos governos de direita em Portugal*. Lisbon: Edições um de Outubro.

Sammis, Elizabeth. 1988. Limits of State Adaptability: The Formation Consolidation, and Breakdown of the Portuguese Dictatorship (1926–1974), Ph.D. Disserration, University of California, Los Angeles.

Schmitter, Phillippe. 1975. Liberation by *Golpe*: Retrospective thoughts on the demise of authoritarian rule in Portugal. *Armed Forces and Society* (November) 2:5–33.

Soares, Mário. 1979. *Confiar no PS, apostar em Portugal*. Lisbon: PS.

Stoleroff, Alan. 1989. Labor Law Reform and Wage Regulation, Class Struggle and the State: Labor and the Cavaco e Silva Governments. Paper presented to the IV International Meeting on Modern Portugal, University of New Hampshire, Sept. 1989.

# Chapter 4

# Democratization and the Greek State

*Stylianos Hadjiyannis*

---

In recent times Greek political developments have offered many surprises. A military coup d'etat in 1967 by relatively obscure army colonels abolished parliamentarism. The junta rebuffed a counter coup led by King Constantine late in that year and forced him into exile in England. In 1973 a coup within the junta replaced the original coup leaders. In 1974 the new military regime collapsed. The conservative civilian government that took over restored democratic norms. In a national referendum late in 1974, voters overwhelmingly opted for a constitutional republic, thereby electorally voiding the almost 150-year tradition of monarchical rule. In 1981 Andreas Papandreou's Pan-Hellenic Socialist Movement (PASOK), a self-proclaimed Marxist- Socialist party proposing to lead Greece on a democratic road to socialism, came to power. Its election interrupted a long succession of rule by conservative governments and military regimes, and its tenure in the 1980s raised important theoretico-praxis questions regarding the realization of its proposal.

These seemingly disjointed and abrupt political turnabouts capped a turbulent and muddled national historical experience that included: a 400-year subjugation under the Ottoman Empire; a bloody eight-year revolutionary war for independence against the Ottomans starting in 1821; the formation in 1833 of the modern Greek state under foreign-born King Otho of Bavaria, who was chosen for and imposed upon Greece by the then Great Powers (Great Britain, France, tzarist Russia); a more than a century-long almost fanatical drive for irredentism, resulting in many regional wars and disputes whose repercussions were still evident in the 1980s (e.g., between Greece and Turkey over the island of Cyprus and the Aegean Sea); a bitter Nazi occupation during World War II (1941–45); a devastating civil war (1946–

49); and a foreign-instigated economic "miracle" growth in the 1960s that a decade later became a chronic economic "malaise."

This history has shaped a distinct Greek culture, an economy, and a political system of power relations. Poulantzas' work in general and of Greece in particular offered a debatable but challenging view of the rise and fall of the 1967 junta in the context of the Greek social formation and its position in the international division of labor. My study revisits that decisive national experience in order to evaluate aspects of Poulantzas's exegesis. It also updates post-1974 Greek politico-economic events to test Papandreou's and Poulantzas' assumptions and strategies to achieve a democratic transition to socialism.

## THE RISE AND FALL OF THE 1967 DICTATORSHIP

The July 24, 1974, downfall of the seven-year-old junta was attributed to self-inflicted wounds triggered by the junta's ill-planned and ill-fated coup d'etat against Greek-Cypriot President Archibishop Makarios in order to force the island of Cyprus to become part of Greece (Stern 1975, 1977). The sequence of events unleashed by this plot proved critical for the Athens regime. As Turkish forces invaded Cyprus, Greece mobilized for war. Unprepared to deal with the military crisis, the junta ceded power to a hastily assembled civilian government.

For Poulantzas, the junta's fall was not so much the result of the military crisis, but the outcome of a longer internal process that had fractionalized the unity of the regime and alienated it from its supporters. This process stemmed from the massive infusion of foreign capital into Greece in the form of state aid by the United States and Western Europe in the 1950s, and multinational direct capital investments in the 1960s. This capital helped create a "dependent industrialization," an industrial progress albeit "under the aegis of foreign capital and at its instigation" (Poulantzas 1976, 14). Poulantzas assumed an ongoing expansion of the capitalist mode of production (CMP) over the social formation. He expected that the CMP would reproduce itself "on a massive scale" and hasten the "dissolution of precapitalist relationships" (Poulantzas 1976, 14). This apriorism made him overestimate the nature and size of the CMP in Greece and its affects on the totality of the nation's social formation. It was an assumption that the reality of the 1970s and the 1980s proved wrong. It also biased Poulantzas' theoretical treatment of that period's events.

Poulantzas built upon previous writings on the movement of monopoly capital from advanced to peripheral nations to explain Greece's position in the international division of labor. Lenin (1979) wrote earlier in this century of a trend toward capital and production centralization and the formation of finance capital in the imperialist nations. Through the extraction of surplus from the periphery toward the imperialist center, the latter found it more lucrative to export capital rather than products to the former given the absence of large markets there. Poulantzas correctly observed that since the 1950s finance capital aimed also to exploit labor on a world scale by installing, as was the case of Greece, capitalist relations of production inside peripheral social formations (1976, 11–13). The center no longer wanted to dominate peripheral nations from the "outside" by merely reproducing relations of dependence. Rather, it needed to establish its dominance "directly within" the periphery (Poulantzas, 1976, 46) in order to "raise the rate of exploitation so as to counteract the tendency for the rate of profit to fall" (1976, 62)—e.g., the introduction of new technology increases the value of surplus accrued beyond necessary labor by making workers produce more in less time. Concurrently, the host state acts to create the right conditions for this new "trend" through the use of monetary, investment, and fiscal policies (Chilcote 1984; Palloix 1978).

For Poulantzas it was important also to understand the ways by which the material framework of a host state internalized the internationalization of capital (1976, 20–23). More than the creation of the "right conditions," the host state is itself forced to undertake changes (e.g., the imposition of the 1967 dictatorship) to adapt to the internationalization of capital process. The nature of the change depended on how the massive introduction of the CMP altered Greece's social formation. For Poulantzas the state is neither a "thing" immune to changes nor a "subject" directing changes. Rather, it is "a relationship of forces, or more precisely the material condensation of such a relationship among classes and class fractions, such as this is expressed within the state in a necessarily specific form" (Poulantzas 1978a, 128–29). A state's form (e.g., a dictatorship, a parliamentary democracy, or a monarchy) mirrors each time the specific setup of a social formation's class articulation. The state is a changing entity, subject to the periodization of capital as, for instance, the transition from merchant to industrial capital affects the relative power of the capitalist class fractions defined by each capital. Ascendant class fractions translate their newly found economic power into political power, challenge existing power bloc alliances, and eventually alter the nature of the state.

Poulantzas narrowed his focus on what he considered the most important consequence of the internationalization of capital: the capitalist class and the kind of capitalist state created to reflect this class. Subsequently, he placed the rise and fall of the 1967 junta regime in the context of his famous power bloc dichotomy: the comprador fraction and the vaguely identified, and only "tendentially differentiated" from the comprador, domestic bourgeois fraction. Both fractions were dependent and subordinate to foreign capital, exemplified by their place in the kind of industrialization process pursued. The comprador acted as middlemen for the implantation and reproduction of foreign capital in Greece, and concentrated in finance, banking, shipping, and petroleum refineries. The industrialization process enabled the domestic fraction to accumulate capital by converting money received from selling commodities into capital. By the 1960s this fraction became quite visible in light industry, construction, and in many other sectors related to the comprador fraction and foreign capital. Both fractions' external ties limited their politico-ideological role, a situation unlike that of the genuine national bourgeoisie found in imperialist nations that were independent of foreign demands in developing national resources and industrializing (Poulantzas 1976, 42–54). To control the industrialization process underway, the more dominant comprador fraction, reflecting the needs and goals of its imperialist superiors, instated the junta. The junta banned all political parties, outlawed trade unions and worker strikes, and rescinded most civil rights. The junta offered a safer climate for capital accumulation, evidenced by increased foreign capital investments after 1967 (Poulantzas 1976, 17).

Poulantzas validly linked the internationalization of capital with internalization, the periodization of capital with the rise of new classes, and changing class articulations with the form of the state. Yet he misjudged many essential aspects directly related to his premises. More precisely, the bourgeois dichotomy, the impact of the crisis of capitalist accumulation abroad and in Greece on the political legitimacy of the various regimes in question, the nature of the Greek CMP and its relation to class formation and articulation, and the logic of authority rather than only the form of the Greek state—aspects that also, as we shall see, conditioned post-1974 developments.

The analytical importance of the bourgeois dichotomy in accounting for the rise and fall of the junta is dubious and unsubstantiated by concrete empirical data. It is true that the unity, aspirations, and political power of the capitalist class were stressful even during the booming economic period of the 1960s. But the source of trouble was between itself as a whole and the dominated classes. The popular agitation in the early 1960s threatened the valorization of Greek and foreign capital. But more important, it threatened the legitimacy of the established regime. Worker demands fortified the electoral fortunes of the bourgeois-liberal Center Union (EK) party, a clientelistic party under the leadership of Georgios Papandreou (Andreas' father). The narrow constraints of the postcivil war, anti-Communist hysteria led elements of the dominant class to interpret their diminishing popular support and Papandreou's liberal reformation attempts as a direct challenge against their very political authority. They tried to thwart the EK party from wrestling state power from the ruling, also clientelistic, bourgeois-conservative National Radical Union (ERE) party. Various means to do so were devised, including: utilizing slanted electoral plans favoring the dominant party, engaging in polling frauds such as double voting and registering already dead people, and intimidating voters. These efforts failed. The EK party came to power in 1963 and again in 1964. Many bourgeois politicians used a variety of parliamentary tricks to weaken the legitimacy of the EK government, including a constitutional crisis initiated by the palace in 1965 that caused the EK government to fall (Thermos 1974). Political turmoil marked the next two years. Short-lived governments decreed by the palace ruled against the wishes of the majority of Greeks. Early in 1967 it became clear that the EK was expected to win the upcoming emergency elections.

A few days before the elections, on April 21, 1967, a small group of unknown colonels usurped state power. The colonels did not have the support of the comprador bourgeoisie. As Stern (1977) argued convincingly, the coup by the junior officers surprised many people. It occurred only days before a coup by the palace and the top army echelon was to materialize. The rumored coup's leaders would have had the support of the oligarchy, the traditional power bloc of Greece's social formation that included the palace, top army generals, the maritime aristocracy, and the heads of Greece's two top banks, the National and the Commercial, which among them controlled most of the nation's economy (Petras 1987, 4–5). The actual coup was grudgingly accepted—attested to by the showdown with the king later in 1967 and his exile to England—and given a try.

The eventual acceptance of the junta showed that although intrabourgeois fighting might threaten the power of fractions in the capitalist class as Poulantzas claimed, they do not threaten the authority of this class as a whole over the subordinate classes. To expect a complete agreement on policies to be pursued such as the imposition or the downfall of the junta among the components of one fraction against the wishes of the components of a rival fraction assumes a lot regarding the logic and purpose of the dominant class in Greece. Although there is a rounded singularity to such an expectation, the reality is often more confused and complicated.

The lesson derived from the rise of the dictatorship is that when any nation's capitalist class is faced with perceived or real interclass challenges to its authority, family feuds become secondary or are quickly resolved through internal compromises to face the threat. The choice of strategy followed in each case to respond to the threat is not clear-cut nor widely accepted. The choice is determined by a variety of factors such as the degree of sophistication available to legitimize actions; the nature of domestic and external realities and contradictions; and the evolving nature of the components of the capitalist class. In 1967, faced with a choice of a possible threat to property or repression, the Greek capitalists welcomed repression. This model aped similar ones considered successful then in Latin America and elsewhere in the world. The junta "solution" legitimized the abolition of parliamentary politics by proclaiming to save Greece from a usurpation of power by communism, a claim that also secured U.S. geopolitic interests in the area (Petras 1977, 12).

The rigidity and subsequent blunders of the junta, the wide popular dissatisfaction against it, and the fear among the power bloc that a revolt against the junta could turn into a revolt against the power bloc, all combined in 1974 to dismantle the junta. This multilateral coincidence of "interests" helps offer a different explanation than Poulantzas' intrabourgeois hegemony and Stern's military crisis regarding the junta's fall.

By the early 1970s, according to Poulantzas, a rearrangement in the balance of forces between the United States and the European Economic Community (EEC) affected Greece's power bloc. Although North American hegemony was never challenged, the "rearrangement" polarized Greek capital along its divergent lines of dependence toward either American or European capital. It is not clear what the "rearrangement in the balance of forces" between the two international superiors accomplished at the international level. Nor did Poulantzas make clear how it occurred. He also assumed a lot regarding the unity of the EEC members as a counterforce to North American designs. Expanding this framework to explain events in Portugal and Spain, as the previous chapters show, made his analysis even more debatable. What occurred was a worldwide recession after the 1973 oil crisis that severely tested the health of the existing global capitalist system. But after the initial shock, the recession coordinated rather than rearranged intraimperialist relations to overcome the crisis. For Greece, however, the recession meant the beginning of the end of the economic "miracle."

The declining demand for its products, overseas labor force, and mercantilist activities made Greece's export-oriented, foreign technology- and capital-dependent economy suffer inordinately throughout the 1970s (Petras 1982, 9). This economy could not recover from this shock even in the 1980s. It exhibited a malaise that defied orthodox cures. Poulantzas ignored the political issue at stake attendant to the economic downturn. In doing so, his analysis remained static, unable to offer any guidance to subsequent events. Instead, the crisis threatened again the legitimacy of Greek capitalism and the growth of the capitalist class in general. The economic crisis could become a legitimacy crisis. The junta was caught in the middle and became the scapegoat. Getting rid of the junta rather than of the capitalist path was by far the most consensual and less painful solution. A change of regime toward one in line with bourgeois democratic norms of the Western European type could at once satisfy public outcries for liberalization and divert public attention from politico-economic legitimacy questions. The trouble was how to overthrow the junta.

Poulantzas focused instead on his problematic structuralist argument that the "rearrangement" polarized the Greek power bloc. Making his thesis even more complicated, the polarization did not occur along monopoly and non-monopoly lines. Instead, he merely asserted, the situation resembled a paralyzing intrapower bloc struggle for hegemony as whole sections of monopoly capital pursued a strategy of integration into the EEC, whereas other sections remained strongly pro-American. Nonmonopoly capital was equally divided and stalemated. As fractions of the power bloc vied for overall dominance within the bloc, their hegemony fights affected the junta. Having severed all "transmission belts" of political representation and expression, the junta was at the same time caught in the middle of a power bloc reshuffle and was unable to accommodate power bloc differences. The junta's inability to organize the contradictions of the power bloc translated into a crisis of the structure and material framework of the junta apparatus. The junta's suppression of free political discourse alienated the ascendant domestic fraction by denying it the opportunity to translate its economic power into political power. The 1974 Cyprus crisis offered the pro-European domestic fraction a significant breakthrough in the fight against the pro-American side. It dismantled the junta and forged a bourgeois democratic pluralist regime, presumably more open to shifts in the power bloc (Poulantzas 1976, 90–126).

Does a focus on power bloc developments alone explain fully the function of the state? In later, modified Poulantzian views of the state, the state functions to protect the interests of the power bloc as a whole and to accommodate shifts in the relative power of fractions within it in order to maintain the bloc's unity. Power bloc disunity necessitates the organizational role of the state (Poulantzas 1978a, 133). Does this lead us to assume that the non-organizational junta regime was a rogue one? If it ran amok by not reflecting the nature of the power bloc, then the crisis was not structural but functional. It is then more important to explain not what the junta did or did not do but why it did so. In short, its logic of authority despite its "purpose." As Poulantzas later conceded, if a state's form is the reflection of the hegemonic fraction in the power bloc, this reflection also encompasses the politico-ideological role of the state vis-a-vis the dominated classes (Poulantzas 1978b). Contradictions between the dominant and dominated classes directly affect the contradictions among the fractions found in the power bloc. For example, political and economic demands by the dominated classes against exploitation through worker strikes, sitins, slowdowns, calls for higher wages, and social agitation directly contribute to the tendency of the rate of profit to fall and reduce capital valorization for the dominant class. Ways to handle demands by the dominated classes while maintaining political domination cause conflict within the power bloc. How to handle demands and resolve the conflict explains why it is not self-evident that the bourgeoisie prefer a "just" or "welfare" state rather than a dictatorship (Poulantzas 1978a, 12–27). Thus what Poulantzas termed "the strategic terrain" of the state includes all intra- and interclass struggles in society at all levels—economic, political, or ideological-cultural. The correction in his later works to include the societywide affects of the internalization of the CMP and the logic of state authority is hereby noted. The junta regime collapsed not only because of intrapower bloc disunity but also as a response to interclass struggle. His corrections also have problems. In a counternegating cause-effect reasoning, he told us the state functions to organize the power bloc, that it cannot do so adequately, that no one knows how to respond to social conflicts, and so on. And then he half-admitted that interclass struggle was at the root of events.

Poulantzas acknowledged class struggle in his case study but drew limited conclusions about it. Whereas there was intrapower bloc dissatisfaction with the junta, the latter was also the target of a struggle waged by the dominated classes that intensified its predicament. Although military regimes were not new to Greece, the 1967 junta relied heavily on violence and brutal force to suppress dissent. The resort to violence hindered the ability of the regime to control the popular movement and thus to control and "direct its own transformation" (Poulantzas 1976, 95). Any "controlled liberalization on the part of the state" to appease elements of the bourgeoisie became "a gaping hole through which the popular movement rushed in." The attempt, for example, to grant the university certain "freedoms" to secure the "neutrality of the intelligentsia and the youth" degenerated into the 1973 Polytechnic of Athens uprising (Poulantzas 1976, 94–95). Yet its suppression did not lead to liberalization but to a coup within a coup. A more repressive regime led behind the scenes by the head of the military police replaced the original colonels. Increased repression did not only affect the domestic fraction as Poulantzas claimed, but dominated and dominant classes alike. For different reasons the latter feared a popular revolt against the junta, and the former felt a revolt was inevitable. With the leaders of the dominated classes exiled or in jail, the popular struggle found expression mostly through the leadership of the bourgeoisie who set both the agenda and direction of change.

The military crisis thesis cannot by itself acount for the collapse of the junta. The military men already in power should have been more qualified than civilians to face the threat posed by Turkey. The real threat was not only war against Turkey but a potentially more explosive political crisis. The general war draft swelled the army with men over whom there was no careful control. Arming the population against an external enemy could also arm it to challenge the junta, which for many was the real enemy. The possibility for an armed revolt against the junta loomed more menacingly than the external threat. Some officers of the nation's largest force, the northern army unit, were rumored to be issuing ultimatums for the abdication of the junta and to be marching toward Athens rather than toward the border with Turkey. These rumors were neither confirmed nor denied by those involved.

Yet the perception that a civil war could ensue if the junta refused to comply was a dire threat no member of the power bloc cared to even contemplate. To diffuse the political crisis, the junta had to fall. To diffuse the military crisis, some arrangement for peace with Turkey should be pursued. On July 24 an interim civilian government replaced the junta. A few days later in Geneva, it negotiated a settlement with Turkey, ceding a divided one-third Turkish-, two-third Greek-controlled Cyprus. A divided Cyprus remained a thorn in subsequent relations between Greece and Turkey, a source of trouble for regional North Atlantic Treaty Organization (NATO) unity, and a divisive issue of U.S. policies in the Eastern Mediterranean.

The events of 1974 showed that when faced with a threat to property or liberalization, the capitalists as a whole opted for liberalization. Yet what both the 1967 and 1974 events shared was the resolve and ability of the dominant class as a whole to maintain its rule. To ensure continuation of control, this class sought a political change under the pretext of democratization; the safest way to pacify popular spirits without disturbing existing power relations. As Poulantzas correctly pointed out, this (and Spain's) nonrevolutionary transition from a military to a democratic regime precluded the "telescoping of stages," or the revolutionary skipping of the democratic stage toward a transition to socialism—even Portugal's more revolutionary transition was ultimately compromised. Yet this "solution" set the context of politics up to Papandreou's 1981 victory.

## THE TRANSITION TO BOURGEOIS DEMOCRACY

Appearances notwithstanding, democracy as a concept and practice was vague and largely alien for most Greeks. From 1946 to 1967, Greeks voted in national elections nine times. Each time their choices were limited. The defeat of the Communist forces during the civil war virtually banished Communists from politics (Yannakakis, 1969; Tsoukalas, 1969; Mouzelis, 1978b). Skewed electoral plans, anti-Communist propaganda, and outright suppression by the police, especially in rural areas, ensured dominance by conservative governments (Tsiokos 1981; Svoron 1984). Greek democracy was disfunctional because dominant domestic (e.g., oligarchy, army) and foreign (especially North American) interests wished it so (Papandreou 1970; Petras 1977; Rousseas 1975; Stern 1977). In 1974 the same interests equated democracy with the desire to get rid of the junta, the scapegoat enemy, and worry about the details later. The issue of socialism was never discussed even among Communists who tried to recover from a split in 1968 into two factions: the Communist party of Greece Interior (KKes) whose members were found in Greece; and the Communist party of Greece (KKE) made up of members who were abroad mostly in socialist bloc nations as the result of the civil war and subsequent red-baiting (Poulantzas 1976, 161–62).

The change from an authoritarian to a democratic regime was more a top-down political rather than a structural change. The democratic appearance did not necessarily free the state from its legacy as a societal power displaying a logic of authority bent on forcefully imposing its rule over society. The 1974 transition was like an orderly shift of power from the military to civilians that "took months to complete while the structure of the military and police apparatuses, the mainstay of the junta, was, for almost a decade (and beyond), not substantially altered" (Tzortzis in *Ta Nea,* July 29, 1986: 6, parenthesis this author's).

The resolution of the 1974 crisis helps us conceptualize some aspects of the state and its function in society. Greece's junta regime acted against both dominant and dominated classes, the difference in treatment being one of degree. The 1974 "democratic" regime tried to hide its overall support for the dominant classes behind "progressive" legislation and "welfare" measures aimed at favoring all social classes. Still, it could not solve the contradictions inherent in its role since ultimately the state must side with the interests of the dominant class as a whole. Furthermore, contradictions intensify because the dominant interests are not always unified or clear-cut except when faced with a common threat. The result would be state policies full of "fissures and gaps" based on a "terrain of compromise" among the dominant class and its foreign allies that is "permanently open" (Poulantzas 1976, 159–60). The state also has to account for the struggle of the popular masses against it and the interests it represents by trying to accommodate or suppress them. In this respect the 1974 change was contingent upon the long-term neutralization of interclass struggle coupled with intrapower bloc unity and support. The rest of the 1970s proved that this double-fold aim was unattainable.

The significance of the 1974 "democratization" process becomes clearer when contrasted with the 1967 military solution. The acceptance of the junta was at best an opportunistic way to maintain political domination. The 1974 "solution" was a highly sophisticated maneuver whose main objective was to legitimize and perpetuate the Greek model of development (thus benefiting the bourgeoisie) under the pretext of democratization. This updated version of regime legitimation occurred through ideological control rather than repressive means. It was made possible by state control of the broadcast media and bourgeois control of most of the larger newspapers rather than the boot and the bayonet. Concurrently, certain concessions were granted to the dominated classes: reintroducing the trade union; legalizing the Communist party; abolishing censorship; and drafting in 1975 a new "just state" constitution coupled with "welfare state" undertones. The new constitution intended to make it easier to achieve social consensus and cohesion (Manesis 1986).

In foreign affairs, an important concession was withdrawal from NATO in 1974. Two reasons accounted for this move. First, most Greeks were convinced of the complicity of the United States in aiding the junta (Stavrou 1977). Even in the United States, despite

> Congressional attempts to suspend military assistance to Greece, and despite Congressional recommendations that the continuation of friendly relationships with the Greek dictatorship could permanently damage long-term U.S. interests in Greece should the military government be overthrown, the policy decision (by the Nixon administration) was to conduct business-as-usual (Craig 1976, 14).

Second, the majority of Greeks interpreted the junta's blunder over Cyprus as American-inspired. In the face of open agression by Turkey (another NATO member!), the lack of NATO or U.S. response to solve the crisis (and side with Greece!) unnerved many Greeks (Hitchens 1975; Stern 1977). The reaction generated anti-American outcries that amounted to "a lid blown off the gas-tank," and to "the radicalization of the public" (Elephantis 1981). No government could ignore the popular demand to free itself from foreign "fingers"—a popular name given to external influences. The symbolic withdrawal from NATO—Greece rejoined the alliance in 1979 on allegedly renegotiated terms—pacified spirits and supported the legitimacy of the new regime.

Democratization also introduced a false sense of increased prosperity and international prestige. Greece could play a greater role in regional economics by replacing Lebanon as a major banking stage for the Middle East following the latter's devastating civil war in 1975. It was also associated with the potential (and in 1981 actual) entrance into the EEC. In his defense of Greece's case for joining the EEC, New Democracy (ND) Economics Minister John Pesmazoglou (1976) argued that Greece's economy was more dynamic than that of some EEC nations. He believed that Greece was able to become an independent and competitive economy, one that EEC integration could bolster even more. This erroneous conclusion assumed, as in many respects Poulantzas also did, that Greek capitalism was a genuine artifact: its crisis the result of external conditions and economic mismanagement by the junta; and that a rational managerial policy could overcome the crisis.

Authority legitimation was clearly evident in the drive to distance the new regime from the legacy of the junta. The campaign slogan "Karamanlis or the tanks" in 1974 more than anything else gave Constantinos Karamanlis' conservative ND party 54 percent of the votes and 220 out of 300 seats in parliament—the disproportionate number of seats gained was the result of an ND electoral plan favoring the larger party. The slogan was a masterful false dilemma. Karamanlis, after all, had been invited from self-exile in France by the dying junta and a committee of civilian prejunta politicians to head the transitional government. Poulantzas argued that the Karamanlis "card" was only one choice among many considered, a choice that tentatively revealed the slight edge the domestic bourgeoisie had over their rivals and that implicitly proved the alleged hegemony crisis that he observed (1976, 34–40). There is no doubt many choices existed; to expect otherwise would have been irrational amid the confusion of the times. But more important, did the Karamanlis choice prove Poulantzas' conclusion right? Not really. Karamanlis' subsequent actions were not directed in fighting this or that power bloc fraction but, as implied by his slogan, in legitimizing the bourgeois democratic regime and thus the interests of the bourgeois class as a whole.

An experienced politician himself, Karamanlis began a slow but steady junta personnel replacement in state apparatuses, which in effect enabled him to appoint his people in all kinds of key positions. In the end, he made it seem that the new democratic state was his achievement (see, e.g., Woodhouse 1982). For the majority of Greeks even late in the 1980s, Karamanlis and the new democratic state were almost inseparable. His skillful political stewardship neutralized opposition by incorporating it into parliamentary democratic procedures (e.g., elections, parliamentary debates), and by turning interclass struggle into interpolitical party conflict. In this new arena, the ND party enjoyed overwhelming advantages. Apart from Karamanlis' notable personal charisma, these included: command of more resources than rival parties; eventual control of most state apparatuses; and the institution of nationwide organizational party structures to replace antiquated clientelist norms. The ND party, moreover, was pitted against a demoralized, unorganized, weak, and splintered Left represented by PASOK and a hastily assembled coalition of the two Communist parties with some smaller parties. The 1974 elections resurrected most of the prejunta political parties, including most leaders of the prejunta past. These elections indicated a longing to achieve some continuation with the past if only out of a hope for a new beginning. With the bourgeoisie finally feeling secure with Karamanlis, and his electoral strength unchallenged by the Left, it seemed as though the double-fold aims of the 1974 resolution could be achieved.

## THE ISSUE OF DEMOCRATIC SOCIALISM

Even small concessions are added gains for the dominated classes, a step forward, an expansion of political and economic horizons. They present the opportunity to provide input or even to enter into the strategic terrain of the state where the real battles are waged. In this way, the post-1974 democratization paved the way to new developments as the contradictions of any process of development wait for their turn to unfold themselves. As such, that period was also notably marked by the formation of Papandreou's PASOK in 1974 as the only newcomer in Greek politics. His party held the promise of new vistas, exemplified by PASOK's meteoric rise from relative obscurity (13.5 percent of the votes) in 1974 to become government in 1981 (48.7 percent). Many analysts have described PASOK's political nature (e.g., populist, nationalist, social democratic, Third World socialist, etc.), but there is little understanding of PASOK's evolving nature and its contribution in Greek politics. PASOK legitimized socialism by making for some time the possibility of an electoral and legislative transition to socialism for Greece popularly acceptable; after 1984 it played a major role in discrediting this idea. It is true that in its early pronouncements PASOK gave many indications of being a militant populist party (Mouzelis 1978b; Poulantzas 1976; Elephantis 1981). Yet PASOK did risk political capital by campaigning openly in 1981 for a socialist transition even though it was not theoretically clear what was meant by such a transition and how to achieve it (Diamandouros, Kitromilidis, and Maurogordatos 1984). The result of the 1981 election was not only a triumph for Papandreou and his party in particular, but for the Left and socialism in general. An unprecedented 61 percent voted for the Left and the Right's fortunes declined to an all-time low of 37 percent. The election was a significant and novel development in Greece: professed supporters of socialism became government for the first time in Greek history, and the dominant class did not obstruct this leftward power shift.

Papandreou appeared to engulf many of Poulantzas' strategies for this road to socialism. Poulantzas was at odds with the more dominant Third International perception of the state. The latter saw the state as an entity to be destroyed by a revolutionary frontal attack in a situation of dual power with a second power such as a soviet state formed outside the existing state. For Poulantzas, the battle to destroy the "enemy" hidden behind the democratic facade of the "capitalist state" must concurrently be waged within the state's structural materiality (apparatuses) and from outside this materiality, an area he called societal materiality. It is possible for a socialist party through such democratic rules as participation in elections, voting results, interparty coalitions, and so on to rise to power. Becoming government is only one, albeit important, step forward, a further inroad in the "strategic terrain" of the state. A new battle is then waged. Its nature is underlined by the fight within the state's apparatuses between the forces of socialism against interests opposed to it (Poulantzas 1978, 252–53). This fight is qualitatively different than intrapower bloc infighting characteristic of nonsocialist government states; involving an indetermined period of time during which changes in existing capitalist relations of production are aimed toward relations where labor and the means of production are united. This union must be accompanied by the gradual expansion of working class control over every level of economic, political, and social structures. Under this process,

> rational social consciousness imbued with the spirit of justice comes to shape social decision-making and resource allocation. Both control and consciousness are made possible by the public ownership of the means of production; neither are guaranteed by it (Selden and Lippit 1982).

No such transitions can occur uninterrupted by opposition nor without the danger that progressive legislation can deteriorate into social-democratic reformism. Poulantzas (1978) maintained that the transition should evolve through a series of "real breaks with the politics of the past." Given the correct configuration of forces, there will be a real "climax" beyond which the reality of socialism or the triumph of the democratic road to socialism can be realized. This democratic and peaceful road to socialism invalidates the need for a proletarian revolution. In the context of Greece, as we shall see, it would also invalidate the common theoretical description of socialism; that is, under socialism the bourgeois-capitalist state is transformed into a worker's state and bourgeois democracy becomes a proletarian one (Chilcote 1984). The absence of a large proletariat, the lack of open revolt against the bourgeoisie, and the necessary coalition of different classes and class fractions to provide electoral support for Papandreou precluded him, even had he desired, from taking any necessary steps toward forming a proletarian state in the near future. It also precluded the adoptation of the existing Soviet-type socialist state.

Whereas the battle takes place inside the apparatuses of the state, the Socialist party must concurrently engage in societal battles: by increasing democratization and popular input at the grassroots level; and by supporting and directing mass movements. In short, Poulantzas presupposed a thoroughly democratic regime, openly in touch with popular demands. For the above process to begin, Poulantzas argued, the nature of the "enemy" must first be understood, that is, this road to socialism demanded most of all an understanding of the capitalist state, taking advantage of its bourgeois rules, and ensuring the widening and expansion of bourgeois democracy as a necessary step toward socialism.

Starting from a theoretical base, Poulantzas was more concerned with strategies and party policies as his theoretical base was structured by his politial experience: growing up in Greece's political turmoil in the 1950s and 1960s; engaging in France's political life in the late 1960s and 1970s; joining the KKes in post-1974 Greek politics; and even running unsuccessfully for a KKes parliamentary seat in the 1977 national elections. During the latter period, he was enmeshed in the dominant debates among the Left in Greece. These debates included such questions as which party out of a pack of at least three would lead the fight for socialism; which would make the decisions; and which would draft the strategies. These issues were far from settled. Intra-Left bickering on these and related issues most clearly distinguished the politics of the Left in Greece for many years. Poulantzas' later writings reflected this reality. Under different guises, this reality was also evident in France, Italy, Portugal, and Spain during that period. The election of socialist leaders in all these nations in the early 1980s reinforced the prospects for a democratic transition to socialism. In the late 1980s, this idea appeared discredited, in effect begging to ask why.

With the above as a guide, I expand upon some of my arguments regarding recent politico-economic events. Although the Greek experience cannot be used to describe other nations' experiences, it can provide general lessons for other nations. Issues pertinent to Greece such as development and crisis, dictatorship and democracy, capitalism and socialism, and so on, are also pertinent elsewhere in the world.

## THE LIMITS OF BOURGEOIS DEMOCRACY: 1974–81

### The Articulation of Modes of Production

Poulantzas overestimated the nature and size of the CMP and its subsequent affects on the totality of the Greek social formation. As stagnation and pessimism in the 1970s replaced the spurt at industrialization and the optimism of the 1960s, a whole different view took form regarding Greece's dependent capitalist development. This new situation revealed the limits of dependent industrialization and the power of the classes it defined.

The much-heralded Greek economic "miracle" of the 1960s turned out to be largely an illusion. That there was a "miracle" was itself miraculous. It was based more on economic affluence rather than economic development. The crisis of the 1970s led many social scientists to conclude that the CMP, or relations of production based on wage earners who own nothing but their labor power and private owners of the means of production, did not define the totality of Greek reality. Rather, two or more modes of production coexist and define the Greek social formation (for the theoretical sources of this perspective, see Foster-Carter 1978; Chilcote and Johnson 1983). The Greek CMP coexisted and dominated a vaguely defined precapitalist mode of production. The latter displayed relations of production in which no labor power was involved. The direct producer did not sell his labor to capital in exchange for wages. And production was based on single commodity production for the market.

Poulantzas assumptions notwithstanding, the CMP remained confined mostly to large urban areas with almost half of Greek industries based in or near the Athens basin; restricted to certain sectors of the economy such as in medium and large export-oriented industries; and dominated mostly by foreign interests (Mouzelis 1978a, 38–40). Most foreign investments were directed to such key, export-oriented industries as petroleum refining (96 percent control), natural gas bottling (86 percent), transport equipment (60 percent), metallurgy (57 percent), and chemicals (45 percent) (Kafatou 1979, 113–15). The new industries were of the enclave type; that is, foreign capital entering "into the local productive processes in the form of wages and taxes to ensure exports of raw material or goods" (Chilcote 1984, 165). Such practice provided foreign companies with the added advantage of using the neutral Greek label to penetrate new markets (e.g., Arab or African ones—see Poulantzas 1976, 24). Out of the top 100 Greek industries in 1972, 17 had foreign links, and of the top 25, nine were outright controlled by multinationals. Three out of the top five businesses were daughter companies of multinationals (Sarlis 1984, 32).

The precapitalist mode persisted in several forms of small-scale commodity production and small agricultural units (Vergopoulos 1975) producing for local and large urban markets. These units remained inefficient and open to exploitation. The terms of exchange were determined by middlemen who utilized such capitalist rules as cornering specific areas for themselves in a monopoly fashion, imposing arbitrary terms of exchange, and forcing producers to comply or perish. The continuation of family-operated, small-scale production units made production of local market consumer goods unable in the long run to compete against foreign products. This situation became especially acute with every opening of the local market to foreign products as Greece geared to join the EEC in the late 1970s.

The perpetuation of such an articulation rather than its eventual dissolution in favor of the dominant mode played into the hands of the capitalists (Mouzelis 1978a, 45). They kept the precapitalist mode chronically in debt and appropriated (or transferred) large parts of the latter's surplus to themselves through the medium of exchange and finance. Underdevelopment persisted because of a lack of what Mouzelis called an "organic integration" between the two modes. I see no sufficient evidence to prove this abstraction or that the capitalist sector gained from this surplus appropriation in the long run. This situation hindered the CMP from achieving its further development, thereby diminishing its potential for a wider accumulation of capital.

## The Historical Antecedents of Internalization

The answer lies with the way Greek society in general internalized the CMP, as well as with the nature and components of the kind of development pursued. As such, I fault Poulantzas for narrowing his observations regarding the modification of politico-economic structures by internalization to mostly on the power bloc and the form of the state. A wider societal focus is needed instead to explain the adaptation of "outside" relations, political and economic behavior by all social classes, and the nature of the state. The internalization of the CMP in the 1960s affected the whole society and distinguished the social formation of the 1970s from those of the past that had unfolded within a basically unchanged context. The formation of the 1970s had a changed context that allowed the rapid political shifts and caused the developmental bottlenecks to occur.

This observation is directly related to Poulantzas thesis. He argued that Greece's specific dependence was the result of two aspects particular to that nation: one, the maintenance of a primitive capital accumulation based on trade and merchant activities in the Eastern Mediterranean area; and two, the blockage thesis. Due to many reasons, an endogenous industrial capital accumulation at the right time never occurred. But he never defined the "reasons" nor the "right time." Comparing these "aspects" with the totally different experiences of Spain and Portugal weakened his thesis even more as Lopez, Sammis, and Nataf explain. Both aspects did take place, and they highly determined subsequent developments, but I disagree with Poulantzas' interpretation of them.

To explain the "reasons" and the "timing" of those aspects, let us digress back to the late eighteenth and early nineteenth centuries when Greeks were still subjugated under Ottoman rule. It can be argued that most of Greece's modern socioeconomic makeup was the direct result of the highly decentralized Ottoman rule. The Ottomans recognized very diverse peoples on the basis of their theocratic linkages (Moslems, Orthodox Christians, Jews, etc.) and along linguistic lines (Greek, Slavic, Armenian, etc.) rather than on the basis of their ethnicity (Stavrianos 1981, 126). The Ottomans allowed for a large degree of local autonomy and for the coexistence of various ethnic groups in the same area, especially in large cities of the empire. Local autonomy led to a kind of rule that ultimately came to be based on interpersonal local allegiances. Local autonomy fed mistrust toward the distant, alien, and not clearly understood centralized authority structure of the imperial court, which, after all, was considered the "enemy." With the formation of the modern Greek state, the local leaders (archons) encouraged and perpetuated the mistrust for central authority—this time against the Athens central government ruled by a foreign king. They did so in order to perpetuate their power in the new state. The central authority relied on the urban population as a support base in trying to break the power of the archons. The tension between the towns and the countryside resulted in chronic and constant constitutional and political instability and the undermining of a national consensus (Mouzelis 1978a). This explains the absence of mass political parties and the perpetuation of interpersonal allegiances until recently. Whereas the "archon" rule was defeated in the beginning of the twentieth century (Tsoukalas 1981), local and group allegiances remained strong (Kourvetaris and Dobratz 1984).

The second aspect of Ottoman rule, the coexistence of many ethnic groups, made it difficult to determine clear national boundaries as the Ottoman Empire began to break apart in a long but steady decline of a century or more. Conflicting territorial claims by newly formed or forming Balkan nations and Turkey itself on the basis of ethnic majorities led to arbitrary irredentism. A long turbulent regional historical experience full of overt and covert conflicts and wars marked regional politics. As many as 10 such wars and conflicts occurred. Many treaties (e.g., the Treaty of Lausagne in 1923) were signed only to be disputed later (e.g., regarding control of some Aegean islands). This situation, called the Eastern Question, was also complicated by outside great powers or modern superpower interference according to their changing strategic stakes in the area (see Petropulos 1968; Couloumbis, Petropulos, and Psomlades 1976; Papacosmas 1979). Greek irredentism, conditioned and constantly changed by varying domestic politico-economic interests, was incorporated under the concept of the "Megali Idea" (Great Idea; see Tatsios 1984; Dakin 1972). In the 1910s the Great Idea received its clearest expression in Prime Minister Eleftherios Venizelos' dream of a "Greater Greece of two continents and five seas." It can be argued that the 1974 coup against the Cypriot government and the events unleashed by it were part of such a past.

The fight between the town and the countryside and the Great Idea provided early, convenient ideological tools with which the establishment involved the masses to its own intraestablishment disputes. In doing so, the establishment neutralized the class formation potential of the masses by preventing them from developing their own class-based consciousness. Instead, the masses developed a consciousness of support for their class superiors amid conditions of chronic poverty.

The clash between the Venizelos definition and a more narrow one offered by the palace in the 1910s and 1920s created another ideological intraestablishment dispute amounting to "Dihasmos," a nationwide split. The split generated an animosity of civil war proportions and marked the political life of the nation for decades. Cold War anticommunism succeeded "Dihasmos" as another such tool against the masses; itself witnessing a substantial eclipse with the post-1974 opening. Thus, whereas up to the 1970s there had been many social conflicts of huge proportions, social power relations were basically unchanged and unchallenged.

Greece's turbulent and particular history as a nation set the context of its economic development. Greek mercantile activities abroad had ensured, even under Ottoman rule, a primitive accumulation of capital in the past two centuries or so. This capital was mostly stored in foreign banks. After independence, constant regional wars, Nazi occupation, a civil war, and recurrent political turmoil were not conducive to storing this capital in Greece. In attracting parts of it, the state offered many concessions to the owners of this wealth. Given the turbulent climate, however, the incoming capital was not willing to engage in risky or unfamiliar ventures such as in large-scale industrial investments and production whose profits would not be realized for many years. Instead, it was invested in land and housing construction to safeguard against currency devaluations, and continued with its traditional and profitable middlemen and merchant pursuits. Some of it went for conspicuous consumption of imported luxury items in order to flaunt wealth. Such short-term profit return investments created a large rentier capital sector that supported a whole range of related professions (Petras 1984), and a few extremely wealthy shipowners, merchants, and landlords. But an indigenous capitalist growth and the formation of an independent national bourgeois class did not take place.

The unwillingness rather than the inability of Greek capital to transform itself deepened Greece's external dependence and blighted its sovereignty. Deprived of local sources, the state relied on foreign capital for development. Administering this capital proved spasmodic and mismanaged, made even dependent progress impossible, and benefited mostly a few middlemen. Between 1823 and 1893, for example, only 6 percent of foreign loans secured went for productive purposes, domestic and foreign middlemen kept 35 percent, and 59 percent financed wars and repaid past debts on exorbitant interest rates (Dovas 1980, 20–21).

In the 1930s Greece was near the bottom of Europe's standard of living. It had a predominantly agricultural economy noted for its primitive production methods and low yield per acre making it difficult to sustain a population of 7 million, and a legacy of huge trade deficits and mounting foreign debts (Polk 1947; 531). Compounding its misfortunes, Greece experienced the "dreadful decade" of the 1940s (Carey and Carey 1968; 124) marked by Nazi occupation and a civil war. By 1949 nearly a tenth of the population were refugees and a third were either wholly or partially dependent on state aid (Papandreaou 1962; 17); more than a fourth of all buildings were in ruins; and despite huge foreign aid (mostly North American), total national income was estimated at around 80 percent of the prewar figure (Stavrianos 1952; 212). By carving out a secure place to amass profits, the Greek capitalists had narrowed and often blocked the state's options to achieve development.

## Miracle or Mirage

The massive infusion of foreign capital in the 1950s and in the 1960s constituted the major source of industrial capital in Greece. The foreign interests found a fertile ground for profits unhindered by local capital-owning competition. The astonishlingly preferential treatment of foreign capital by the state revealed the continued unwillingness of Greek capitalists to make full use of their capital in developing industries. In order to attract foreign investments, the government enacted Legislative Decree 2687 in 1953, which, along with a plethora of lesser supportive decrees, provided concessions and incentives to foreign capital (An Economic Observer 1972). In the case of the French aluminum company Pecheney, the government, a partner in the venture, supplied electricity at low cost. In the case of an Alcoa smelter (40 percent government-owned) plant, an energy saving device was not installed because the state provided power at lost cost (McNall 1980, 116).

Foreign-owned assembly plants and hotels do not lead to genuine industrial breakthroughs. Apart from providing some jobs and wages, foreign investors were more interested in exploiting Greece's comparative advantages (cheap labor, natural resources, holiday resorts, and so on). Lucrative concessions governing the repatriation and volume of foreign companies' earnings offset generous tax-free incentives to reinvest profits and keep this surplus in Greece. Profits made in Greece often took advantage of both initial investment and reinvestment incentives by recycling most of the same money all the time. Foreign capital also used laws intended to promote domestic capital investments, especially in the area of export incentives. Likewise, domestic capital profitably utilized laws drafted for foreign capital by treating Greek shipowning capital as foreign (Dovas 1980; 180–82).

In general, there was a coincidence of interest among the Greek capitalists, the state, and foreign capital. The Greek capitalists profited even more by merchant, middlemen, and marketeering activities by operating under and around foreign concerns. The latter enjoyed a free hand in production and penetrated regional markets. The state expediently advertized its role in promoting general welfare, modernization, and industrialization. But although appearing to act in unison, each part had in reality narrow goals within each individual sphere of interest that merely perpetuated rampant opportunism and the plundering of the economy. Development was attempted through a compilation of ad hoc efforts rather than a coordinated and sustained drive to do so. It was thus the lack of "organic integration" inside the troika that led to the lack of "organic integration" between the CMP and the precapitalist mode observed by Mouzelis (1978a) that hindered the CMP from expanding over all of the social formation. The troika's marriage of convenience based on a shared desire to profit and a common hatred of communism aimed to solidify its power rather than expand the CMP.

On the Greek side were the "victors" of the civil war, the same interests and their right-wing politicians that could not stay in power 30 days without American support; and a power elite of 1,800 that lived in luxury while the rest of the Greeks "milled around in rags and tatters" (Stavrianos 1952; 4). It was the same state that tried to hide its authoritarianism by promising modernization and economic affluence in an effort to heed the advice of a 1947 report by the Food and Agriculture Organization (FAO) of the United Nations, which asserted that "not until government arrangements can be worked out which have the confidence and support of the great mass of the Greek people can clear and consistent economic programs be established (Stavrianos 1952, 13). It was evident that the economic problems of Greece would not be solved solely by a technological solution involving only the development of the means of production, of natural resources, and agriculture. Any future economic progress depended more on a socio-political transformation, one that would include extensive and even radical changes in relations of power. Instead, the "miracle" witnessed the persistence and even the tightening (for example, the 1967 junta) of political suppression.

On the foreign side, President Truman assured the U.S. Congress that American aid to Greece would give the United States the chance to totally control Greece's economy (Acheson 1965, 292). The aid aimed to integrate Greece into the West (Kariotis 1979) not so much to help the nation "free" itself from outside "pressure" as the Truman Doctrine argued (LaFeber 1976, 54), but to strengthen the overall interests of the United States. It was the beginning of a new U.S. foreign policy that coupled the drive for strategic superiority with economic dominance on a global scale: any limitation to free trade could be overcome by an emphasis on the threat the Soviet Union posed for the United States. The immediate result of the U.S. involvement in Greece reflected this twofold policy. The infrastructure reconstruction started in the 1950s created roads and port facilities that ensured better troop movements in case of war with the socialist bloc and facilitated entrance into and exit from Greece of products and raw materials. Roads were inadequate in meeting Greece's domestic needs even in the 1980s.

Aggregate economic indicators appeared to support the claims of national economic progress and contributed to the illusion of affluence. The GNP increased 5.6 times from 1950 to 1980; per capita income multiplied 30.6 times (from $143 to $4,377; and exports, representing only 24.4 percent of imports in 1950, rose to 69.7 percent in 1980 (Kintis 1981, 29). For Fotopoulos (1978, 27), industrial products among total goods exported jumped from 2 percent in 1954 to 42 percent in 1973. For Krimpas (1982), the share of agriculture in total output fell from over 60 percent pre- World War II to about 15 percent in the 1970s.

A different picture emerges when different statistics are considered. For example, the "miracle" that conservatives claimed had been achieved did "not mean that the country entered the path of economic development . . . (rather, the "Right") had failed to create employment opportunities that would have allowed Greeks to remain in their country" (Tsoukalas 1981, 128). But why should the Right try to create employment opportunities in the first place? The Right was more interested in maintaining its rule while trying to gain political capital for whatever progress it could point its fingers to. Moreover, assembly plants do not necessarily mean that more jobs would be created. Beyond an initial job creation, capitalism must constantly try to eliminate labor from the production process. It must do this in order to lower production costs in terms of wages and benefits, and to do away with the problems associated with labor such as strikes, and absenteeism—failing to do so peacefully, the bayonet was used. Foreign investments, instead, had a limited, if not negative, multiplier effect on the economy. They did not do much to satisfy domestic market needs or meet basic human needs (e.g., production for the local market, educational improvements, and health care provision). Market needs were satisfied by imported goods, a practice amounting to xenomania, and human needs by trips abroad. As one example, in 1983, after two decades of a steady increase, there were 41,086 Greek students in foreign universities, representing nearly a third of all Greek students (Vrettos 1983). These numbers placed Greece at the top of student exportation among Western nations, a dubious distinction since it involved a foreign currency and brain drain.

Lack of employment opportunities at home, freedom from cultural norms, and aspirations for easy riches abroad have historically prompted many Greeks to leave their chronically impoverished country. The "development" of the 1960s, however, created a wave of emmigration of unprecedented intensity and size. Migration in search of employment mainly to Western Europe, the United States, and Australia reached catastrophic dimensions. The amount justified the expressions "biological decay of the nation" or the "hemorrhage of the working capacity" (Kalligas 1978, 170–76). For Kalligas, emmigration trends reached their peaks during the dictatorship even though working class reserves had been exhausted in the previous years. In the two-year period (1968–69) alone, 145,000 people emmigrated, a number equivalent to the total increase of the Greek population. Between 1958 and 1976, one million Greeks, a tenth of the population, left for Western Europe (Mouzelis 1980, 22). Most were in their youth. Their absence skewed the population toward older age, handicapped Greece's defense potential, and depressed its productive ability.

The state made no effort to institute skill development programs, nor to modernize and expand higher education. Instead, the junta reversed all the educational reforms of Georgios Papandreou's government and treated even legitimate student demands for modernization as a challenge to its rule. Had there been a genuine desire toward growth, educational improvement, an integral part of industrialization, would have been a major priority. Instead, lack of skill development impeded the work force from attaining a higher level of technological expertise and deprived future generations of Greeks of a competitive edge in foreign and domestic markets.

The "miracle" did not lead to income equalization. By 1973, 40 percent of the lower classes earned only 9.5 percent of the national income compared to double that income for the same population percentage in England (Fotopoulos 1978, 83; see also Kafatou 1979). Basic industrial wages rose from 22 drachmas per day in 1951 to 1,314 drachmas in 1984, yet in real terms, given that in the late 1970s and early 1980s inflation hovered around 20–26 percent, this increase represented a dubious gain for workers. Since 1973 unemployment figures began to rise and in 1988, after seven years of PASOK rule, stood at 13 percent.

Increasing trade gaps, widening budget deficits, and mounting foreign debts were not threatening nor clearly evident under the junta, which offered little accountability of its economic policies. A healthy world economy carried the Greek economy along with it. Mass immigration kept unemployment levels artificially low. Foreign competition did not lead to domestic layoffs because little was produced that could be threatened by it. Imports provided service-oriented employment, from middleman management to secretarial work to distribution and maintenance. And immigrant remittances, a thriving merchant marine industry, and tourism were substantial foreign currency inflows.

The 1973 oil crisis and its negative impact on the world economy was the first major indication of the fragile status of Greece's economic fortunes. The oil crisis became more serious when the 1974 opening unleashed suppressed demands for a new politico-economic system of power relations. Democratization at home and worsening economic conditions in the emigrant nations led many political exiles and immigrants to return. The returnees put added pressure on the system to accommodate their demands for employment and state aid (e.g., pensions, health care, education). Moreover, as Petras (1984) noted, whereas Greeks abroad willingly took risks in almost all economic ventures, upon returning home they engaged mostly in land or building acquisitions and other related risk-free professions or investments associated with the prevailing rentier capital. Such nonproductive pursuits offered little to the development of a viable economic structure in the long term. In contrast, they generated inflation by driving up land prices, which the domestic Greeks could ill-afford, or by introducing new consumerist patterns, which the locals sooner or later imitated. Although there was a surge in foreign money entering Greece with the returnees, the traditional source of foreign exchange through remittances began to decline. For many who remained abroad, ties with the old nation slowly disappeared as their old folk at home died. By the 1980s, remittances continued their downward trend.

The downfall of the merchant marine industry was another unexpected economic reversal. Basing its profits mostly on the oil business, this industry went into a tailspin after 1973. Competition by other nations also dealt a blow to its declining fortunes. Unemployment among sailors ran high and deprived the economy of more foreign currency because merchants were paid in U.S. dollars. Related to this decline was a similar drop in Greek shipbuilding, a traditionally large employer. The tourist industry grew in unstructured and inefficient ways, and was negatively affected by external conditions such as changing tourist preferences, the declining value of the dollar, terrorist acts, and nuclear accidents (e.g., Chernobyl) in other countries.

The restricted nature of the CMP and the continuation of rentier capital and small-scale single commodity production explain employment patterns prevalent in the 1970s and 1980s. In 1981, 65.7 percent of nonagricultural workers were wage-earners—compared to 95 percent in Sweden. This percentage placed Greece at the bottom of the scale among the 28 member-nations of the Organization for Economic Development and Cooperation (OECD). Almost half of those worked in the public sector where placement was based mostly on "rousfeti" (clientelistic rettribution—Tsoukalas 1986, 185–90). Many others engaged in nonproductive occupations, evidenced by ownership of small retail shops on every street throughout Greece. The owners produced nothing and overexploited themselves and their families by working long hours. The tourist industry presented another opportunity for small-scale, seasonal employment (hotels, souvenir shops, travel agencies). But the best bet was public sector employment. Wages there were secure. Legal constraints on dismissal offered no incentive to be productive for fear of job loss. This norm gave rise to a giant yet cumbersome and inefficient bureaucracy. Its main motivations were to expand even more and deflect blame. Some earned a living by providing services to citizens trying to deal with archaic and often incomprehensible bureaucratic standards. The result was a nonproducing, service-oriented work force earning money through overpricing, market manipulation, tax evasion, side deals, and in general mimicking on a smaller scale similar patterns dear to their class superiors. In short, a para-economy evolved, outside the control of the state, above normal or legal parameters, and based on low productivity and the perpetuation of individual advantages—a condition that later plagued even genuine efforts by Papandreou to instill a collective consciousness on Greeks.

Such employment patterns gave rise to an amalgam of various substrata with high inequalities of wealth among them that could be grouped under one large, highly conspicuous petty bourgeois class. In the 1970s this "class" played a decisive role in electoral outcomes as it searched for a political party of its own. Its numerical strength and internal divergence made it important to woo and difficult to satisfy politically and economically. It sided first with the ND party and remained dissatisfied and highly fluid for the rest of the 1970s. In 1981 large segments of this class joined PASOK. Its divergence biased any strategy and theory regarding the transition to, or the definition of, socialism.

By comparison, the manufacturing workers peaked to around 41 percent in Athens in 1971 and declined to 34.2 percent in 1983 (Tsoukalas 1986, 180). This low percentage was in an area that concentrated 35 percent of all Greeks; 47.3 percent of all private, 24.4 percent of all public, and 47 percent of all industrial investments; 48 percent of industrial production; 49 percent of industrial employment; and 73.5 percent of all businesses employing more than a 100 workers (in *Ta Nea,* July 24, 1986, 12). In the countryside where the precapitalist mode was widespread, this percentage was even lower. An observer would be hard-pressed to find two members of a family who worked in some sort of factory job. Similarly, the traditionally conservative peasants saw their numbers diminish fast since the 1960s. Urbanization in search of state services and immigration in search of jobs were trends of near catastrophic proportions for the countryside and the urban centers alike. Agriculture could not support urban needs and urban dwellers faced a worsening quality of life. Athens became the most polluted city in Western Europe (Schwenk 1986, 181) with life-threatening levels of air and noise pollution; almost a quarter of its residential houses were built without zoning; its public parks and recreational spaces were nearly nonexistent; traffic congestion was monumental and constant; and public transportation was outdated and inadequate.

At the same time, monied affluence in terms of wages, remittances, tourism, and the merchant industry provided the fuel for a consumerism of explosive dimensions during the 1970s. This tendency to consume mostly imported gadgets was reinforced by the political opening in 1974, and also by exposure to foreign consumerist patterns following the nationwide expansion of television, foreign films, returnees from abroad, tourist inflow, and so on. The way consumerism unfolded in the Greek context made it certain that neither ND nor PASOK policies could satisfy. Greeks did not necessarily consume more than they could afford. Even in the late 1980s, only a very limited number of people used credit cards. It was a cash-buying consumerism based on what might be called diminishing expectations of consumption that cut across class lines. If a person did not have enough cash to buy a house, the money would be spent to purchase a luxury car. If one could not afford that, a less expensive car was chosen. If not a car, then a color television set, and so on down the scale. Such consumption did not satisfy higher expectations, although more Greeks appeared better off than in previous times. Beneath the nonrealization of higher expectations implied in an economic downturn laid a latent, embryonic class formation consciousness waiting to be tapped. Papandreou managed in 1981 to tap into these latent feelings but was unsuccessful in satisfying them once in power. These consumerist patterns hindered the accumulation of savings capital and deprived the state of this important source of capital. State efforts to attract savings by offering high interest rates (up to 21 percent in some cases in the 1980s) met with actual or perceived traditional fears regarding currency stability. Such fears in the past had acted to convert currency into property, preferably buildings; evidenced by their inclusion in the widespread social norm of dowry.

Skewed economic affluence for industrialists, middlemen, profiteers, speculationers, and importers of foreign goods in an ever-enlarging domestic market set higher consumer standards in the 1970s. Others quickly aped them. Ever-widening trade deficits ensued. ND efforts to improve exports in order to close the gap failed as imports far outstripped each single year's exports. Although legislation offering export incentives was enacted, the management, production, and distribution of goods were spasmodic, inefficient, and of low quality. Greece was forced to borrow from abroad to finance its state deficits, making it more dependent and vulnerable to foreign whims. Currency devaluations to improve the competitiveness of its exports failed to improve foreign sales and acted further to increase the amount paid for imports. Crude oil became the biggest foreign exchange drain. Demand for it and its price increased multifold because of the imported car-buying craze that swept Greece in the 1970s, and the 1973 and 1979 oil crises. Currency declines made the hoarding of foreign currency lucrative, created a black market, and forged clandestine networks to smuggle surplus Greek currency abroad.

## The Political Implications of the Economic Crisis

ND politicians viewed the crisis as the result of the oil crisis and irresponsible fiscal management by the junta. These assumptions avoided a critical focus on the disfunctions of the Greek model of development. They conveniently obscured real problems that might be more than the dominant classes were willing even to admit. A re-evaluation of the capitalist path and power relations was at stake. In avoiding these issues, the new regime disassociated itself from the junta and the politics of the past; maintained the illusion that the way out of the crisis was better management by new state technocrats; and played up the seasoned belief among Greeks that most of the country's misfortunes were foreign-influenced and over which the new government had no control. Placing blame elsewhere allowed the new regime to reverse most of the concessions initially granted to the dominated classes without paying the price for it. Wide-ranging austerity measures such as wage cuts, layoffs, higher service provision rates and taxes, and antistrike legislation met with little social resistance.

In regard to the overall direction of the economy, an almost blind belief in non-Greek, pro-Western, "catching up" paths to development involving modernization and the shedding of traditional practices ruled supreme. Krimpas (1982) argued that Greece's continuous economic malaise could be corrected only by upgrading policies based on rational adjustments such as institutional and administrative reform and full integration with the EEC. By believing so, blame was placed on the popular masses who had no input in policy-making and who suffered the most. There was no mention of the enormous wealth accumulated by capitalists and foreign interests (Mouzelis 1980; Nikolinakos, 1977). Blaming the chief beneficiaries and architects of the "mirage" was thus avoided.

Politically, the need to "construct a democratic system in line with what was considered to be a healthy and fast-developing society" received priority (Manesis 1986, 10). But political overhauling and "democratization" unsupported by an economic cure were equivalent to building a structure on shaky foundations. Nor was society healthy. The economic crisis prevented the evolution of the social formation into clearly defined classes that could buttress the formation of a Western European-type bourgeois democratic state. The "fissures and gaps" in policies that Poulantzas observed in the early 1970s deepened by the end of the decade. The dominant class and its political representative, the ND party, could not cure the "malaise" with any imaginative prescription. Instead, they merely echoed assumptions that in the 1960s had appeared as true and tried sources of progress. But the desire to rationalize the economy and open it up to private initiative and the free market so that "Greece belongs to the West," as an ND party slogan put it, remained unrealized. Such proposals were more talk than action. The ND government continued to rely on the *rousfeti* practice to enlarge its electorate base and to return favors; expanded the state's role by necessary intervention in the economy; caved in to conflicting capitalist class demands; and overall provided no clear or sustained strategy for a rational way out of the crisis.

The government continued with its strategy of deflecting blame. This ploy failed to convince the public as each year revealed that the previous year's ND government's own cures failed to ensure recovery. The government then blamed the personnel responsible for the policies enacted. A summary dismissal of this personnel was presented as a solution. Proclaiming triumphantly new measures to cure all ills that in effect were more of the same formula, the newcomers really waited their turn to be blamed by future appointees. The misplacing of blame elsewhere fed upon a social psychology that viewed crises and their resolution as an abstraction, outside any person's control (Vergopoulos 1986). This psychology contributed further to the regime's inability to deal with the crisis.

This governmental malfunction alienated both dominant and dominated classes. Rather than splitting along EEC and U.S. lines of dependency and allegiance, as Poulantzas argued, the capitalists as a whole had reached another cul-de-sac. Many among them were even threatened by the anticipated EEC integration. Although there might be gains from access to European production techniques and markets, they felt that the ND party could not be trusted to protect their interests. Beyond wishfully assuring Greeks of the positive aspects of joining the EEC, the government had no EEC policy to ensure the survival of the Greek economy. According to ND Defense Minister Evangelos Averof's candid confessions in 1981, the ND government had neither a general plan for the economy nor "the trust of the business section regarding the future course of the economy and the government's political economy" (*Ta Nea,* July 9, 1986, 6). Averof observed budget deficits as high as 52.2 percent of anticipated government revenue in 1981; domestic public borrowing derived mainly from public savings, depriving financial sources for private businesses and narrowing private initiative ventures; and foreign currency deficits and foreign borrowing to repay past debts were locked in an ever-worsening vicious circle. Averof finally stretched the need to "strengthen the climate of (public) trust toward the state, to support private initiative," and to "repay (the state's) obligations toward its citizens (*Ta Nea,* July 9, 1986, 6). That same year the ND government was voted out of power. While Karamanlis was prime minister, "lack of trust" and dissatisfaction were largely muted. But when he removed himself from electoral politics to become president of the republic in 1980, ND's electoral fortunes declined sharply.

The petty bourgeoisie were similarly disenchanted as their lot progressively worsened. The freezing of prices and wages while inflation increased reduced their profit margins and purchasing power. The peasant population was largely ignored in national politics. Underrepresentation radicalized them away from mainstream politics. As conditions worsened, the state blamed the dominated classes for their inflationary demands for wage increases or consumerism. This strategy favored monopoly capital, the main supporter of the ND government, which wanted a disciplined work force. The option of another junta to discipline the work force was unacceptable within the democratic facade on the 1970s. Monopoly capital found in austerity measures a convenient tool to do so. One-sided austerity measures undermined the concessions granted earlier on to the dominated classes. As large interclass majorities became unhappier with ND policies, the economic crisis turned into a political one. The double-fold aim noted previously appeared to be crumbling.

## The Politics of the Left

Feeling that the ND government had abandoned their politico-economic representation, many Greeks searched for a political party that would help them. A poll taken just before the 1981 election showed that 28.8 percent of the voters were liberals, 15.3 percent were conservatives, 14.6 percent socialist non-Marxists, 14.2 percent socialist Marxists, and 4.1 percent Marxist-Leninists (Loulis 1984/85, 380). In the same poll, 53 percent named high inflation (around 26 percent) as their main worry. Papandreou's victory in the 1981 election could thus account for large blocs of liberals shifting to PASOK out of dissatisfaction with the stale economic policies of the ND. Papandreou welcomed all in a "wide alliance" of "classes and social layers," which "are the object of dismal exploitation" by the capitalists and by "middlemen, retailers, the banking system, and the multinationals" (CMS 1981, 12). This kind of political stance earned him the label of a nationalist: a person motivated by a loyalty and a devotion to his nation; an attitude of national consciousness exalting one nation above all others; and a belief in the virtues of one's culture rather than of other nations or supranational groups (Kegley and Witkoff 1981, 365 fn). His nationalism was evident in his oft-repeated slogan of "Greece to the Greeks." He was also labeled a populist as he appeared to make the popular sector (the working class, the petty bourgeoisie, and the peasants) a main participant in any national political coalition and a major beneficiary of public policy. Despite a "considerable variation in the degree to which populism is competitive and democratic, it is clearly 'incorporating' by being based on a multi-class coalition" (Collier 1979, 19–24).

Describing Papandreou as a nationalist-populist leader missed the mark by far. He was a politician few in Greek politics could rival. He could interpret the social formation of Greece and inflate latent feelings. But more important, to expand his popular support he had to update socialist messages in line with his audience. His audience necessitated different strategies toward, and definition of, socialism possible for Greece. The "wide alliance" he envisioned was in tune with the nation's multivaried and divergent amalgam of not clearly defined classes. He projected himself as being fiercely intent to side with Greece's interests in general and more specifically with the "nonprivileged many." He would not cede to foreign interests and their local allies whom he called the "privileged few." As a slogan it worked wonders. Since no other statistics or labels described such definitions, even members of the dominant classes of an economy in crisis could feel nonprivileged, in effect tapping into the feelings of higher expectations.

His unorthodox theoretical social definitions confused Marxist analysts who then declared Papandreou's ideology unclear. But this social schema was far-reaching and enlightened even though it confounded Marxist analysis. Electoral strength means incorporating many classes. Both the ND and PASOK did so, and both claimed to represent all classes. Neither was a populist party. Incorporation in the abstract cannot be a guide in understanding PASOK. It was Papandreou's social dichotomy rather than incorporating appeal that most clearly marked his early position. The embryonic interclass challenge implied by the "privileged few/nonprivileged many" schema redefined the nature of politics in Greece and chipped away the kind of social accord dominant in past social formations. Concurrently, he professed to achieve socialism through democratic procedures, thereby reflecting the democratic norms taking hold in the late 1970s. Both the dichotomy and democratic socialism diluted the nature of his radical messages as things stood in the early 1980s.

This strategy enabled him to attract large numbers of voters along non-ideological interclass lines. His nationalist-populist disguise enabled Papandreou to escape the phantom of the Communist "threat." His "super-patriot" stance kept his opponents from pinning on him the derisive "Communist" epithet. Even though he called himself a Marxist-Socialist, none could accuse him of being a puppet of the Soviet Union. His stance allowed Greeks of nonleftist beliefs to vote for him and to espouse some of his socialist programs (in the context of nationalism). It was possible to accept a situation where a vote for PASOK did not make one a "second-class" citizen (in the context of being branded a Communist—Mouzelis 1978b, 71). This stance neutralized the potential opposition of army officers. As a further check on army reaction, he also assumed the position of minister of defense.

Personality aspects also boosted his appeal. He was the only politician wearing turtlenecks rather than the traditional shirt and tie. He was popularly referred to by his first name, Andreas, which became his trademark, thus distancing him from his family's name but not from the clientelistic style of Center Union politics. His eloquence as a speaker, his sharpness as a thinker, and his personal charisma could not be doubted even by the opposition. And, as a member of parliament for the ND party told this author privately, Papandreou had a kind of sex appeal that attracted women voters to his image.

Papandreou's quick dominance of the Left was due to default by the traditional Left. The Communists split into two fiercely opposed groups in 1968. Subsequently, the KKE, the larger of the two, could not shed its legacy of missed opportunities, mistakes, outdated slogans, and beliefs in working class domination that alienated other classes from it (Satiropoulos in *Ta Nea,* July 28, 1986, 9). The KKE appeared to address a distant past rather than the present. Its heroic fight against the Nazis, its role in the civil war, and its many years of being prosecuted after that had a narrow appeal. For the majority of younger Greeks living in a changing social reality, these issues were distant and not quite relevant. Even among many older working class members who voted for the KKE out of a long-held respect for the undoubtedly patriotic role of the Communists in the past, their behavioral patterns, especially in consumption, could not reconcile with KKE slogans. The working class, moreover, remained small and divided in its party allegiances. Other classes refused to ally with a party that still proclaimed the dominance of the working class in any alliance it might enter. The KKes, the smaller of the two, was more of the Eurocommunist type found in France or Italy. More enlightened in its messages, it still maintained its Communist lexicon. Its updated messages alienated hardcore Communists, and the Communist lexicon could not compete with PASOK's diluted socialist phraseology in attracting non-Communist voters—in 1987 it dropped its Communist epithet and called itself the Greek Left (E. AR.) to no avail. Caught between PASOK and the KKE on the left, its appeal suffered accordingly. In the late 1970s and throughout the 1980s, it remained mostly a party of leftist intellectuals. The Communists in general clearly failed to open up and to expand their political power base.

Papandreou appeared to have done so. But whereas Poulantzas advocated also the need to democratize the base by allowing more grassroots input into the party machinery, Papandreou was from the start of PASOK's formation a most authoritarian figure who constantly expelled from his party any who dared to dissent. Papandreou's authoritarianism and the bitter fights between parties for electoral dominance and survival precluded the formation of bottom-up democratization in PASOK. Faced with a tightly controlled and militant PASOK and in order to control internal dissent, other parties' machineries were forced to become more centralized and authoritarian. Party weaknesses were covered up. Open intraparty debate was shunned because it could be adversely interpreted as a sign of leadership default.

Political conflicts turned into interparty struggles waged under conditions of often extreme fanaticism among their supporters and encompassing all social aspects. For example, more than any other time in Greece's history there were interclass mass movements by all kinds of issue-oriented groups. But such movements as student, feminist, pacifist, anti-American, and ecological did not remain independent for long. These movements caved in to interparty bickering and made to reflect party strength at the national level. Heavily dependent on party money, organizational ability, and leadership, these movements inevitably split into many party-affiliated factions fiercely opposing each other. Because of the show of strength involved with any movement issue, even small, local, or unimportant issues would soon turn into national issues, if only to prove a point. Unhappy with this situation, many people from all classes became nonactivist, choosing instead nonpolitical pursuits such as consumption and entertainment.

The compound effect of the economic, socio-cultural, and political insecurity and lack of consensus directly affected the superstructure of the state. Itself mirroring this societal fluidity but always lagging behind, the new state was forced to expand into all aspects of life to alleviate the crises. At the same time, it was itself a main source of these crises. Its clientelistic, bureaucratic structure could not at once side with the bourgeoisie and neutralize the masses. The sustained economic crisis made this aim difficult to handle.

## The Logic of Authority of the Greek State

The power of the state makes the capture of state power the inevitable goal of any social class or class fraction wanting to present its specific interests in terms of the general interest. In theory, the state as an institution and its role in society

> has grown increasingly important in every society, from advanced industrial to Third World primary-good exporter, and in every aspect of society—not just in politics, but in economics (production, finance, distribution), in ideology (schooling, the media), and in the law enforcement (police, military) (Carnoy 1984, 1).

The post-1974 Greek state played a most important social role by virtue of its size and its intervention to handle the many crises. Yet the more it tried to do so, the more it distanced itself from social realities. The post-1974 state resulted from a political rather than a revolutionary change. The transition from a dictatorship to a right-wing democracy was really a superficial change of state personnel. This change maintained the logic of state power and its role in society (*Ta Nea,* July 29, 1986, 6). For Tzortzis, the state's main function to maintain its power conditions its "function in socio-political affairs" even as in the process the state also affects the direction of social changes. Tzortzis, unlike Poulantzas, viewed the growth of the Greek state not as a part of society but under a logic that separated state and society, a logic not significantly altered after 1974. As argued earlier, this assumption stemmed from the traditional enmity between the state and localized group interests. In trying to establish its power over a reluctant society, the state asserted its authority by suppressing or excluding most societal expressions of dissent. Under this logic, opposition to state policies by issue groups or political parties was seen as a challenge to the state per se. By handling most such cases as a challenge to itself, the state helped transform even minor expressions of dissent into nationwide antagonisms.

But challenge is constant in a developing society faced with a variety of crises. The inflexible refusal of the state to deal with social problems explains in part the fierceness with which parties fought each other over all issues. The democratic opening inevitably allowed for freer and more open forums of debates regarding accountability of state policies. The airing of popular discontent became widespread in the late 1970s. But the opposition found it difficult to express its views through what Poulantzas called the strategic terrain of the state. Instead, it did so in the area Poulantzas termed the terrain of societal materiality. This intensified social contradictions and hindered the formation of the consensus needed to solve national problems.

In 1974 the state tried to adapt to a society wanting to forge a democratic political system. By 1981 the state had failed to do so. Yet it was not the state that needed to be overhauled in order to catch up with society, as Manesis (1986, 10) argued. The need was to change the logic of state power, which meant the logic of those exercising state power. If this could happen, then the state would mirror society and be responsive to the latter's needs. This could not happen because the economic crisis did not allow the capitalist class to solidify its position in society and in the state. As this class remained stalemated, flowed along with the economic malaise, and overall muddled through, so did its representatives in the state.

Pluralist elections and the orderly or peaceful transfer of power in 1981, prompted many analysts to proclaim the "maturization" of Greek democracy (see, e.g., Macridis 1984). Indeed, elements of the 1975 constitution did recognize certain economic and social rights (articles 16, 21, 22, and 23) attesting to a just and welfare state as well as providing for an interventionist state: the establishment of economic planning, the protection of the environment, and the potential to nationalize industries (articles 17, 24, 79, and 106) (Manesis 1986, 34). Yet, at the same time the new state could not escape its legacy. The 1975 constitution included elements of the strong state of the past: the maintenance of the Greek Orthodox church as the official state religion (article 3), the constitutional protection of foreign capital (article 107), and the imposition of limits on civil liberty in case of "abusing" those liberties (article 25) among other (Manesis 1986, 34). The electoral plan approved in the 1974 elections enabled the ND party's 54 percent electorate vote to translate to 220 out of 300 seats in parliament. This outcome gave it the numbers to enact into law any bill introduced by the ND and, of course, to ratify the new constitution that it had itself drafted. But top-down legislative acts did little to ensure that the state reacted to societal realities. Nor did it mean that such acts would be followed in practice, or that the state's (i.e., its personnel's) logic would be altered.

Society welcomed the elements of a just and welfare state and shunned the authoritarian elements. It respected or ignored the state. Anarchy and chaos reigned as different social interests interpreted the laws arbitrarily. Respect for the authority of the state suffered accordingly, which further exacerbated the latter's intolerance and intransigence. With political parties as the only outlet of expression, huge rallies supporting this or that party and an intensification of campaign battles often turned an ugly face (Diamandouros, Kitromilidis, and Maurogordatos 1984). The party became a substitute for the state. Each party, together with its party-affiliated newspapers, defined a different societal reality than that of its enemies. As most Greeks shifted to PASOK, this party's view of reality took wider hold. For PASOK, the state was equated with the ND party and thus should be changed and become more open to grassroots democratic input. Yet, PASOK's plan ammounted to a mere change of personnel, a solution that changed neither the logic of the state nor social reality.

## THE LIMITS OF THE GREEK ROAD TO SOCIALISM: 1981–88

### Intentions and Realities

Papandreou's democratic road to socialism had a lot in common with Poulantzas' path. In an introductory speech at a 1980 conference sponsored by the Center of Mediterranean Studies (CMS) in Greece, Papandreou reaffirmed his Marxist orientation. But in achieving socialism, he denounced Western European types of social-democratic reformism and voiced his dissatisfaction in accepting as models existing socialism found elsewhere. Instead, he called for a "third road," a socialist political economy that would take into account Greece's "specific historical objective and subjective conditions" and the nation's "position in the world economy." The road to socialism would be the priority of all socio-political and economic aspects. It would occur within "truly democratic frameworks" (CMS 1981, 9–16).

He differed from Poulantzas on Greece's position in the world economy. Poulantzas saw Greece as a link along the imperialist chain. Papandreou saw Greece as a dependent nation in a metropolis-satellite relationship. In his study of Chile and Brazil, Gunder Frank (1967) set forth the theoretical assumptions regarding such a relationship, and in a later work (1969), he widened this analysis to include the rest of Latin America. Wallerstein (1974) used a similar scheme in terms of a core, semiperiphery, and periphery framework to trace capitalism's expansion since the sixteenth century into a world system, and he elaborated on this scheme in a later collection of essays (1979).

According to Frank, all nations were incorporated into a world capitalist system. The metropolis experienced a capitalist development. As the matropolis extracted and appropriated surplus generated by the satellite, the latter witnessed a development of underdevelopment. The political consequence of this setup was the formation of a ruling class in each satellite nation. This class acted as a local link between the metropolitan centers and its nation. It had a stake in maintaining these ties by appropriating part of its national surplus before passing the rest to the metropolis. This situation created relations of political and economic dependence on the part of the satellite. The satellite could achieve independence only when it severed the domestic and external links. Wallerstein's most notable addition to Frank's thesis was his semiperiphery category to account for satellite nations that managed some development from underdevelopment. This addition fitted the case of Greece (Pollis 1984). It also fitted previously core nations (e.g., imperial Spain and Portugal) recently delegated to a semiperiphery status (for a more detailed analysis and critique of Frank's and Wallerstein's theses, see Brewer 1980; Chilcote and Johnson 1983; Chilcote 1984).

Papandreou and his followers pointed to Legislative Decree 2687 in 1953 as one example in establishing Greece's dependence on the metropolis and the regime of xenocracy (foreign rule) characteristic of the post- World War II period. As explained earlier, the benefits offered to foreign capital, including the constitutional protection in article 107 of the 1975 constitution, made foreign investments in Greece very lucrative.

The privileged few comprised the link between Greece and the metropolis. Along with the parties representing them (the ND or the Right), they undermined national interests by giving in to foreign demands. At the same time, they enriched themselves by exploiting the nonprivileged majority. For Papandreou, national liberation necessitated a "double struggle": against the local ruling class and against its metropolitan superiors. The successful conclusion of the struggle of the dominated classes against the ruling class in Greece would also lead to national liberation from foreign control (Papandreou 1975, 77–78). This world view helped Papandreou develop his social dichotomy schema.

He incorporated the twin aim of "class struggle" and "national liberation" in the 1981 campaign slogan of *allaghi* (change). Theoretically, *allaghi* was another somewhat unclear and all-encompassing concept. But in the context of Greece's society, it nonetheless proved to be an electorally successful slogan. *Allaghi* meant that PASOK would first replace the ND party in power and then set policies that would delink Greece from its ties of dependency. Sensing that the concept of *allaghi* was the best strategy to defeat the ND party, all parties of the Left and the liberal center quickly adopted it. Even though there was a basic disagreement in regard to both defining the kind of change advocated and its results, all parties claimed a share in ensuring that change would be "authentic and real" (Diamandouros, Kitromilidis, and Maurogordatos 1984). The force of this concept marked the politics of PASOK in power and defined the political experience of Greece under Papandreou.

The victory presented a unique opportunity for the formation of an inter-Left coalition of interests at the top of the political power. By allowing a wider incorporation of progressive elements to share power, Papandreou could have strengthened his position in the battle within and outside the "terrain" of the state against interests contrary to socialism. Once in power, Papandreou shunned any cooperation with the Left, relying instead on his party's parliamentary majority. His authoritarian legacy and "ambition" inhibited the realization of his "professed" goals, isolated him from the parties to his left, weakened his electoral base and that of all the parties of the Left, and played by default into the hands of the Right.

Papandreou's election represented, according to PASOK members, a "step" in a "series of steps" required to achieve socialism (Kostopoulos 1983). The next "step" would be to change existing pockets of conservative strongholds by replacing bureaucrats appointed by the ND with socialist personnel. The changing of the guard would assure the eventual democratization of state apparatuses. Three tactical routes were proposed: one, the decentralization of state power and apparatuses by the creation of many decision-making bodies such as locally elected councils more responsive to local needs and problems (Kostopoulos 1983, 16), or workers' syndicates and cooperatives (Nikolinakos 1984, 73); two, the simplification of bureaucratic rules concerning state power and public life; and three, the democratization of the state's repressive apparatuses (e.g., the army and police). These measures would enhance popular input into the state and provide fuel for further reforms in the drive toward a more complete socialism, the break with foreign interests (e.g., the EEC, United States, and NATO), and the promotion of national independence (Nikolinakos 1984, 68–73).

Concurrently, Papandreou's political economy plans involved three initial changes toward reorganizing Greece's economic structures. The gradual "socialization" (a Papandreou concept distinct from nationalization) of the nation's major public sectors (transportation, energy, banking), and monopolized private sectors (trade, large industries, etc.). Socialization would institute a plan to allow control of these enterprises by workers, state, and management, to improve performance and meet social needs. An overall five-year (1983–87) Program for Social and Economic Development based on the promotion of national independence, popular sovereignty, and social justice would promote socialist reforms. Private ownership was legitimate if it were not a monopoly using exploitative and speculative practices (Kostopoulos 1983, 87–105; see also Pollis 1984; Clogg 1983).

The roads to socialism for both Papandreou and Poulantzas were fairly similar. Eight years later and after being re-elected to power with only a drop of less than three percentage points in popularity, Papandreou could not realize his "socialist visions" nor assuage the economic crisis. Initially, Papandreou's government blamed the long years of ND misrule and pre-1981 change of power "scorched earth" tactics that drained most state treatures (Marinos 1983, 3) for all of Greece's woes. After eight years in govnmernment, Papandreou often blamed his ministers and routinely and promptly replaced them. "Cool spirits and patience" were needed for stabilization (austerity) measures to work in 1986, declared Economics Minister Kostas Simitis (*Ta Nea,* July 2, 1986, 19). Simitis paraphrased the theme of his ousted predecessor, Gerasimos Arsenis, who since 1981 never tired of repeating that his yearly measure would work if only Greeks would be patient and tighten their belts. Arsenis later joined a small but steadily growing group of other PASOK members of similar fate to form in 1986 the Greek Socialist party (ESK).

Mishandling problems and inability to achieve results was evident in many areas. For example, little if nothing was done about the smog problem of Athens, the "most polluted city in Western Europe" (Schwenk 1986, 181), which had reached alarming levels and threatened the health of many residents. After 20 teams of scientists took years to study the problem, plans were allegedly drafted to deal with air pollution. Before they were implemented, the minister in charge was abruptly replaced in 1985. The newcomer discarded the old plans, initiated studies of his own, and by 1988 was still drafting new measures and asking Athenians "to be patient" (*To Vima,* June 12, 1988, 17).

Papandreou acted quickly to solidify his personal grip on political power by amassing in himself most of the authority of the state, thereby overcentralizing rather than decentralizing authority or expanding democracy. It was an overcentralization and personalization of authority without internal or external "counterbalancing mechanisms" to resist such abuses of authority (Manesis 1986, 45). One such mechanism had been the powers given the president by the 1975 constitution. Early in 1985 Papandreou refused to endorse the re-election of President Karamanlis, who then retired from public affairs. Christos Sartzetakis, a Papandreou ally, became the new head of state on March 30, 1985. According to the constitution, the president is elected by members of parliament. The election of Sartzetakis became possible after Kostas Alevras, the president of parliament and a PASOK member, cast the deciding vote. The ND contested the constitutionality of Alevras' vote and thus Sartzetakis' legitimacy. A constitutional crisis was avoided as upcoming parliamentary elections to elect a constituent assembly diverted attention. After the June 1985 elections, the new parliament amended the constitution mostly in regard to stripping the presidential office of many of its powers. Sartzetakis became mainly a ceremonial head of state. At the same time, Papandreou's narrow majority in the new parliament enabled him still to dominate the legislature. His control over his party's parliamentarians, and his absolute control of PASOK's central machine, allowed him thus to rule almost without any opposition. Amending the constitution to reflect narrow political needs and personal ambition, however, did nothing to enhance the "goal" of democratic socialism or ease the lot of the masses.

Overconcentration of power led to the almost inevitable situation in which the state was identified more and more by one person (Papandreou). He was then ultimately blamed for all of Greece's misfortunes. He, at other times, was the refuge of last resort for the solution of all crises by virtue of his power. In either case, supporters and foes alike presented him as responsible for solving or causing, respectively, anything from economic crises or summer forest fires to international conflicts or even traffic jams. Papandreou diverted attention from himself by blaming everything on the continuous resistance to his "progressive" policies by the ND party and its newest leader, Constantinos Mitsotakis. The deep personal animosity between these two men traced its roots to the leading and antagonistic roles they had played in the 1965 constitutional trickery by the king to dissolve the EK government. As if nothing much had changed two decades later, Greek politics were still marked by the bitter, mud-slinging battle between the same men.

Instead of supporting labor and the popular masses that had provided him with a near mandate, Papandreou often did the reverse. In 1986 a new law weakened labor unions by severely curtailing their right to strike in state-run industries that employed large numbers of union members (Travlou-Tzanetakis in *Ta Nea*, June 24, 1986, 6). The General Confederation of Workers of Greece (GCWG) was already weak and divided into factions representing in descending order the three parties of the Left (PASOK, KKE, KKes). Unable for many years to develop its own syndicalist identity, after 1974 the GCWG fell prey to partisan politics and interests. Each faction identified its goals with those of the party with which it was affiliated (Kravaritou-Manitaki 1986, 288). The result was a workers movement that subsumed its interests in favor of party interests. After 1981 the dominant PASOK faction supported government policies, whereas the smaller factions opposed the state at every turn, thereby transforming general economic demands into inter-Left political conflict (Kravaritou-Manitaki 1986, 288–89). Rather than incorporate opposing opinions and demands, the state tried instead to control the GCWG through personnel appointments in decision-making positions. Along with other strong-arm tactics, this increased authoritarianism infuriated the other factions. They countered with overt and covert confrontational stances such as boycoting negotiational forums and paralyzing strikes. Intra-GCWG animosity could be observed by the fact that on the May 1, 1986, commemoration of the 100th anniversary of the Chicago workers' uprising, two different observances occurred: a different one by the PASOK faction, and another belonging to the two Communist parties and ostracized PASOK members. Ironically, only the previous day Papandreou called May 1 "a symbol of unity and solidarity among the workers of the world, a day of struggle, mobilization and workers rights" (quoted in *Ta Nea*, April 30, 1986, 2). In other areas, changes to upgrade workers rights legislation were unenforced. In 1981 legislation to provide equal rights for women was enacted. In 1986, however, stewardesses in the state-run Olympic Airways were still discriminated with lower wages, intimidated by male employees and pilots, and asked to provide bodily measurements when applying for the job (Kanta in *To Vima*, July 6, 1986, 6).

Papandreou's "change" became a cosmetic solution to complex societal problems. He proved that there was not much difference between himself and his ND predecessors in returning political favors, or *rousfeti*, and appointing Left-leaning individuals to replace Right-leaning ones. In higher education, for example, many academic seats were offered to leftist professors. They described their appointments as "realism and justification of one's struggle" (Panousis in *Ta Nea*, June 21, 1986, 6). For Panousis, himself a professor, such appointments did not substantially alter the very structure of an archaic higher education system because such "hot issues and problematics" as the rejuvenation of universities (the subject of visionary declarations and support for PASOK during the 1981–83 period), deteriorated, once the new appointees were in place, into reversals, apathy, agony, and new dilemmas (*Ta Nea*, June 21, 1986, 6).

As an editor supportive of socialism and working for a pro-government newspaper told this author, Papandreou had rescinded in practice all his socialist visions even though he still used socialist slogans. This made the editor's job equivalent to trying to "defend the indefensible" in presenting stories through a socialist perspective (Athens, June 17, 1986). Socialist phraseology was more evident in the drafting of new legislation. But it seemed as if new laws were enacted only to disappear. Another editor wrote that new laws were always enacted that either "voided, changed, completed, upgraded, modernized but never enforced previous laws" (*Pondiki* August 8, 1986, 14). The only notable exception was the commitment to maintain and indeed advertize internationally PASOK's increased protection of and incentives for foreign capital investments in Greece (see the pamphlet distributed by the Hellenic Development Corporation 1985). PASOK's own Legislative Decree 1262/1982 supplemented both LD2687/1953 and article 107 of the 1975 constitution. Rather than eliminate xenocracy, Papandreou was reinforcing it.

As with all elections since 1981, the October 1986 campaign for municipal elections resembled more a "theater of the absurd." There was a need to solve local and municipal problems by electing to office those who were "best-suited to upgrade local self-rule and to improve the quality of life in the city." But those issues were advanced in terms of "general political or political party strength" (Linardos in *To Vima*, July 6, 1986, 7). Linardos concluded that, whereas democratic rules necessitated "party strategies," the attention to "notches" of popularity rather than to the issues at hand threatened democracy.

Long an advocate of a direct and simple proportional plan to replace the skewed ND electoral plan, Papandreou did so only in the 1984 Europarliament elections. He resisted calls by other parties to use the same plan in the 1985 national elections. His party devised a plan for these elections that skewed results even more than the 1981 ND one (see Table 4.1).

Two reasons accounted for this plan. It translated an anticipated lower popular vote for PASOK into an artificially induced majority in parliament

**Table 4.1**
**1985 National Election Results**

| Parties | 1[a] Votes % | 2[b] Seats | 3[c] Seats | 4[d] Seats |
|---|---|---|---|---|
| PASOK | 45.82 | 161 | 137 | 158 |
| ND | 40.85 | 126 | 123 | 130 |
| KKE | 9.89 | 12 | 30 | 11 |
| KKes | 1.84 | 1 | 6 | 1 |

[a] Votes (%) received.
[b] Allocated parliamentary seats under 1985 plan.
[c] Seats under 1984 direct proportional plan.
[d] Seats under 1981 plan.
*Source: Pondiki*, June 2, 1986, 20–21.

and marginalized smaller parties (especially the Communist parties). Both reasons were evident in the campaign slogan "PASOK or the right" aiming to rally leftist voters behind PASOK so that the votes of the Left would not be split. The continued adoption of this plan in future elections could polarize Greek politics into two large parties (i.e., PASOK and ND) by minimizing the presence of smaller parties in parliament. It could direct voter support toward the main parties to ensure that voting offered some representation. The tendency toward a two-party system in which the contenders significantly moderate their views to attract the majority of voters in the political center could stabilize Greek politics into an orderly interchange of power between two parties having few substantial differences, if any, in their respective agendas. Such a scenario would allow Papandreou to contribute notably to the legitimacy and perpetuation of bourgeois democracy in Greece rather than to the legitimacy of socialism. This twist of purpose could thus most clearly mark his tenure. Yet, the marginalization of many voters deprived of meaningful representation and, conversely, the inordinate importance of smaller parties to break possible electoral ties by the two main parties could also destabilize politics. In the first case, the absence of the safety valve provided by interest groups in securing economic and political representation in advanced capitalist nations, could create a permanently disgruntled social segment. In the second case, the reluctance to compromise and form coalitions among the parties of both Left and Right could lead to short-lived governments and continued political uncertainties.

Efforts to gear the economy toward meeting social needs managed the reverse. The Public Electricity Utility (DEI), only too eager to switch off electricity in cases where a resident defaulted on payments, lent capital and provided electricity to large private industries that often refused or were unable to pay their bills (the company was owed more than $200 million in

1986 exchange rates; *Pondiki*, July 11, 1986, 15). The powerful centralized authority of the state did nothing to force payment.

A group of industrialists, politicians, economists, and editors met to determine the degree of productivity and competitiveness of the Greek economy. They concluded that Greece's problem was connected directly with "the state of investment activities, the pace of technological development, organization apptitude, and work quality contribution of society as a whole" (*Ta Nea*, July 2, 1986, 19). For Thodoros Papalexiou, president of the powerful Confederation of Greek Industrialists (CGI), the health of industry has been "attacked from all sides," especially by "world recession, inflation, and domestic insecurity created by certain directions of the state's political economy" (quoted in Papandropoulos 1983, 3).

The irony was that such "enlightened" opinions came from the very people who also refused in practice to undertake the kind of measures they believed were necessary. According to industry analysts, "the present insurmountable problems of Greek businesses are the result of their own, uncontrolled credit procurement policies in the past" (Papandropoulous 1983, 3). Liberal lending to industrialists by the state in the past lessened the incentive by the former to invest their own capital in their companies. Piling up debt did not mean more capital would be available to invest in modernizing plants and streamlining production. Instead, most of the loans were "squandered in all kinds of other ventures"—presumably in consumerist pursuits, illegal export of surplus currency, or loan-shark activities. In doing so, "industries collapsed but the industrialists were enriched" (Karamanolis and Tsouparopoulos in *Kiriakatiki*, October 7, 1984, 6).

In 1985, 35 industries were on the verge of bankruptcy, unable to pay a total of $1 billion accumulated debt to the state. These industries employed 25,000 workers. Their solvency involved more than an economic problem: the PASOK government could not allow 25,000 workers to become unemployed without paying a high political cost. PASOK created the Organization of Reconstruction of Industries (ORI), a state holding company to oversee the functioning of these 35 so-called problematic enterprises. The ORI reserved the right to include in its ranks future industries that might become problematic—by some accounts between 200–500. The ORI in effect became the nation's single largest industrial concern. The state's rehabilitation of the problematics appeared as "an opportunity to promote worker participation in management. But there have been no examples of true worker management stemming from this policy" (Schwenk 1986, 170). Moreover, other industrialists strongly criticized the ORI. They interpreted its role as a ploy to kill private initiative and force capitalists out of their factories. They accused the state of unfair interference with the functioning of the free market by offering advantages to the 35 industries (Schwenk 1986, 170).

Whereas turnarounds might occur, by 1988 state control of the problematics was itself problematic. This revealed how avoiding a political cost turned into an economic cost that threatened to become a worse political cost. The problematics continued to be a drain on state budgets even though, according to the undersecretary for industry, Vaso Papandreou (no relation to Andreas), "it would be more cost-effective to shut the problematics and simply keep on paying workers their wages" (*To Vima*, August 10, 1986, 8). Any attempt to do so, however, would be interpreted by most critics as a show of weakness and an explicit admission that the ORI had failed.

Tax evasion remained rampant despite periodic efforts to correct this problem. For example, according to Finance Minister Dimitrios Tsovolas late in 1986, the government was going to investigate 130,000 upper income individuals and almost 800 companies for tax evasion, and estimated to net 130 billion drachmas ($1 billion) in recovered tax revenue (*Ta Nea*, July 3, 1986, 19). As in past such efforts, no revenue was recovered. In 1987 government reports of a more ambitious and determined nationwide tax evasion hunt saturated the media for many weeks in advance. On the first day of the "hunt," it was found that the government "lacked the personnel" by more than half to undertake its task since it was scheduled in the middle of the summer when most Greeks (and tax agents!) were on holidays. The few agents that ventured out found it difficult to gain access to the records of the businesses they visited, and in some cases they were even bodily assaulted by those querried. The "hunt" ended ingloriously. In a candid interview the previous year, the then resigning manager of the Tax Evasion Office, admitted that

> the state, up to October 1981, had defaulted on its power to check the legality of the practices of the big capital in Greece. Thus, when we (PASOK) began to check, large industrialists and importers treated us as if we were illegal. They even accused us of abusing our state power (for checking their records) (parentheses mine, quoted in *Ta Nea*, June 16, 1986, 19).

The continuation of tax evasion and para-economic practices by big capital, and to a lesser extent by all social classes, defied efforts to stabilize the economy through the utilization of orthodox economic measures (e.g., freezing wages, investing in technological upgrading, and so on). According to some estimates the para-economy produced almost 30 percent of the GNP (Papayannakis to *To Vima*, November 10, 1985, 6)—other, less-confirmed estimates placed the figure as high as 60 percent. If the state were able to tax and control the para-economy, it could significantly improve budget deficits and state treasuries. Many argued that the para-economy was the only successful economic strength of the nation and thus should not be prosecuted. But most of the para-economy was based on nonproductive, middlemen activities that merely accumulated personal capital for further consumption (*To Vima*, June 29, 1986, 33). Deriving profits mostly from imports, middlemen had important stakes in continuing "the nation's external dependency" for consumer products evident by the rise of imports from 19 percent of the GNP in 1970 to almost a third in 1984. They resisted state attempts to control imports in favor of domestic production and limited the range of options to overcome national dependency. Greece itself became one giant "problematic enterprise." Borrowing from abroad to pay for imports became compulsory rather than optional as more than 70 percent of new loans were spent to satisfy interest payment on past ones. The middlemen's fight against state control was aided by EEC rules that encouraged open economies and free trade (Giannitsis in *Ta Nea*, March 15, 1986, 6).

Regarding tax evasion and illegal export of foreign currency by businesses, the following two cases among many uncovered shed some light on the size of para-economic practices in Greece. Artificial overpricing of imports by many food-importing businesses through the branches of the Dutch Algemene Bank Nederland N.V. in Athens exported illegally millions of dollars. This deprived the state of millions in reserves and revenues (Roussis in *Ta Nea*, April 28, 1986, 21). And the Athens branch of Chase Manhattan Bank during 1982 and 1983 illegally loaned money to 56 industrial and business concerns in Greece. The precise nature of those transactions, especially in the area of exports, remained clouded in controversy (Roussis in *Ta Nea*, November 2, 1984, 20).

In many such cases overindebtness by capitalists became the burden of the state. It created a situation that can be described as welfare for the rich; rather than go out of business the capitalists relied on the state to bail them out. Rather than a threat to their interests, many capitalists found in PASOK an unexpected protector and ultimate guarantor of their fortunes. Elsewhere, half-baked efforts by the state to control the para-economy raised outcries by many capitalists. They charged that the state deliberately attacked certain firms to justify takeovers. They pointed to the case of Heracles Cement Company, the largest in Europe, which was brought under state bank control after controversial charges of fraud and illegal export of foreign currency were levied but later dismissed (Schwenk 1986, 169–70). The company was eventually handed back to its owners.

Papandreou proved unable to restore the economy. According to a report by the United States Federal Reserve Bank in 1985, the Greek economy exhibited the highest-ever current accounts (18 percent of the GNP) and budget (10 percent of the GNP) deficits; foreign debt (state and private) increased from $7.1 billion (18 percent of the GNP) in 1980 to more than $15 billion (47 percent of the GNP) in 1985; state borrowing, accounting for 19 percent of the GNP, made Greece the highest state debtor among all OECD nations; the ability to repay the debt worsened from 11 percent of the GNP in 1983 to 30 percent in 1985; the need to borrow money to cover public spending needs doubled during the first year of PASOK rule and by 1985 increased by a further 170 percent; and businesses took a loss each year since 1983—the top 2,300 main industries, representing 80 to 85 percent of Greece's industrial strength, had a net loss of $280 million in 1984, more than double the loss recorded in 1983 (*To Vima,* June 29, 1986, 6–7).

After eight years of PASOK rule, the possibility of a Greek road to socialism through democratic procedures remained illusive. Given the professed intention to achieve such a transition, could it be that this road was impossible in the case of Greece? If so, what made it impossible? Yet, if the transition to socialism was an "objective possibility" (Offe 1978, 28) requiring an indeterminate period of time, which may "occupy and even define whole historical epochs" (Sweezy 1972, 1), how can we be sure that the 1981–88 period did not lay the foundations of a future socialism?

## Reforms and Dependency

Answers to these questions cannot be derived from the period under examination. Government policies since 1981 assumed that structural economic reforms through better management and utilization of resources would reinvigorate the ailing health of Greek capitalism (Pollis 1984, 101–111). Such an assumption simplified the complex problems of political economy and idiosyncracies of the Greek economy as a crisis of the CMP. Focusing only on Greece's restricted CMP narrowed the definition of "structural reforms" from the whole plexus of production realities to a linear techno-managerial solution utilizing orthodox CMP-oriented economic formulas that essentially missed the real problems and were not very different from the ones unsuccessfully utilized by the past ND governments. Moreover, the desire to improve the CMP, as we see, protected the interests behind the CMP more effortlessly and conveniently than any ND government could have done.

Improving the CMP before any necessary "steps" were taken to structurally substitute capitalist relations of production with socialist ones could have been seen by Papandreou as a necessary precondition for a transition, exposing thus a significant gap in the strategy proposed by Poulantzas. Poulantzas' theoretical discourse on the subject (1978a, 252) focused mostly on political struggle rather than class struggle at the economic level. The success of socialist parties within and outside the strategic terrain of the state in forming political alliances and ensuring grassroots democratization appeared more important than the outcome of economic class struggle. It seems instead that in the case of Greece, the most important problematic was the creation of socialism, with its goal of raising material standards for the majority of the population, within a restricted capitalist matrix experiencing a sustained economic crisis. Material improvement for the masses would offer them concrete benefits and would predispose them to support socialist programs. Such support would translate into electoral majorities and provide the fuel for further changes. This dialectic interplay of economic affluence and political power could thus lead to democratic socialism. Yet, the one without the other can lead to a derailment of goals and a reversal of intentions.

In contrast, Papandreou's attempt to do precisely that raised equally important obstacles that perhaps preclude the possibility that a democratic transition could occur, assuming that the transition was his goal. A techno-managerial reform of the Greek CMP proved incompatible with even hints of socialist phraseology and "reforms." The initial wage increase of 12 percent, which by itself did not significantly raise the already low material benefits of the dominated classes, found the capitalists strongly resenting it. Moreover, as Dimitrios Konstas, a professor of political science told me (Athens, June 20, 1986), the extra income was not saved or used to consume domestic products that would have generated profits for domestic industries, fueled investments, and increased employment opportunities. Rather, coinciding with the freer entrance of EEC products, the extra income was spent on imported goods, which further depleted foreign reserves and forced the state to borrow more money from abroad.

Further, it undermined foreign and domestic trust by investors and capitalists who refused to comply with Papandreou's economic policies, resulting in disinvestment and capital flight abroad by Greek capitalists. Efforts to attract some of that capital forced the government to comply with capital demands for differential treatment and compromised its ability to continue with popular reforms. But more important, efforts to develop Greece's CMP before any transition was attempted only strengthened the fortunes and political clout of the very capitalist class Papandreou proclaimed to eliminate in order to achieve socialism. By aiding capital, Papandreou alienated the popular classes. Efforts to raise the competitiveness of Greek capitalism presupposed measures that included: lowering or freezing wages to cut production costs; exploiting workers by demanding improved productivity; and importing technology to improve the quality of production that made workers redundant thereby increasing unemployment.

Indeed, since 1984 budgets introduced austerity measures, curtailed worker benefits, and in general called on the popular classes to be patient until measures were given a chance to work. According to Georgiou (1985, 35–36), the 1985 wage level was equal to that of 1978. Georgiou observed that whereas the price index of most consumer goods was almost equal to that of Italy or West Germany, Greek wages were half and one-third that of Italian and West German workers, respectively. And PASOK's social spending was not significantly higher than ND spending to justify the former's contention that under PASOK the working class achieved its "class struggle goals." Georgiou argued that PASOK, rather than alleviate the fortunes of the wage earners had, instead, under the phraseology of socialism-populism, subjugated the dominated classes to the demands of capital much more effectively than ND governments. The combination of diminishing expectations, the perception that measures were one-sided, and the belief that PASOK was aligning with the capitalists turned explosive. In 1986, more so in 1987, and in 1988, massive nationwide strikes occurred that each time further worsened the economic and political fortunes of the nation.

The inability of PASOK to transform Greece's political and economic nature stemed also from the very dependent position that the nation occupied in the world economy. Poulantzas never made it clear whether his strategies for a socialist transition applied to imperialist or dependent nations. Greece's position in the imperialist chain differentiated it from that of, for example, France in gauging those two nations' potential for a democratic transition. Greece's external ties and foreign dependence placed many limits on its ability to pursue any policy that might appear threatening to the imperialist core. According to Gunder Frank, a participant at the Center of Mediterranean Studies (CMS) conference in 1980, efforts to restructure the Greek economy would also bring about countermeasures by metropolitan nations (CMS 1981, 205).

The option of tanks in the streets as a countermeasure against Papandreou was out of the question even if he were to pose a significant threat. Such a move would undermine the legitimacy of any new regime. Instead, more sophisticated and thus more effective ways were used such as drying up credit and investment, capital flight, stirring up the Turkish threat, international media campaigns to discredit Greek "socialism," and applying pressures through NATO and EEC policies. A recent novelty was the issuance of a travel "advisory" by U.S. President Ronald Reagan in 1985, warning American tourists to stay clear of Greece because of terrorism. Reagan used the occurrence of terrorist incidents to charge Athens airport with security lapses. Although the charges remained unsubstantiated, the "advisory" amounted to "a tourist-political war" full of threats and warnings to the Greek government—including the loss of sorely needed tourist currency (*Pondiki* June 21, 1985, 8–9).

Papandreou tried to minimize his vulnerability by taking advantage of EEC capital outlays. From 1982 to 1985 Greece received $2.5 billion in direct aid and secured many benefits from EEC investments in infrastructure (*To Vima,* July 29, 1986, 35). His pre-1981 calls not to join the EEC became a policy of renegotiating the terms of Greece's membership to reflect the nation's economic weakness vis-a-vis the rest of the EEC nations. Remaining in the EEC benefited mostly the agricultural sector as the price for its produce increased to meet EEC standards. The peasants responded with overwhelming support for PASOK. The struggling domestic and petty bourgeoisie and wage earners in the urban centers, however, continued to be adversely affected by the onslaught of superior EEC products and higher prices for domestic products. Many among those who had supported PASOK in 1981 felt that PASOK reneged on its promise to rid Greece of foreign influences and income inequalities. Many re-evaluated their political allegiances. PASOK's re-election in 1985 was more the result of the marginalization of the two CPs by the electoral plan devised rather than a show of genuine popular support. In the 1986 municipal elections, Athens, Peireus, and Salonika voters, representing a major bloc of Greek voters, opted for ND mayors. This trend in the cities was ahead of a lesser but steady erosion of support in the countryside.

Papandreou also followed an "independent, multidirectional, Greek-oriented" foreign policy that turned into multialienation from traditional allies without winning any significant new friends. But such overtures as the Five Continent Peace Initiative (an effort of participation to mediate between the superpowers for nuclear arms reductions), solidarity with Third World and Arab states, and refusal to condemn the downing of the Korean airliner by the Soviets were not fueled by some blind intention to oppose the United States and EEC metropolitan centers as critics charged. By adopting an "independent" stance, Papandreou aimed to turn Greece into a regional small-scale imitator of the metropolis. In effect, he envisioned the similar role advocated by the previous ND governments. Most important, it became obvious that he shared the same assumptions with the ND regarding the nature of the economic crisis and its resolution. Moreover, whereas the ND championed democratic capitalism, PASOK claimed to want democratic socialism. Yet both shared the desire to use the state to protect and regulate capitalism as well as making it a major entrepreneur. As such, PASOK's and ND's efforts were not qualitatively different. The only difference was in the ends professed.

For example, by using the power of the state Papandreou courted the allegiances of Greek capital to expand the regional role of both. He explored opportunities for Greek products to penetrate markets where Greece enjoyed a comparative advantage (i.e., Arab and North African ones). His intentions were revealed by significant state expenditures and tax incentives in such private and public export-oriented industries as weapons and war-related technology, construction products, cement, textiles, pharmaceuticals, and so on. Under Papandreou, trade with the Middle East and North Africa witnessed the fastest expansion (Schwenk 1986, 209). Increased trade was coupled with sustained and determined diplomatic support for the Arab nations intending to draw Arab capital to Greece. Arab investments, it was assumed, would strengthen confidence to and reveal support for his foreign and economic policies. For example, after mediating between Libya and France over Chad in 1984, Papandreou pronounced that Libya's Moammar Kadafi would invest $1 billion in Greece, although the details of the agreement were not fully disclosed. As it turned out, this was another one of Papandreou's empty claims. As with the Kadafi case, however, significant Arab investments did not materialize, which, although sobering for Papandreou, could be a positive aspect for the nation as a whole in the long run. The illusion of continued affluence based on imported capital would only reinforce the social psychology that the crisis was an abstraction as long as the state could, temporarily, balance its books with new capital.

The drive to solicit the allegiance of capital was evident in the change of language used. As explained by Undersecretary for Industry Vaso Papandreou, the problems of Greek industries stemmed from the lack of an industrial class!. Business-minded people were sorely needed in the economy. The government was willing to "open a dialogue" to ensure their cooperation and contribution to the economy. National priorities far superceded "political criteria and ideological differences" in a wide alliance between businesses and the state. Finally, for her, the definition of "leftist politics was to have a competitive economy and healthy businesses whether they were private, public or socialized" (*To Vima,* August 10, 1986, 8–9).

The industrialists reciprocated accordingly, although some suspicions remained. A new board of directors in the Union of Industrial Products Exporters (UIPE), encompassing 200 industries accounting for 80 percent of exports, and an important member of the Confederation of Greek Industries (CGI) announced that exporters had "a great responsibility to prove true the government's most recent doctrine that 'industrial exports meant industrialization in general'" (Kraloglou in *To Vima,* August 3, 1986, 7). Members of the CGI, commenting on earlier indications of change in PASOK's political economy, agreed "with the government regarding the weak points of industry and the 'medicine' it offers, but we disagree with the 'dosage' and the nature of the 'therapy' prescribed" (quoted in *To Vima,* September 29, 1985, 42). Whether such statements by the state and capitalists underlined a tendency toward closer cooperation in the future remained to be seen.

## The Strategic Terrain of the State

Unable to improve Greece's economy to favor the dominated classes and "forced" to accept capitalist demands, Papandreou found himself vulnerable at the political level as well. His entrance into the strategic terrain of the state led to unfamiliar territory in much the same way as the "right" discovered itself in the unfamiliar role of opposition. The 1981 election enabled him to assume control of parts of the state apparatuses such as administration, parliament, government radio, and television. Through replacement of personnel, he aimed to expand his power base throughout all the machinery of the state. More concentrated control did not result in more actual power for Papandreou. Constant bickering among his ministers made it difficult for him to mediate all disputes and to achieve compliance with his wishes evident by: 10 Cabinet reshuffles in six years; and lack of consensus on long-term policies (Linardatos in *To Vima,* December 1, 1985, 3). In-fighting was also evident by changing five different managers in the state-owned Olympic Airways in four years, and so on in other public sectors, and by resignations—for example, four in one day at Channel 1 of the Greek Broadcasting Company (*Ta Nea,* April 20, 1986, 18). Moreover, he isolated himself more and more. Ministers experienced difficulty in consulting him (*Pondiki,* August 1, 1986, 6–7).

The more seasoned Right was only temporarily set back. Conceding parts of the state did not eliminate it from all centers of power within the state. Unable to challenge Papandreou at the top of power, the Right began a war of attrition against PASOK's policies. Incessant resistance at the level of policy implementation where ND's long years of *rousfeti* practice had filled most middle- and low-level bureaucrats with its supporters was one way. Papandreou's directives from above did not necessarily lead to compliance. Mismanagement, apathy, nonimplementation, and wars of attrition among bureaucrats created a divided state and hindered the success of most state programs. In 1986 Papandreou admitted the "fact" of conservative "cocoons and locii existing still" within the state that sabotage the implementation of the politics of *allaghi*. He urged his supporters to maintain vigilance, daily struggle, and faith in the principles of socialism to overcome this resistance (quoted in *Ta Nea,* April 11, 1986, 17).

"Face-lifting," top-down efforts to modernize and rationalize the Greek bureaucracy by a change of personnel at the top, did not do much to face lift societal norms regarding public employment. The standard operating procedures of doing nothing persisted and even worsened among new and old bureaucrats and was imitated by the private sector. According to research by the German magazine *Der Spiegel* (reprinted in the *To Vima,* July 7, 1986), "Greeks are the highest paid idlers in Europe" because only 200 working days make a year—down from 308 in 1979. These "working days" were in reality even fewer when national holidays (e.g., memorial and holy days), and repeated strikes are taken into consideration. As many Greeks sardonically often told this author, getting a job did not imply a desire to work or to contribute to production but an "altruistic effort" to help reduce unemployment figures. The result of such attitudes was drops in productivity (44 percent of EEC standards in 1986) when yearly increases of 9 percent were needed to "catch" with the EEC in the near future. This could not be achieved unless and in part.

> the whole system of vacation, memorial days, holidays, semi-holidays, semi-memorial days, onomastical celebrations, short absences from work, and many

> other neo-hellenic inventions that form the idler-syndrome, or, better, in neo-Greek, the “copana”, (is) re-evaluated (editorial, *To Vima,* July 20, 1986).

## The Terrain of Societal Materiality

The battle waged in the societal materiality was equally compromised. PASOK could not improve the economy nor completely overcome its enemies within the state. At the same time, PASOK could not alter the logic of state power to accommodate social realities. Opposition parties and their affiliated newspapers began to attack PASOK policies ceaselessly. The KKE pointed at “turns to the right” as PASOK appeared to “lose” its “third road to socialism” and obeyed instead “monopoly capital demands (Kotzias 1984). The ND accused PASOK of a drift toward totalitarianism and the socialist bloc. Paraphrasing the slogan *allaghi,* the ND called for *apallaghi* (ridance) of PASOK from government. PASOK responded by increased authoritarianism, using a variety of excuses to justify its actions: occasional cases of repression were presented as isolated instances; state mismanagement was treated as blunders by individuals; power centralization was explained as necessary to ensure “socialism” against determined opposition; and the suppression of strikes was seen as necessary responses for the achievement of national objectives. In the process, the period’s political discourse was colored by exchanges of “risk-ladden rhetoric” and Cassandra-like warnings of imminent “destabilization dangers” to democratic principles by all political and economic contenders (Linardatos in *To Vima,* November 10, 1985, 4). For Pretenderis, post-1981 opposition politics amounted to a “war against the state,” a “civilized one” along ideological and theoretical issues but a “war” nonetheless (*To Vima,* November 11, 1984, 5).

The government’s authoritarianism was countered by increased confrontational tactics by opposition parties. By doing so, it pre-empted the KKE from forming a “pluralist and democratic” para-state that would enable it to amass popular support to challenge the PASOK superstate as an alternative road to socialism. The inability of the Left to democratize and cooperate made it vulnerable to the Right. Being traditionally clientelistic and authoritarian, the Right did not share this problem of the Left. By equating the continuous crisis of the economy with the state, and the state with Papandreou and his party, the Right imitated successfully Papandreou’s pre-1981 strategy against the ND government.

Whereas in pre-1981 times the state represented the Right, after 1981 it was the state of the Left. In neither case was it the state of the Greek society as a whole. The result was continuous societal polarization rather than consensus, anarchy rather than order, and muddling through rather than overcoming obstacles through the sweeping transformations envisioned by both Papandreou and Poulantzas. This situation invited more authoritarianism and "strong" leaders at the helm of the state. They in turn created more mistrust for centralized authority. This apparently inescapable viscious circle at the political level combined with a paralyzing crisis at the economic level adversely affected the health of the Greek society in the 1980s. Unemployment, underemployment, or meaningless employment prospects alienated many young Greeks. These resulted in a renewed exodus abroad, in sharp drops in marriages and births, in a plethora of anarchist groups, and in Kamikazi-like motorbike rides. Fast-paced changes, job insecurity, imported television shows, crime, and the severing of traditional norms confused many older Greeks. Environmental disasters and worsening quality of life conditions, disrupting strikes and foreign enemies (e.g., Turkey), and in general a plethora of real or perceived threats made for a society besieged by psychological fears. Escape or safety valves invited more authority, which is the other side of repression and military regimes. Other valves included a return to traditionalism, increased nationalism and isolationism, personal distructions (tavernas, discos, alcohol), and driving norms that have resulted in the highest per capita accident rate in Europe.

The deterioration in practice of the professed aims by Papandreou exposed also certain gaps in Poulantzas' strategies during the transition. It is not clear in Poulantzas' writings exactly how a socialist party can win battles within the capitalist state against the traditional occupants of this territory. They, by definition, command more resources than the legislative power of the socialist party. Since the rules of battle are established by bourgeois democracy, the socialist party is forced to obey rather than establish new ones to lessen the odds against it. This can be corrected by the ongoing "series of breaks" with the politics of the past such as legislative measures that slowly institute socialist rules. But in bourgeois democracies governments are in power on probation and subject to reelection every few years. Whereas the socialist party must win the "hearts and minds" of the population, the opposition must try to slow the implementation of progressive legislation. The battle then becomes a race against time until the next elections. It is subject to many influences such as: the state of the economy; the nature of the political debate; social norms; and interstate relations. All these conditions make for a more complicated strategy than merely the need to democratize the base or to legislate socialism. Papandreou, for example, failed to improve the economic crisis that enabled him to achieve power in the first place. The way politics were conducted forced him to react rather than act. Social values and practices hindered the democratization of the state and society. Finally, Greece's dependent position reinforced rather than severed external ties.

In the process, the democratic transition to socialism remained as compromised as all other aspects of Greek realities. But more than just a socioeconomic malaise, Greece exhibited a crisis of ideology and of conceptual language. Slogans and political ideas relevant in the 1970s did not necessarily reflect sentiments and issues of the 1980s and beyond. For example, the KKE's emphasis on labor exploitation did not reconcile with Greek consumerism and culture; PASOK's "third road" to socialism was an abstraction compared to being able to host the 1996 Olympic games (the 100th anniversary of the modern Olympics started in Athens); production improvement as a national priority was a generality next to planning a summer vacation on a Greek island, etc. The slogans of the Left that were forged in the past and reflected poverty, political persecution, and civil wars could not be fully grasped by many among the young. As with the older generations, the young inhabited a society more concerned with pollution, traffic jams, and vacationing rather than with the distant past.

Critics from the Left could argue that such behavioral patterns and priorities were the result of false consciousness. This could be true, yet at what point does false consciousness become a reality? The experience of this reality should be taken advantage of rather than be discarded as bourgeois propaganda. It is from within this reality that new political language should arise. The achievement of socialism, more than a political or economic strategy, involves the utilization of language that reflects social realities and evolving historical conditions. The overhauling of Greece's politico-economic and social crisis could not be achieved unless the political language were overhauled. The language used to determine whether Greece belonged to Greeks, the West, or the East was a schematic abstraction compared to the language needed to deal concretely with new concerns and paradigms. This need was clearly evident in the post-Chernobyl age: nuclear catastrophes, scarcities, super-power rivalries, defense buildups, and a variety of interrelated problems that directly affect not only superpowers, economic metropolises, and Third World nations but every person at the human level. The language used should not take its cues from the lessons of a past that the present will surely nullify but from the future toward which humanity moves unprepared to face. And unless language was changed, no political party, especially not PASOK, could even attempt a transition toward a system of power relations where human needs could be satisfied.

## The 1989 Elections

The multiple, interrelated problems identified above reached new heights during 1989, the repercussions of which would surely be felt well into the 1990s. That year witnessed two highly contested and ultimately inconclusive elections for parliament (on June 18 and November 5 respectively), ending each time with limited-mandate, caretaker governments—a third election was tentatively scheduled for mid-April 1990.

The electoral results were a letdown for all actors and social forces following the tremendous amount of energy, resources, mud-slinging attacks, and mass mobilizations that were expended. In both cases, the New Democracy party, capturing the plurality of votes, fell just short from being able to form a government of its own. PASOK saw its fortunes decline to around 40 percent despite massive attacks against its past record and a plethora of allegations of scandalous behavior levelled against its leader and many of its top members by all opposing parties. The Coalition of the Left and Progress, comprised by and ostensibly signifying the end of the schism between the two Communist parties, received about 12–13 percent. Although the Coalition dropped the communist label, tried to embrace the whole left spectrum, and utilized the concept of progress, it did not significantly improve its popular standing.

Shifting through the political impasse for deeper meanings and messages, it became evident that the polarization of society had solidified even more. The near absolute hold of the party leaders over their parties and constituents made it difficult for any party to make inroads into the domain carved by others. At the same time, the rigidity of control made it difficult to ensure meaningful inter-party compromises in order to form viable governments. For example, the unlikely and unexpected coalition between the New Democracy and the Coalition of the Left and Progress after the June election in support of an interim government became possible for all the wrong reasons: in order to use the new Parliament to persecute Papandreou and other PASOK officials for alleged scandals rather than use the opportunity to bring about broad changes in the conduct of politics and economic policies. Also, the post-November election compromise by all three main parties to support a neutral government was an expediency toward another round of elections after exploratory mandates to form a government had failed.

In the meantime the nation remains besieged by social and economic problems with no direction from above or better yet driven by misdirection, confusion, and near abdication of leadership responsibility.

## References

Acheson, Dean. 1969. *Present at the Creation: My Years in the State Department,* New York: Norton.

An Economic Observer. 1972. Greece: A case of neocolonialism, *Monthly Review* 24 (December): 23–37.

Brewer, Anthony. 1980. *Marxist Theories of Imperialism,* London: Routledge and Kegan Paul.

Carey, Andrew, and Jane Carey. 1968. *The Web of Modern Greek Politics,* New York: Columbia University Press.

Carnoy, Martin. 1984. *The State and Political Theory,* Princeton, NJ: Princeton University Press.

Center of Mediterranean Studies (CMS). 1981. *Metavasi sto Sosialismo,* Athens: Aletri.

Chilcote, Ronald. 1984. *Theories of Development and Underdevelopment,* Boulder, CO: Westview Press.

Chilcote, Ronald, and Dale Johnson (eds.). 1983. *Theories of Development: Mode of Production or Dependency?,* Beverly Hills: Sage.

Clogg, Richard. 1983. PASOK in power: Rendezvous with history or with reality. *World Today* 39 (November): 436–42.

Collier, David (ed.). 1979. *The New Authoritarianism in Latin America,* Princeton, NJ: Princeton University Press.

Couloumbis, Theodore, John Petropulos, and Harry Psomiades. 1976. *Foreign Intervention in Greek Politics,* New York: Pella Press.

Craig, Phyllis. 1976. The U.S. and the Greek dictatorship: A summary of support. *Journal of the Hellenic Diaspora* 3 (October): 5–15.

Dakin, Douglas. 1972. *The Unification of Greece, 1770–1923,* London: Ernest Benn Limited.

Danopoulos, Constantine. 1983. Military professionalism and regime legitimacy in Greece, 1967–1974. *Political Science Quarterly* 98 (Fall): 485–06.

Diamandouros, P., M. Kitromilidis, and Th. Mavrogordatos. 1984. *I Ekloyes tou 1981,* Athens: Estia.

Dimitras, Panayiotis. 1982. Tournant Historique en Greece. *Esprit* 1: 141–45.

Dovas, Yannis. 1980. *Ikonomia tis Elladas,* Athens: Sihroni Epohi.

Elephantis, Angelos. 1981. PASOK and the elections of 1977: The rise of populism, in Howard Penniman (ed.): *Greece at the Polls: The National Elections of 1974 and 1977.* Washington, DC: American Enterprise Institute.

Foster-Carter, Aidan. 1978. The modes of production controversy. *New Left Review* 107 (January–February): 47–78.

Fotopoulos, T. 1978. Exartimeni Anaptixi ke Ekviomihanisi, in Spiros Papaspiliopoulos (ed.): *Meletes Pano sti Sihroni Elliniki Ikonomia.* Athens: Papazisi, 61–121.

Frank, Andre Gunder. 1967. *Capitalism and Underdevelopment in Latin America: Historical Studies of Chile and Brazil,* New York: Monthly Review Press.

———. 1969. *Latin America: Underdevelopment or Revolution.* New York: Monthly Review Press.

Georgiou, Panos. 1985. I "Taxikes Aretes" tou PASOK ke i Ekloyes. *Sholiastis* 29 (August): 36–37.

Hellenic Development Corporation. 1985. Foreign Investments in Greece, pamphlet.

Hitchens, Christopher. 1975. Detente and destabilization: Report from Cyprus. *New Left Review* 94 (November–December): 61–73.

Kafatou, Sarah. 1979. Politics in a dependent country: Contemporary Greece. *Socialist Review* 44 (March–April): 103–30.

Kalligas, K. 1978. O Dramatikos Klonismos tis Ellinikis Ikonomias, in Spiros Papaspiliopoulos (ed.); *Meletes Pano sti Sihroni Elliniki Ikonomia*. Athens: Papazisi, 51–60.

Kariotis, Theodore. 1979. American economic penetration of Greece. *Journal of the Hellenic Diaspora* 6 (Winter): 85–95.

Katris, Ioannis. 1979. *O Prodomenos Laos: To Hroniko Mias Pentaetias, 1975–1980*. Athens: Papazisi.

Kegley, W. Charles, Jr., and R. Eugene Witkopf. 1981. *World Politics: Trends and Transformations*. New York: St. Martin's.

Kintis, Andreas. 1981. *Anaptixi tis Ellinikis Viomihanias,* Athens: Gutenburg.

Kostopoulos, Sotiris. 1983. *PASOK—2 Hronia,* Vols. A and B. Athens: Kaktos.

Kotzias, Nikos. 1984. *O Tritos Dromos tou PASOK,* Athens: Sihroni Epohi.

Kourvetaris, George, and Betty Dobratz. 1984. Political clientelism in Athens, Greece: A three paradigm approach to political clientelism. *East European Quarterly* 18 (March): 35–59.

Kravaritou-Manitaki, Yota. 1986. I Ergasiakes Shesis stin Ellada, in Aristovoulos Manesis and Costas Vergopoulos (eds.), 287–306.

Krimpas, George. 1982. The Greek economy in crisis, Ralf Dahrendorf (ed.): *Europe's Economy in Crisis*. New York: Holmes and Meier.

LaFeber, Walter. 1976. *America, Russia, and the Cold War, 1945–1975*. New York: John Wiley and Sons.

Lenin, V. I. 1979. *Imperialism: The Highest Stage of Capitalism*. New York: International Publishers.

Loulis, C. John. 1984/85. Papandreou's foreign policy. *Foreign Affairs* 63 (Winter 1984/85): 375–91.

McNall, Scott. 1980. Greece and the Common Market. *Telos* 43 (Spring): 107–21.

Macridis, Roy. 1984. *I Elliniki Politiki sto Stavrodromi: To Sosialistiko Pirama*. Athens: Greek Europress.

Manesis, Aristovoulos. 1986. I Exelixi ton Politikon Desmon stin Ellada, in Aristovoulos Manesis and Costas Vergopoulos (eds.), 15–60.

Manesis, Aristovoulos, and Costas Vergopoulos (eds.). 1986. *I Ellada se Exelixi*. Athens: Exantas.

Marinos, Yannis. 1983. En Opsi tou Neou Proipologismou. *Ikonomikos Tahidromos* (November 24), 3–7.

Mouzelis, Nicos. 1978a. *Modern Greece: Facets of Underdevelopment*. New York: Macmillan.

———. 1978b. The Greek elections and the rise of PASOK. *New Left Review* 108 (March–April): 59–74.

———. 1980. Modern Greece: Development or underdevelopment? *Monthly Review* 32 (December): 13–25.

Nikolinakos, Marios. 1977. *Meletes Pano ston Elliniko Kapitalismo*. Athens: Nea Sinora.

———. 1984. *Dokimia Ya Ena Elliniko Sosialismo*. Athens: Nea Sinora.

———. 1981. *Global Rift: The Third World Comes of Age*. New York: William Morrow.

Stavrou, Nikolaos. 1977. *Allied Politics and Military Interventions: The Political Role of the Greek Military*. Athens: Papazisi.

Stern, Lawrence. 1975. Bitter lessons: How we failed in Cyprus. *Foreign Policy* (19): 34–78.

———. 1977. *The Wrong Horse: The Politics of Intervention and the Failure of American Diplomacy*. New York: Times Books.

Svoron, Nicos. 1984. *I Episkopisi tis Ellinikis Istorias*. Athens: Themelio.

Sweezy, M. Paul. 1972. Toward a program of studies of the transition to socialism. *Monthly Review* 23 (February): 1–13.

Tatsios, Theodore George. 1984. *The Megall Idea and the Greek-Turkish War of 1897: The Impact of the Cretan Problem of Greek Irredentism, 1866–1897*. Boulder, CO: East European Monographs.

Thermos, Elias. 1974. Conflict and prospects in Greek politics. *East European Quarterly* 8 (June): 203–21.

Tsiokos, Thanasis. 1981. *To Kathestos tis Exartisis ke i Anagi tis Allagis*. Athens: Sihroni Epohi.

Tsoukalas, Constantinos. 1969. Class struggle and dictatorship in Greece. *New Left Review* 56 (July–August): 3–17.

———. 1981. *I Elliniki Tragodia*. Athens: Nea Sinora.

———. 1986. Ergasia ke Ergazomeni sti Protevousa Aristovoulos Manesis and Costas Vergopoulos (eds.), 163–241.

Vergopoulos, Costas. 1975. *To Agrotiko Zitima stin Ellada*. Athens: Exantas.

———. 1986. Ikonomiki Krisis ke Exsihronismos stin Ellada ke ston Evropaiko Noto, in Aristovoulos Manesis and Costas Vergopoulos (eds.), 61–106.

Vrettos, Spyros. 1984. I Arithmi Miloun gia tin Ekpedefsin Mas. *Ikonomikos Tahidromos* (February 7): 17–19.

Wallerstein, Immanuel. 1974. *The Modern World-System Vol 1. Capitalist Agriculture and the Origins of the European World-Economy in the 16th Century*. New York: Academic Press.

———. 1979. *The Capitalist World Economy: Essays*. New York: Cambridge University Press.

Woodhouse, C. M. 1982. *Karamanlis: The Restorer of Greek Democracy*. Oxford: Clarendon Press.

Yannakakis, Ilios. 1969. The Greek Communist Party. *New Left Review* 54 (March–April): 46–54.

Offe, Claus. 1978. Notes on the future of European socialism and the state. *Kapitalistate* (7): 27–37.

Palloix, Christian. 1978. *I Diethnopiisi tou Kefaleou*. Athens: Nea Sinora.

Papacosmas, Victor. 1979. Post-Junta Greece in Historical Perspective. *Indiana Social Studies Quarterly* 32 (1): 122–41.

Papandreou, Andreas. 1962. *A Strategy for Greek Economic Development*. Athens: Contos Press.

———. 1970. *Democracy at Gunpoint: The Greek Front*. New York: Doubleday.

———. 1975. *Imperialismos ke Ikonomiki Anaptixi*. Athens: Nea Sinora.

———. 1981. Introduction, in cms, 9–16.

Papandropoulos, Athanasios. 1983. Pia i Lisi ya tis Provlimatikes, *Ikonomikos Tahidromos* 49 (December 8): 3–7.

Papaspiliopoulos, Spiros (ed.). 1977. *Meletes Pano sto Sihroni Elliniki Ikonomia*. Athens: Papazisi.

Pesmazoglu, Ioannis (John). 1976. Greece's proposed accession to the EEC. *World Today* 32 (April): 142–51.

Petras, James. 1977. Greece: Democracy and the tanks. *Journal of the Hellenic Diaspora* 4 (March): 3–30.

———. 1982. Greek socialism: Walking the tightrope. *Journal of the Hellenic Diaspora* 9 (March): 1–15.

———. 1984. Isodimatiko Kefaleo. *Ikonomikos Tahidromos* (March 8): 27–30.

———. 1987. The contradictions of Greek socialism. *New Left Review* 163 (May–June): 3–25.

Petropulos, John. 1968. *Politics and Statecraft in the Kingdom of Greece*, Princeton, NJ: Princeton University Press.

Polk, George. 1947. Greece put us to the test. *Harper's* (195): 529–34.

Pollis, Adamantia. 1984. Socialist transformation in Greece. *Telos* 61 (Fall): 29–47.

Poulantzas, Nicos. 1976. *The Crisis of the Dictatorships: Portugal, Spain, Greece*, London: New Left Books.

———. 1978a. *State, Power, Socialism*. London: New Left Books.

———. 1978b (ed.). *I Krisis tou Kratous*. Athens: Papazisi.

Rousseas, Stephen. 1975. Memoire on the second solution. *Journal of the Hellenic Diaspora* 2 (March): 22–35.

Sarlis, Dimitris, 1984. *I Politikes Plevres tis Entaxis tis Elladas stin EOK*, Athens: Sihroni Epohi.

Schwenk, Millicent H. 1986. The economy, in Rinn S. Shinn (ed.): *Greece: A Country Study*, 3rd ed. Washington, DC: Foreign Area Studies, American University, 157–221.

Selden, Mark, and Victor Lippit (eds.). 1982. *The Transition to Socialism in China*. Armonk, NY: Sharpe, Inc.

Stavrianos, L. S. 1952. *Greece: American Dilemma and Opportunity*, Chicago: Henry Regnery.

# Chapter 5

# The Theory and Practice of Transitions: Struggle for a New Politics in Southern Europe

*Ronald H. Chilcote*

---

Our three cases of regime transition to democracy in Southern Europe (chapters 2–4) allow for an appreciative but critical assessment of the thinking and analysis that Nicos Poulantzas contributed to comparative study. Although he was particularly influenced by French philosophy, once he assimilated the thought of Gramsci, "tensions were introduced into his analysis that continued to work themselves out for the rest of his life" (Jessop 1985, 23–24). These tensions, as noted below, influenced his evolving theoretical and political perspectives of societies in transition to democracy, social democracy, and democratic socialism. Whereas his earlier work was largely theoretical and abstract, especially his *Political Power and Social Classes* (1973) and *Classes in Contemporary Society* (1975), in *The Crisis of the Dictatorships* (1976) he combined theoretical perspective with political experience. The result was a challenge to traditional thinking about Spain, Portugal, and Greece, an effort to evolve a class theory of the state, and an attempt to confront the problems involved in a democratic transition: "In returning again and again to the problems of the democratic transition he engaged in continual self-questioning and eventually modified all the fundamental strategic positions with which he was identified" (Jessop 1985, 310). It is clear that his attention to democratic socialism was more than a critique of Leninism or of right Eurocommunism; it also was recognition of the practical politics to come: "Poulantzas, whatever his optimism that a democratic socialism was worth struggling for, was also pessimistic about the prospects of achieving it" (Jessop 1985, 310). His insights prompted a rethinking of the dilemmas and contradictions of democratic socialism. He also stimulated analysis that linked a class theory of the state to capitalism on a world scale. Thus struggle between dominant and popular classes and internal dissension between bourgeois fractions could be tied to divergent lines of dependence with regard to U.S. or European capital, to the rupture with the Third World (especially in the Portuguese case), and the eventual integration of these countries into the European Common Market.

This concluding chapter begins with a summary of the emphases that Poulantzas gave to each case study and how his analysis related to ensuing political and economic developments. This includes a comparison of the case studies, with attention to similarities and differences in the experiences of Spain, Portugal, and Greece. Finally, we examine several questions that emanate from our understanding, and assess the prospects for socialism and Marxism in contemporary Europe.

## SUMMARY ANALYSIS

Fred López has examined the decade in which Spain transformed from a military dictatorship and exceptional form of capitalist state to a parliamentary democracy. In chapter 2 he analyzes Poulantzas' interpretation of the Franco dictatorship, revealing strengths and weaknesses of the argument while emphasizing class relations and struggle among classes and how this activity affected bloc formation and hegemony in the challenge to preserve and to oppose the regime. He also examines opposition during the democratic transition and looks at the links between the political and economic contradictions in the economic growth during the 1960s and the emergence of an opposition in the trade unions, political parties, student movement, and the Catholic church. Regional distinctions and influences are accounted for in his analysis, in particular the drive for regional autonomy that accompanied demands for democratization.

In the analysis Poulantzas offered on Spain, López identifies important contributions. First, Poulantzas separated important political and strategic questions from his more general theoretical concerns, relating them to Marxist thought and revision of that thought. The results were relevant to Southern Europe and Latin America where exceptional capitalist states or military-authoritarian regimes were prevalent during the period. Second, he examined the class character of the dictatorship, the causes of the regime's collapse, and the democratization process and its relation to national liberation struggles in dependent capitalist systems. Third, he analyzed the transition to the democratic period within a new phase of imperialism and internationalization of capital in which European capital challenged the hegemony of U.S. capital. Fourth, he emphasized class relations and the role of the state as a mediator of class conflicts and stabilizing influence on the social formation.

Poulantzas argued that the decay of the Franco dictatorship was caused by the redistribution of the balance of forces (the Catalan and Basque bourgeoisies and a section of state capital) within the power bloc in favor of capital oriented toward Europe. Both the comprador and domestic bourgeoisie supported the dictatorship, although the former, concentrated in banking and finance, was subordinate to foreign capital and served as an intermediary for penetration and reproduction of foreign capital within the country, and the latter was partially autonomous from foreign capital. The domestic bourgeoisie favored European capital and democracy in contrast to the privileged position of the comprador bourgeoisie, which favored the exceptional capitalist state and its ties to U.S. capital. Because of its dependence on foreign capital, the bourgeoisie was weak in the face of imperialism so that the hegemonic position of finance capital was undermined by contradictions within the power bloc, leading to an opening toward parliamentary democracy. In this process the domestic bourgeoisie exploited the nationalist manifestations of the petty bourgeois liberal professionals and intellectuals.

Poulantzas felt that the alliance between the domestic bourgeoisie and popular classes in Spain precluded the possibility of a transition to socialism. Thus the transition to parliamentary democracy was a victory for the domestic bourgeoisie and a weakening of the workers' movement. Poulantzas envisioned the state as a mediator of conflict and a stabilizing influence on the social formation; the exceptional capitalist state emerges to reorganize the hegemony of the power bloc and control over society.

Spain's economic transformation was a consequence of its reinsertion in the world capitalist economy, facilitated by relations with the International Monetary Fund, World Bank, and Europe. The ensuing "dependent industrialization" was characterized by increased consumer purchasing power, urbanization, and the proletarianization of the peasantry. Popular struggles challenged the regime, creating a crisis of hegemony within the power bloc.

López objects to the proposition of Juan Linz that the Franco regime was "authoritarian" and ideologically situated between totalitarianism and democracy; instead he believed that the regime represented the outcome of an intense struggle between forces of Left and Right. Poulantzas believed that the fractions of the bourgeoisie oriented to the EEC and the United States were at odds with each other and destabilized the hegemony in the power bloc, which led to the crisis of the dictatorship. López argues that the resulting instability allowed the domestic bourgeoisie (especially Basques and Catalans) to distance itself from the regime and therefore from foreign capital. He also questions Poulantzas' assumption that the exceptional capitalist state emerges only when a crisis of capital accumulation or political legitimation must be resolved and querries why Poulantzas does not explain why the exceptional capitalist state persists once the crisis is resolved. He feels that Poulantzas was incorrect in his analysis of the ideology of the Franco dictatorship and underestimated the effectiveness of the regime in neutralizing the masses through a national popular ideology. Poulantzas also failed to consider how intrabloc relations varied so that the Greek example may have been applied inappropriately to Spain and Portugal; further, Poulantzas neglected analysis of strategies and tactics of the major Left parties and discounted the role of the opposition in the transition to democracy by emphasizing internal divisions within the ruling class.

Whereas in the case of Portugal Poulantzas argued that the domestic bourgeoisie remained hegemonic throughout the revolutionary period, Dan Nataf and Elizabeth Sammis (chapter 3) believe that he incorrectly identified the domestic bourgeoisie and associated the monopolistic groups with the comprador bourgeoisie; they state that some of these monopoly groups constituted a monopoly domestic bourgeoisie that was not motivated to seek an alliance with the popular masses (who demanded decolonization and nationalization of their assets). They conclude, in contrast to Poulantzas, that the domestic bourgeoisie did not participate actively in the overthrow of the dictatorship and therefore was unable to control the democratization process. Instead the popular masses, they feel, challenged the political power of the monopoly domestic bourgeoisie, the comprador bourgeoisie, and the large landowners.

Poulantzas argued that the domestic bourgeoisie emerged with foreign capital and European influence, and it sought political liberalization and the support of popular masses to wrest control from the comprador bourgeoisie and the landowners; this was not possible under the dictatorship but was carried out under the revolutionary period; further, that a socialist transition could not take place during 1974–75 under the domestic bourgeoise, which controlled the democratization process in a way that precluded the possibility of dual power and assault by the working class and popular forces against the state. Nataf and Sammis suggest that democratic socialism, which combined elements of parliamentary democracy with revolutionary gains, was the order of the day as antimonopolistic sentiment put socialism on the agenda.

The domestic bourgeoisie favored a reorganization of the power bloc to exclude the large landowners, thus distancing itself from the dictatorship, whereas the comprador bourgeoisie continued its support. Nataf and Sammis ask if a comprador bourgeoisie really existed because it was not clear that some large economic groups were controlled by foreign capital and had more to gain by European integration. They also show how the groups increased their industrial investments and suggest that Poulantzas misidentified segments of the dominant class.

Nataf and Sammis level other criticisms. Poulantzas correctly identified a division between the comprador and domestic bourgeoisie, but incorrectly identified elements of each segment. In general, nonindustrial groups comprised the comprador bourgeoisie, and industrial groups made up the monopoly domestic bourgeoisie, which in turn was differentiated from the nonmonopoly domestic bourgeoisie. Whereas some family and bank groups were in the comprador bourgeoisie and involved in speculative activities, associated with foreign capital in the colonies, and hurt by the bank nationalizations and the granting of independence to the colonies, not all monopoly holdings were associated with this class, a distinction left unclear by Poulantzas. Both monopoly and nonmonopoly holdings were incorporated in the domestic bourgeoisie and oriented in part to the domestic market as well as the European one. Thus a monopoly domestic bourgeoisie with interests similar to those of the comprador bourgeoisie was distinguishable from a nonmonopoly domestic bourgeoisie, which exercised influence in the revolutionary period but was not decisively influential as politics consolidated around the representative electoral process and hegemony came into question. Given this split in the domestic bourgeoisie and the lack of hegemony, Sammis and Nataf believe that a transition to a democratic socialism (implying a political hegemony among popular mass forces on the Left if not an effective socialization of the private means of production) was possible. Thus Poulantzas distorted the class analysis and failed to see any outcome for the Left because of the impossibility of a dual power situation.

Poulantzas also misjudged the coup by underestimating the issues of concern to the military and overestimating the revolutionary movement's links to the Europeanists and underestimating the movement's sympathy to the popular masses. On the question of democratization, Nataf and Sammis find Poulantzas' analysis of February 1975 and his postscript more than a year later to be confused. He stressed conflicts within the dominant class, yet from March to November 1975 there were important conflicts between the dominant class and the popular masses. They believe that Poulantzas tended to emphasize continuity throughout the period.

They go on to suggest that Poulantzas might have placed more attention on the extent to which the domestic bourgeoisie had lost power. There could have been more emphasis on the strategic implications of the April 1975 elections for the constituent assembly. Here Poulantzas was correct in assessing the contradictory strategies of the Socialists and Communists and their different conceptions of socialism, but he ignored the possibility of a Left electoral majority. However, they believe that he misrepresented the role of the Socialists as subservient to the interests of the domestic bourgeoisie, and they conclude that the Socialists could have brought about the transition to socialism in a liberal or bourgeois democratic rather than revolutionary way.

They discuss the lack of hegemony under the Portuguese party system after 1976, noting that the bourgeoisie and the supporting classes lacked clear direction, even though the party system remained remarkably durable throughout the period into 1988. In their conclusion, they state that a principal problem was resolving internal dominant class contradictions and division under representative democracy while continuing to involve or coopt segments of the popular masses. There were contradictions within the popular masses, for example, over the question of representative democracy versus dictatorship of the proletariat, the ties with Europe, and divisions in the labor movement, whereas the collapse of the domestic bourgeoisie allowed the possibility during the revolutionary period of a shift of state power decisively in favor of the popular masses. Instead a mixed capitalist system evolved, and the failure of the capitalist class and the popular masses to assume a convincing role in the process left open the intrusion of international capital. Thus Poulantzas overemphasized the role of the domestic bourgeoisie both during and after the revolution, and he underestimated the possibility of a transition to socialism even though the Left failed to agree on a common project leading to socialism. They argue that the Left's failure did not allow the domestic bourgeoise to assert political and economic hegemony, and in fact Portuguese politics was dishegemonic because neither the popular masses nor the domestic bourgeoisie was ascendent. This exposed the country to policy options favored by international lending agencies and foreign capital.

Stylianos Hadjiyannis (chapter 4) focuses on the shift from an exceptional state in the form of a military regime to a bourgeois democratic state in Greece. He sees this as an orderly shift of power rather than any substantial change. Poulantzas explained the political crisis as an authority or hegemonic crisis—when the authority of the dominant fraction in the power bloc is challenged as relations of production are affected by change in the form of capital, for example, from merchant to industrial capital.

Poulantzas showed how the comprador bourgeoisie served as an intermediary in the penetration and reproduction of foreign capital in Greece; this capital concentrated in finance, banking, shipping, and petroleum refineries. Divisions between U.S. and European interests within the power bloc, however, resulted in instability in its hegemony and a crisis of authority in the Greek state itself. The domestic bourgeoisie evolved with industrialization, but it was not a genuine national bourgeoisie independent of foreign influence and capital. In the 1960s it was involved in light industry and associated with the comprador bourgeoisie and foreign capital. Poulantzas argued that Greek development was limited by its dependent position on international monopoly capitalism. As international capital penetrates the production process in the host country, the national and international economies link more closely and the host state facilitates conditions for capital formation and reproduction. Hadjiyannis shows that the 1967 military solution was a brutal means of maintaining power, whereas the 1974 democratization process became a more sophisticated effort to legitimize and perpetuate the Greek model of capitalist development and to benefit the domestic bourgeoisie as well as foreign capital.

Hadjiyannis shows how Poulantzas differed from the Leninist strategy of dual power and frontal attack on the state. Unlike his analysis of Portugal, Poulantzas emphasized political strategies and party policies and structured his theoretical base on his political experiences in France and an unsuccessful campaign to win a parliamentary seat in the 1977 elections in Greece. He describes how the importing of metropolitan relations of production were internalized by Greek society in a specific way, resulting in massive consumption of luxury and other goods. He examines patterns of employment, noting that many Greeks opted for nonproductive work, while peasants migrated to urban areas and contributed to the worsening of the quality of life there.

## SIMILARITIES AND DIFFERENCES

We agree with criticism that *Crisis* is but "a preliminary, theoretical attempt to assess the undermining of dictatorial politics in Portugal, Spain and Greece" and that Poulantzas correctly situated individual countries within the world capitalist system; further, whereas Poulantzas avoids a crude analysis of a monolithic ruling class dominating the state, he tends to treat the popular classes or masses in generalized fashion (Cocks 1978, 1124–25). Poulantzas, however, directly confronted mainstream political science with his emphasis on social classes rather than institutional forces. Our analysis follows in this direction. Thus our chapters diverge from other approaches that emphasize only "electoral competition among freely constituted parties" and "classical liberal guarantees of individual freedom," but distinguish between liberalization of an authoritarian regime and prospects for a broad democratization process and also show the contrast between American and European attitudes, with the former emphasizing the electoral process and the latter social and economic participation (O'Donnell, Schmitter, and Whitehead 1986, 16–17).

Whatever our criticism, we must not forget that Poulantzas, like Marx before him, offered his provocative analysis close to and in the midst of rapidly changing events. It is in this spirit that we have provided our own assessment, first, of the decisive moments of transitions from dictatorship to democracy and, second, of the economic and political crisis in the aftermath of these transactions. Thus the fortunes and misfortunes of Andreas Papandreou and his party can be associated with the decline of right-wing rule and the rise of democratic socialism, the government's heavy social spending, and a wave of xenophopia aimed at withdrawal of Greece from both NATO and the EEC. The election of Mário Soares as president of

Portugal was offset by the fluctuating success and failure of his Socialist party and the tendency of the pluralistic political party system to move rightward in the face of the relatively stable but isolated Communist party. At issue was an economic crisis prompted by low productivity, high external debt, inflation, unemployment, and the threat to small and medium businessmen and farmers faced with cheaper and better imports, the consequence of declining tariffs as Portugal integrated with the EEC. Socialists in Spain under Felipe González appeared to consolidate their position only by sacrificing extremist positions and moving to mainstream politics; thus a shift in position brought Socialists to support a 1986 referendum calling for remaining in NATO, thus ensuring party dominance in national politics.

Why by the late 1980s after the three countries had elected socialist regimes were they unable to implement or consolidate their reforms? We have emphasized the internal political and economic crisis in each country: on the one hand, the problem of dishegemony and intra-bourgeois class conflict, the emergence of the political parties and subsequent obscuring of the popular classes and movement; and on the other, inflation, unemployment, and a high foreign debt that limited domestic investment. The failure to implement meaningful changes also can be attributable to international developments, the influence of the Reagan years and conservative regimes in Great Britain and West Germany together with U.S. and EEC pressures to counter the reformist regimes in Southern Europe. For the United States and its conservative West European allies, the central issue was security and maintenance of NATO military bases in Southern Europe. The EEC sought further to integrate the economic community, strengthen interdependency, and ensure its stability within the international capitalist order.

Table 5.1 shows comparisons among the three cases. Our analysis reveals that structural reforms in Portugal were profound in the 1974–75 revolutionary period, especially with nationalization of the banks and large agrarian holdings, which severely affected the ruling classes, whereas reforms after 1974 in Spain and Greece were relatively modest. A regime transition occurred in all three countries, and whereas a transition in the state apparatuses appeared possible in the three situations, in fact institutional apparatuses tended to change in name only, with functionaries carrying on with rules and procedures familiar to the pretransitory period. Although there is no consensus as to when it took place, a transition to capitalism had affected all three countries. And clearly a transition from dictatorship into a parliamentary period of bourgeois politics occurred after 1974. Whereas a transition to socialism was a desire of the socialist regimes that came to power (and in Portugal this goal was written into the 1976 constitution), no socialist transition was implemented in the ensuing period.

Crisis in many forms was evident in Spain, Portugal, and Greece. Class hegemony was insecure in the transitory periods, given the instability among

**Table 5.1**
**Transitions in Southern Europe: thematic emphases**

| Theme | Spain | Portugal | Greece |
|---|---|---|---|
| Reforms | | | |
| Bank Nationalism | − | + | − |
| Agrarian | − | + | − |
| Transitions | | | |
| Regime | + | + | + |
| State | − | − | − |
| Capitalist | + | + | + |
| Democratic | + | + | + |
| Socialist | − | − | − |
| Crisis | | | |
| Hegemony | + | + | + |
| Political | | | |
| Instability | + | + | + |
| Economic | | | |
| Unemployment | + | + | + |
| Emigration | + | + | + |
| Inflation | + | + | + |
| Debt | + | + | + |
| Power Bloc | | | |
| Pre-Coup | | | |
| Domestic Bourgeoisie | − | − | − |
| Comprador Bourgeoisie | + | + | + |
| Popular Classes | − | − | − |
| Post-Coup | | | |
| Domestic Bourgeoisie | + | + | + |
| Comprador Bourgeoisie | − | − | − |
| Popular Classes | − | + | − |
| Influences | | | |
| Regional | + | + | − |
| International | + | + | + |
| US | + | + | − |
| EEC | + | + | + |
| NATO | + | + | + |
| IMF | + | + | + |
| World Bank | + | + | + |
| Third World | − | + | − |

and within the political parties, the unfulfilled demands and needs of mass popular movements, and the serious imbalances in the economies. The return of workers who had emigrated abroad in the period of the dictatorships simply exacerbated the deteriorating economies.

Our chapters here focus on the composition of the power bloc in the periods prior to, during, and after the transitions. As Table 5.1 shows, the comprador bourgeoisie lost influence and the domestic bourgeoisie was ascendent through these periods, whereas the popular classes rose to a position of prominance only in Portugal during 1974 and 1975.

Finally, regional influences were important. In Spain, movements favoring autonomy gained influence in Andalucia, Catalonia, and the Basque country, whereas in Portugal small rural farmers in the north manifested opposition to the revolutionary regime in 1975, and peasants and rural workers acquired land through the agrarian reform or forcibly occupied large farms in the south. Only Portugal related to the Third World, the consequence of its imperial dynasty, the colonial wars in Africa, and the struggle within and outside Portugal to bring independence to the African possessions. After independence, attention turned more decisively toward Europe as all three countries integrated with the EEC. The economic and political relations between the three nations and the United States and Europe impacted on power relationships within the ruling classes. NATO exercised influence through long-standing military treaties, whereas the IMF and the World Bank negotiated agreements relating to the economies and foreign debts of each country.

The introduction to this book raised questions in the search for a class theory of the state (on class, see Carchedi, 1977, and on state, see Carnoy, 1984). From the three case studies we have learned that transitions are constrained by the process of the dominant mode of capitalist accumulation. This process determines the limits of democracy, but due to its own internal contradictions it tends to cause conflicts to rise within the dominant classes. The structure of dominant class interests and the magnitude of the accumulation crisis, the role of the state and the popular masses may vary. Given the ascendency of international interests, the extent of indirect and/or direct control over the state remains high. Under such circumstances, the scope of action for political parties is one of either sustaining the general direction of capitalist accumulation and thus furthering the interests of capital or renegotiating the terms of coexistence between the dominant and popular classes within the emerging model of capitalist accumulation. To the degree that parties persist in this contradictory role, the process of accumulation can proceed in the incrementalist manner of Spain and Greece. Conversely, as in the case of Portugal, when the interests of the dominant classes are internally contradictory, leading to a failure to integrate fully with the accumulation process, the extent of dominant class control decreases. The state gains relative autonomy and attempts first to negotiate and finally to impose a solution to accumulation problems. This imposition may be such that in order to create greater balance between the structure of interests and the prevailing accumulation model, it can transform the dominant class itself. This undermines the structural resistance to the international accumulation process, but may tie into a more general rejection of capitalist social relations. This process will be shaped in large measure by the ability of the popular masses to establish various direct and indirect forms of representation that press the limits of change. The state can be transversed by the conflict among segments of capital as well as competing tendencies within the popular masses. Thus the strengths, unity, and capacity for forging broad alliances among forces of the Left become essential in moving the process from a mere adaptation to the problems of international capitalist accumulation to a process that secures important beachheads for a long-term process of socialist-oriented transformation. These findings, drawn from our comparative analysis, may serve as a basis for study of situations elsewhere.

## ISSUES AND PROSPECTS

Our approach follows in the Poulantzas search for a class theory of the state. We have not refined theory or resolved the conceptual difficulties involved in such an ambitious undertaking, but some categories of class can be identified. The analysis in the three case studies tended to depart from Poulantzas' distinction between the comprador and domestic bourgeoisies. My own preference is to consider the dominant bourgeoisie as tending to be a ruling capitalist class in possession of the major means of production and political power; as a ruling class it is an economic class that rules politically and dominates the economy through control over corporations and financial institutions. This class need not be monolithic and can incorporate varied interests that tend to become cohesive. Among the owners of capital who purchase means of production and labor are the monopolistic bourgeoisie (large owners of industrial and banking capital with ties to foreign capitalists, owners of factories, insurance companies, banks, and large commercial companies who may also be large landowners) or a nonmonopolistic bourgeoisie (owners of industrial and commercial firms who sometimes ally with the monopolist or foreign bourgeoisie, owners of small industrial and commercial enterprise, or middle-size and small farms who tend to be nationalist and sometimes oppose imperialism). The fractions of the bourgeoisie also may be distinguishable by type of capital or possession of means of production, for example, the agrarian bourgeoisie (modern landowners who run farms with machinery, pay salaries to workers and make profits; or traditional landowners who operate large estates, live in cities, and invest little in their land); commercial bourgeoisie (usually large owners sometimes allied with monopolistic or foreign bourgeoisies but also owners of small enterprise); and the banking bourgeoisie (owners of banks). The bourgeoisie may also be distinguishable according to amount of capital (large, medium, and small bourgeoisie).

Analysis of the bourgeoisie, of course, must relate to other classes. For example, the petty bourgeoisie comprises small capitalists who directly or indirectly control their means of production, but, unlike large capitalists, do not possess much capital and may feel oppressed by the bourgeoisie. They may reside in urban areas as owners or tenants of small artisan industries and businesses or as independent professionals or in rural areas as sharecroppers, tenant farmers, and the like. The new petty bourgeoisie, a term emphasized by Poulantzas (1978a), or new middle class (Wright 1978) comprises some professionals, bureaucrats, and managers who influence capitalists, but like workers do not usually own means of production. The proletariat does not own its means of production and sells its labor power for money or wages; it consists of urban workers in monopolistic or nonmonopolistic industries and white collar workers in private or public industry, banks, and so on; or rural farmhands and sharecroppers who earn wages. The peasants may be farmers who do not own their land and usually are associated with precapitalist modes of production, for example, squatters, renters, and unpaid family workers; they also are subsistence farmers who own their land, who do not sell much of their produce for market, and do not hire wage laborers. The lumpen proletariat are unemployed, idle persons.

Beyond the identification of categories of class and ways of analyzing class and struggle (above) or models of class structure (Burris 1987), there is the conceptual difficulty of contending with critics who argue against determinism, reductionism, and static analysis. Writers such as Wright have related their categories to identification of population segments so that positions "are located uniquely within particular classes" yet certain categories of employees are found within "contradictory class locations" (1985, 43). In criticism of his earlier work and that of other theorists, Wright argues that class analysis should rest on relations of exploitation rather than domination. "The marginalization of exploitation both undermines claims that classes have 'objective' interests and erodes the centrality Marxists have accorded class in social theory" (1984, 385). Resnick and Wolff concur in the need to focus on exploitation, and they offer a strong reaffirmation of a Marxist understanding of classes: "Marx's conceptualization stands, we believe, as a critique both of the traditional Marxist theory of class and of the recent efforts to remedy its vagueness and inadequacies" (1982, 1). They argue that Marx provided a basis for complex class analysis drawn from surplus value theory and different from traditional dichotomous theory: "We understand class to be defined narrowly in terms of the specific processes of producing and distributing surplus labor. . . . we understand class to be neither reduced to an effect of any non-class aspect of society, nor are any non-class aspects reducible to the mere effects of class defined in surplus labor terms" (Wolff and Resnick 1986, 112). From Freud, Lukàcs, and Althusser, Wolff and Resnick adapt a use of "overdetermination" or "a seamless cause and effect tying together all aspects of any society" (1986, 115) to explain that Marx understood class not only as constituted by a position in property relations or as a self-conscious position within social conflict, but also as "one particular social process among the many that comprise social life" (1987, 110). They go on to identify two fundamental classes of producers and appropriators and two subsumed classes of distributors and recipients of surplus labor, and they suggest that any individual may occupy all, none, or any combination of these class positions. Essentially, Resnick and Wolff stress the centrality of class as a process in Marxian theory and the need for us to focus on class to understand Marx's method of analysis of exploitation.

We can also ask what kind of transition? In the spirit of Marx and Poulantzas, our essays have critically examined the transition to democracy in Southern Europe. Our objective has not been to contribute to the declassing of the socialist project in Spain, Portugal, and Greece, but to analyze why Socialists in those countries favor political accommodation and therefore have reached an impasse in the long-range process of a transition to socialism.

Transition to representative democracy was apparent in all three cases and the rhetoric of socialism suggested some sort of a political transition that combined democracy with an illusion of a socialist possibility, but no true socialist transition of the political economy occurred because the private means of production were not all socialized and popular classes did not emerge to political power with or without the vanguard of a workers movement or proletarian party or progressive petty bourgeoisie. In the case of Portugal the experiment failed, according to Sammis and Nataf, because the Left popular forces failed to agree on a socialist project that would bring them to power and because the domestic bourgeoisie retained influence even though it had shown support for a progressive outcome. It is clear, however, that capitalism and bourgeois economic interests were in the end decisive, both in the national and international situations. Poulantzas understood the devisive nature of the Left as well as the structural legacy of the dictatorship, which permitted a change in regime but not in the state itself. The regimes evolved from radical possibilities, especially in Portugal, to bourgeois parliamentary, social democratic, or democratic socialist forms. In each case political parties emerged decisively to overshadow the popular forces identified by Poulantzas. Thus attempts at direct participatory democracy succumbed to indirect, representative forms. An essential question was whether solutions could be found for the economic and political crisis in Southern Europe without more popular and direct participatory democracy.

There is also the question of revolutionary strategy in the transition to democracy and the drive toward socialism. We have affirmed that the role of class and class struggle in the search for a theory of the state becomes important in the revolutionary process. In large measure Poulantzas remained faithful to the Leninist conception of dual power; the workers and popular classes had to build their revolutionary base outside the state apparatuses so that the state could eventually be smashed. In the early months of the revolutionary period, Portuguese Communists found themselves in the paradoxical position of occupying the apparatuses of the state as they seized and ran newspapers and journals as well as important governmental agencies. Workers faced the possibility of running industrial firms that had fallen to the state. The delicate balance of forces prompted an evolutionary course for the PCP, but the experience revealed the possibility of a bloodless revolution through penetration and occupation of key state apparatuses, even though the illusory Communist hegemony over some aspects of political life prompted reactionary violence from the Right.

Finally, we must assess the role of democracy in the play of popular forces. What kind of democracy evolves as bourgeois political forces insist on the parliamentary process and the dominance of the political parties. If pluralism is premised on individual choice, bargaining, and compromise, how did this emphasis undermine coalitions, alliances, and the aggregation of groups outside the party system? To what extent did the parties manipulate the popular groups and the labor movement? To what extent does this bourgeois democratic process affect the declassing of the socialist project? And how do these perspectives affect our analyses of the situation?

Whereas critics fault Poulantzas for a simplistic explanation, limited to a few categories, an effective class analysis probably must analyze class as process and overdetermined in the sense advocated by Resnick and Wolf. Such analysis in the Portuguese revolutionary period, for example, would be complex and difficult, yet it would provide the basis for a more exhaustive and incisive account.

Throughout Europe there is a declassing of socialism, a retreat from class analysis, associated with blocs of Left-center political forces, popular reforms, allegiances to socialist pluralism, development of the forces of production through capitalism, and the abandoning of Marxist concepts such as dictatorship of the proletariat and class struggle. Laclau and Mouffe argue, for example that "it is no longer possible to maintain the conception of subjectivity and classes elaborated by Marxism, nor its vision of the historical course of capitalist development, nor, of course, the conception of communism as a transparent society from which antagonism have disappeared" (1985, 4). This "new revisionism" (Miliband 1985) is based on a number of assumptions: the working class has not produced a revolutionary movement; there is little correspondence between politics and economics, and ideology and politics are relatively autonomous from economics; there is no special relation between the working class and socialism; a political force can be constructed out of various "popular" elements; and the struggle for socialism is conceived as a plurality of "democratic struggles" against inequality and oppression. Norman Geras identifies other premises rejected by the new revisionists: structural class position cannot be a primary historical determinant; the metaphor of base and superstructure is theoretically not viable; it is invalid to speak of objective class interests; and that socialism itself is not crucial to social transformation (1987, 40–82). Ellen Meiksens Wood sees a revival of the "new true socialism" against which Marx and Engels directed polemics in the 1840s; she characterizes the movement, in its rejection of economism and class-reductionism, as excising "class and class struggle from the socialist project" (1986, 1).

This shift away from Marxism and the declassing of the socialist project is rooted in the successes and failures of popular movements (feminist, pacifist, ecological, and so on) that supported radical reforms, but often politically compromised on strategies for their implementation. At the same time organized labor was undermined and weakened by the reorganization of capital in the advanced countries. Democratic socialism necessitated alliances of the Socialist Left with parties of the center to counter Communist influence. The compromising of principles in turn led to the breakup of some traditional leftist parties (the Communists in Spain, for example) and to the search throughout Europe for a new Left politics. In the process Western European intellectuals divided over strategy (electoral participation or revolution); stage (bourgeois, national democratic, or proletarian); type of party (coalition or vanguard); alliance (popular or united front; hegemony (dominance or dispersion of political forces); socialism (pluralist, social democratic, or Marxist). Also at issue was the Leninist strategy of mobilizing the working class into a counterstate organization, parallel but external to the capitalist state in the form of dual power, a perspective Poulantzas modified in his later writings, arguing that struggle within the state apparatus itself was necessary to disrupt the balance of forces and bring about a transition to socialism. There is evidence of this shift in *The Crisis of the Dictatorships* and especially in his last book, *State, Power, and Socialism* (1978). In an interview with Henri Weber, Poulantzas made clear that two efforts must be coordinated: first, "a struggle within the state. . . . whose aim is not to substitute the workers' state for the bourgeois state through a series of reforms designed to take over one bourgeois state after another . . . a struggle . . . to sharpen the internal contradictions of the state, to carry out a deep-seated transformation of the state"; and, second, "a struggle outside the institutions and apparatuses, giving rise to a whole series of instruments, means of coordination, organs of popular power at the base, structures of direct democracy at the base [which] would not aim to centralize a dual-power type of counter-state, but would have to be linked with the first struggle" (Poulantzas 1978b, 12–13).

The fundamental problem for the socialist project, certainly in Greece and Portugal, but elsewhere in Europe was the serious economic crisis. Social democratic governments could not contend well with inflation, unemployment, increasing foreign debt, and low productivity; their integration with the EEC surely would affect small and medium firms as big European capital found access to new markets.

In practical politics some Communist parties distanced themselves from the Soviet Union and sought accommodation and alliances with progressive forces. The oil crisis of 1973, the recession of 1974–75, and worldwide overproduction prompted a reassessment. In November 1975 the French and Italian Communist parties affirmed that socialism was a higher phase of democracy and freedom; there must be a continuous democratization of economic, political, and social life; the socialist transformation should involve public control over the principal means of production; small and medium agrarian and industrial producers must participate in the building of socialism; democratization of the state must increasingly give a role to local and regional government; and a plurality of political parties should exist alongside autonomous trade unions.

Fernando Claudín has looked at the emergence of Europe as a capitalist superpower, at the conservative challenge to the social democratic parties that since the end of World War II had served as political mediators between capital and labor, and at the crisis in Southern Europe signified by the collapse of the dictatorships in Spain, Portugal, and Greece. In the south, he believed, the crisis "may make Western Europe in a very direct sense the weakest link of the imperialist system in the present world conjuncture. . . . there is now no mere political instability involving changes of government, but a crisis of the political regime which is tending to develop into a crisis of the social order" (Claudín 1978, 20).

Poulantzas undoubtedly was influenced by his observations of the transition in Spain, Portugal, and Greece. The penetration of popular and Communist forces into the apparatuses of the Portuguese state in 1974 and 1975 implied the possibility of transformation without smashing the state altogether. Stability in a chaotic period necessitated the imposition of a bourgeois parliamentary system and the subsequent decline of mobilized popular forces necessitated a strategy of aligning popular and bourgeois forces to ensure at minimum incremental advances. Ellen Meiksins Wood notes a change in Poulantzas: "As his earlier political stance, with its ultra-left and Maoist admixtures, gave way to Eurocommunism, he moved away from his earlier views on Bonapartism, "ideological state apparatuses', and so on. . . . his theory of the state as well as his explicit political pronouncements shifted from an apparent depreciation of liberal democratic forms toward an albeit cautious acceptance . . . of the Eurocommunist view of the transition to socialism as the extension of existing bourgeois democratic forms" (1986,

27). No doubt Poulantzas maintained his allegiance to Marxism, but his work may have inspired some Left intellectuals in the early 1980s to move beyond the structural interpretations after his death and evolve theory and practice within a post-Marxist terrain. The ensuing debates affected some intellectuals in England and France (see Geras 1987, and Laclau and Mouffe 1987) who pushed for democratic rather than class struggle, and looked for links between liberal and socialist democracy in which the latter was seen as an extension of the former. For Wood (1986) the choice was between the radical democracy of the new revisionists and the socialism of class politics. Activists can function as liberal radicals to reform capitalism or they can try to keep alive the socialist project, and it is this problematic that has been divisive among Left intellectuals and politicians throughout Southern Europe.

## References

Burris, Val. 1987. Class structure and political ideology. *Insurgent Sociologist* 14 (Summer): 5–46.

Carchedi, Guglielmo, 1977. *On the Economic Identification of Social Classes*. London: Routledge and Kegan Paul.

Carnoy, Martin. 1984. *The State and Political Theory*. Princeton, NJ: Princeton University Press.

Claudín, Fernando. 1978. *Eurocommunism and Socialism*. London: NLB.

Cocks, Peter. 1978. Review of Nicos Poulantzas, *Crisis of the Dictatorships*. *American Political Science Review* 72 (September): 1124–25.

Geras, Norman. 1987. Post-Marxism? *New Left Review* No. 163 (May–June). 40–82.

Jessop, Bob. 1985. *Nicos Poulantzas: Marxist Theory and Political Strategy*. London: Macmillan.

Laclau, Ernesto, and Chantal Mouffe. 1985. *Hegemony and Socialist Strategy: Towards a Radical Democratic Politics*. London: Verso.

———. 1987. Post-Marxism without apologies. *New Left Review* No. 166 (November–December), 79–106.

Miliband, Ralph. 1969. *The State in Capitalist Society*. New York: Basic Books.

———. 1985. The new revisionists in Britain. *New Left Review* No. 150 (March–April). 5–26.

O'Donnell, Guillermo, Philippe Schmitter, and Laurence Whitehead (eds). 1986. *Transitions from Authoritarian Rule: Prospects for Democracy*. Baltimore: Johns Hopkins University Press. Citations to volume I on Southern Europe and volume II on Latin America.

Poulantzas, Nicos. 1973. *Political Power and Social Classes*. London: NLB.

———. 1975. *Classes in Contemporary Capitalism*. London, NLB.

———. 1976. *The Crisis of the Dictatorships: Portugal, Greece, Spain*. London: NLB.

———. 1978a. *State, Power, Socialism*. London: NLB.

———. 1978b. The state and the transition to Socialism. *Socialist Review* 7 (March–April, 9–36. Interview with Henri Weber.

Przeworski, Adam. 1985. *Capitalism and Social Democracy*. Cambridge: Cambridge University Press.

Resnick, Stephen, and Richard D. Wolff. 1982. Classes in Marxian theory. *Review of Radical Political Economics*. 13 (Winter): 1–18.

———. 1987. *Knowledge and Class: A Marxian Critique of Political Economy*. Chicago: University of Chicago Press.

Wolff, Richard D. and Stephen Resnick. 1986. Power, Property, and Class. *Socialist Review* No. 86 (March–April), 97–124.

———. 1987. *Economics: Marxian versus Neoclassical*. Baltimore: Johns Hopkins Press.

Wood, Ellen Meiksins. 1986. *The Retreat from Class: A New 'True' Socialism*. London: Verso.

Wright, Erik Olin. 1978. *Class, Crisis, and the State*. London: NLB.

———. 1984. A General Framework for the Analysis of Class Structure. *Politics and Society* 13 (4) 383–423.

———. 1985. *Classes*. London: NLB.

# Index

# About the Authors

*Ronald H. Chilcote* is professor of political science, University of California, Riverside, and managing editor of *Latin American Perspectives*. His research and publications have focused on Portuguese-speaking Africa, Brazil, and Portugal, and his current work, based on field research in 1985–86, 1987, 1988, and 1989, is focused on the Portuguese revolution of 1974–75 (the research published by the Centro de Documentação de 25 de Abril, University of Coimbra). He is the author of *The Brazilian Communist Party: Conflict and Integration* (1974), *Power and Ruling Classes in Northeast Brazil* (1990), and *Theories of Comparative Politics: The Search for a Paradigm* (1981)

*Stylianos Hadjiyannis* is assistant professor of political science, Shawnee State University, Ohio, and has taught at Pomona College and Fullerton College. His essay is based on annual field trips to Greece during 1984 and 1988. He completed his doctoral work in political science at the University of California, Riverside (1987). Currently he is preparing a text on international relations from a Third World perspective.

*Fred A. López III* is associate professor of political science, California State University, Bakersfield. His essay is based on field work in Spain and a doctoral dissertation in political science completed at the University of California, Riverside (1986). He is a coordinating editor of *Latin American Perspectives*.

*Daniel Nataf* is assistant professor of political science at the University of Maryland, Baltimore County. His essay is based on numerous field trips to Portugal. Currently he is revising for publication his doctoral dissertation (University of California, Los Angeles, 1986) on Portuguese democratization, and he has written a forthcoming article on social cleavages and electoral support. His current research focuses on electoral politics, trade unions, and the state in Portugal.

*Elizabeth Sammis* is a legislative consultant to the Maryland State Legislature. She recently completed her dissertation (University of California, Los Angeles, 1988) in sociology on the relationship between the Portuguese dominant class and the state under the Estado Novo.